THE CHILDHOOD OF ART

European Perspectives:
A Series of the Columbia University Press

The Childhood of Art

AN INTERPRETATION
OF FREUD'S AESTHETICS

Sarah Kofman

Translated by Winifred Woodhull

Columbia University Press

New York   1988

Columbia University Press wishes to express its appreciation
for assistance given by the government of France
through le Ministère de la Culture
in the preparation of this translation.

Columbia University Press
New York   Guildford, Surrey
Translation copyright © 1988 Columbia University Press
L'enfance de l'art first edition copyright © 1970 Payot, second edition copyright © 1975
PBP, third edition copyright © 1985 Editions Galilée

Library of Congress Cataloging-in-Publication Data

Kofman, Sarah.
The childhood of art.

(European perspectives)
Translation of: L'enfance de l'art.
Includes index and bibliographies.
1. Freud, Sigmund, 1856–1939—Views on art.
2. Freud, Sigmund, 1856–1939—Views on literature.
3. Freud, Sigmund, 1856–1939—Aesthetics.
4. Psychoanalysis and art.   5. Psychoanalysis and
literature.   I. Title.   II. Series.
BF173.F8K5913 1988   700.1'9   87-25700
ISBN 0-231-06312-1

Book design by J.S. Roberts

CONTENTS

1. The Double Reading   1

2. Fascination by Art: Art as a Cognitive Model
   of Psychic Processes   23

3. Freud's Method of Reading: The Work of Art
   as a Text to Decipher   53

4. Art in the Economy of Life: The
   Metapsychological Point of View   105

5. From Artistic Creation to Procreation: The
   Limits of a Psychoanalysis of Art   149

   Appendix. Delusion and Fiction: Concerning
   Freud's *Delusions and Dreams in Jensen's 'Gradiva'*   175

   Notes   201
   Works of Freud Cited   227
   Index   231

THE CHILDHOOD OF ART

Kofman's title is playing on the French idiomatic expression "c'est l'enfance de l'art," which means "it's elementary, a matter of first principles." As in English, the term "childhood" also connotes here an early stage in something capable of development.

—Trans.

1

THE DOUBLE READING

THE "APPLICATION" OF PSYCHOANALYSIS TO ART

Doesn't Freud himself declare that the interests of psycho-analysis from the point of view of art are very limited indeed?[1] Under these circumstances, the resistance with which attempts to "apply" psychoanalysis to art met and continue to meet might appear unjustified. And yet this undertaking encountered vehement opposition that took the same form as the initial resistance to psychoanalysis: vehement rejection and incomprehension, accu-sations of pansexualism and degradation of the highest cultural values.[2] Therein lies the explanation for Freud's caution, his care in defining precisely the task of psychoanalysis in the aesthetic realm, the polemical character of most of his writings, and the nuances introduced from one work to the other as resistances are overcome. But since the resistances are never abolished once and for all, a more or less deliberate self-censorship persists in Freud's discourse.

These few remarks guide my reading of Freud's texts.[3] They enjoin us to distinguish the works in which he sets out the relations between psychoanalysis and art (noting the differences he intro-duces from one work to the other) from the works where he engages in an "application," and to distinguish what Freud declares in his discourse as a matter of strategy from what he masks more or less consciously. They urge us, therefore, to do a symptomal reading of his text, making it say something more or other than what it says literally, yet basing the reading on the literal sense alone. But once these distinctions are made, do the limits of psychoanalysis in its "application" to art, so often pointed out by Freud, still stand?

Indeed, judging from his *discourse*, Freud seems fascinated by artists, particularly in his earliest works, and imposes very clear limits on a psychoanalysis of art. But "application" itself exceeds these limits and forces him to curb his admiration. Two texts separated by a ten-year period clearly show the nuances introduced from one work to the other.

The 1913 essay "The Claims of Psycho-Analysis to Scientific Interest" says, "Psycho-analysis throws a satisfactory light upon some of the problems concerning art and artists; but others escape it completely." And farther on: "The connection between the impressions of the artist's childhood and his life-history on the one hand and his works, as reactions to those impressions (*Anregungen*) on the other is one of the most attractive subjects of analytic examination" (13:187). But in "A Short Account of Psycho-Analysis," written in 1923, Freud says:

> The researches of psycho-analysis have in fact thrown a flood of light on the fields of mythology, the science of literature, and the psychology of artists. . . . We have shown that myths and fairy tales can be interpreted like dreams,[4] we have traced the convoluted paths that lead from the urge of the unconscious wish to its realization in a work of art, we have learnt to understand the emotional effect (*Affectivewirkung*) of a work of art on the observer, and in the case of the artist himself we have made clear his internal kinship with the neurotic as well as his distinction from him, and we have pointed out the connection between his innate disposition (*Anlage*), his chance experiences and his achievements. The aesthetic appreciation of works of art and the elucidation of the artistic gift (*kunstlerische Begabung*) are, it is true, not among the tasks set to psycho-analysis. But it seems that psycho-analysis is in a position to speak the decisive word in all questions that touch upon the imaginative life of man.

And further on:

> It must not be forgotten, however, that psycho-analysis alone cannot
> offer a complete picture of the world. If we accept the distinction
> which I have recently proposed of dividing the mental apparatus into
> an ego, turned towards the external world and equipped with con-
> sciousness, and an unconscious id, dominated by its instinctual
> needs, then psycho-analysis is to be described as a psychology of
> the id (and of its effects on the ego). If these contributions often
> contain the essence of the facts, this only corresponds to the im-
> portant part which, it may be claimed, is played in our lives by the
> mental unconscious that has so long remained unknown (19:208–
> 209)

In the first text, it is said that psychoanalysis can provide only a
"satisfactory light"; in the second, that it can release a "flood of
light." In the one, there is an avowal of total incompetence to resolve
certain problems, whereas in the other, though it is acknowledged
that certain tasks are not within the province of psychoanalysis, and
that it can only make "contributions," these contributions reveal
the *essence* of the facts, and psychoanalysis speaks the "decisive
word" on man's imaginative life. The latter text is a good example
of Freud's method of self-censorship. For polemical reasons, it is a
compromise between what Freud thinks and what he openly declares; each phrase affirms the opposite of what the previous one
asserted and in that very gesture cancels it, or at least alters it in
a peculiar fashion. The modesty of Freud's declarations, which is
merely apparent, obliges us to read his text carefully. Like all compromises, it must be deciphered.

What happened in the interval between the two texts?
Freud discovered close relationships among the various psychic
productions: myths, tales, literature, and art can be explained *like*
dreams. Freud's method consists essentially in showing the relationship and the distinction between these phenomena. It introduces continuity where there is apparently only a lacuna, a void, a
rupture, or a disjunction, establishing a link between the conscious
and the unconscious, the normal and the pathological, the child
and the adult, the civilized man and the primitive man, the indi-

vidual and the species, the ordinary and the extraordinary, the human and the divine. It links various cultural and psychic productions, representation and affect, and so forth. In this way, Freud effaces all the oppositions inherited from traditional metaphysics. That is why what he *does* is not an "application" of psychoanalysis to art; he does not apply to art, from the outside, a method belonging to a supposedly alien sphere. If the method is coherent, it is because each of its objects of study is but a different repetition of the same. For Freud, works of art are like all other psychic productions insofar as they are compromises and constitute "riddles" to be solved. Thus the interpreter of these productions is a new type of mediator, working on behalf of Eros: to solve the riddles is to reestablish a contact. Moreover, the work of interpretation itself is not cut off from its libidinal roots. In the first text, Freud speaks of an "attractive subject" for analytic examination, and elsewhere speaks in terms of "disturbance" and "fascination," to express art's powerful effect on him and other men.

To render this effect intelligible is precisely what Freud proposes to do, claiming that speculation, far from suppressing fascination, strengthens it. The opposition between intellect and sensibility is abstract; it arises from a psychology of the faculties of which classical aesthetics is the heir, and whose weakness Freud demonstrates. Freud himself could not enjoy without understanding; his lack of taste for music,[5] as well as his taste for literature,[6] can be accounted for in this way. It also explains why, except for his work on Leonardo da Vinci and Michelangelo's *Moses*, he limited himself to the psychoanalysis of literary works. To render intelligible the effects of affect; to establish links between dispositions, the vagaries of life, and production, between works of art and other cultural or psychic productions in general, whether dreams or neuroses; to show their resemblance and their difference—such is the sole task that Freud sets himself, or at least the only one he openly acknowledges. He acknowledges just as openly the limits of psychoanalysis, which are repeated in all his works. Completely outside its province are the "aesthetic appreciation of a work of art" or of the artist's formal procedures on the one hand, which properly belong to aestheticians, and on the other, the explanation of the artistic "gift," genius, and the possibility of creation.[7] Psychoanalysis is said to make a mere "contribution" to art, drawing on the psychology of the id and its effects on the ego. Everything that lies outside the sphere of the id is left to others. What lies beyond this sphere—the work of the artist—depends for its analysis on ego psychology and the science of aesthetics. What lies this side of it— the gift, genius —remains a mysterious enigma that absolutely escapes all scientific knowledge. By virtue of this gift, the artist is an inexplicable being, exceptional and favored by the gods.

Does Freud accept this theological and ideological conception of the artist? That is the question. But does the claim that the "gift" cannot be explained by psychoanalysis amount to an affirmation that it is, by its very nature, mysterious? For Freud, it is biological science that should take up the problem where psychoanalysis leaves off, for it is life that bestows "gifts." (I shall study this problem at greater length in my last chapter.) But does this substitution of life for God repeat differently the same ideological conception of art, or does it introduce a radically new conception? Moreover, if what lies on either side of the id escapes psychoanalysis completely, how could Freud say that its "contribution" sometimes reveals what is most essential about the object of study, and that psychoanalysis is "in a position to speak the decisive word in all questions that touch upon the imaginative life of man"? Wouldn't this amount to removing what is essential to the work of art from the field of psychoanalysis? How, then, are we to understand the fact that psychoanalysis encountered resistance and was so often reproached for having a reductive project? Indeed, the distinction Freud establishes in the text cited above between a "psychology of the id" and a "psychology of the ego" is dangerous, for it contradicts other texts where Freud considers it illegitimate to assimilate the ego to consciousness and the id to the unconscious. The simplistic quality of his exposition offers additional proof of its polemical character and invites a reading of Freud's text that discloses something other and something more than what it literally says.

A SYMPTOMAL READING

Let us refer then to two examples of "applied" psychoanalysis where we can see more clearly the functioning of the opposition between what is openly declared and what is masked in Freud's discourse. "The Uncanny" begins thus:

> It is only rarely that a psycho-analyst feels impelled to investigate the subject of aesthetics, even when aesthetics is understood to mean not merely the theory of beauty but the theory of the qualities of feeling. He works in other strata of mental life and has little to do with the subdued emotional impulses (*Gefuhlsregungen*) which, inhibited in their aims and dependent on a host of concurrent factors, usually furnish the material for the study of aesthetics. But it does occasionally happen that he has to interest himself in some particular province of that subject; and this province usually proves to be a rather remote one, and one which has been neglected in the specialist literature of aesthetics. (17:219)

Freud begins by excluding aesthetics from the sphere of psychoanalysis proper and expressing his indifference toward emotional impulses that result from drives that are inhibited in their aims or sublimated (although the two expressions do not have exactly the same meaning). However, this statement should perhaps be read as meaning the opposite of what it says; that is, as disclosing something like an indirect response to the vulgar belief that psychoanalysis is interested only in the "demoniacal" in man. In his discourse, Freud repeats the distinction between the "lowly" and the "sublime" the better to denounce it, convinced as he is that psychoanalysis has something to say about the "highest" cultural phenomena. As he shows in the study that follows this introduction to "The Uncanny," muted emotional impulses cannot be understood if they are seen as cut off from the uninhibited sexual drives of which they are a diversion. What Freud here attempts to put under erasure is the moral and metaphysical opposition between the "high" and the "low," thereby showing that a "pure" aesthetics cut off from psychoanalysis and reserved for specialists can only be a vain science. At the end of "The Uncanny," Freud states that aestheticians are but fine talkers: the quality of uncanniness, that "remote region" of aesthetics which the discipline generally neglects, and which Freud consequently takes the liberty of studying with no risk of offending it, appears upon examination to be the essential quality of the work of art.[8] Here again, Freud establishes links between the disciplines and stands opposed to a psychology of the faculties. The specialist can only fall and keep men in a state of metaphysical illusion. In the preface to *Totem and Taboo* (1913), Freud writes: "[These essays] seek to bridge the gap (*vermitteln*) between students of such subjects as social anthropology, philology and folklore on the one hand, and psycho-analysts on the other." Freud links these disciplines because there exists an unsuspected unity among phenomena heretofore considered distinct, such as the totemic meal and the Christian communion, the divine and the human, as *Totem and Taboo* is devoted to proving. And Freud writes in "On the Teaching of Psycho-Analysis in Universities," published in 1919:

> The application of this method is by no means confined to the field of psychological disorders, but extends also to the solution of problems in art, philosophy and religion....Thus the general psycho-analytic course should be thrown open to the students of these branches of learning as well. The fertilizing effect of psycho-analytic thought on these other disciplines would certainly contribute greatly towards forging a closer link, in the sense of a *universitas literarum*, between medical science and the branches of learning which lie within the sphere of philosophy and the arts. (17:173)[9]

It is interesting to note that this text dates from the same year as "The Uncanny." It supports my interpretation of the first lines of that work, as does the rest of "The Uncanny" itself. To cite a single example, the uncanny impression produced by the *Tales of Hoffmann*, especially "The Sandman," cannot be understood without reference to the symbolism of dreams. Only an acknowledgment of the symbolic equivalence between tearing out the eyes and castration can account for this effect. A view that simply accepts the text at face value and looks for no deeper secret "does not account adequately for the substitutive relation between the eye and the male organ which is seen to exist in dreams and myths and phantasies; nor can it dispel the impression that the threat of being castrated in especial excites a peculiarly violent and obscure emotion, and that this emotion is what first gives the idea of losing other organs its intense colouring" (17:231). Similarly, such a view renders incomprehensible the fact that in this tale the fear for the eyes is always tied to the death of the father, and that the Sandman keeps coming back as a disturber of love.[10]

Freud thus establishes a link between disciplines and the phenomena under study on the basis of a common nucleus, the oedipal structure. But only the reaction formations to this structure present themselves, as so many differential variations of an invariant, of a postulated type.[11]

What Freud *does* in "The Uncanny" makes possible then another reading of his initial declarations; above all, they must be seen as the denunciation of an aesthetics reserved for specialists and of an ego psychology cut off from a psychology of the id.

Let us refer now to the first lines of "The Moses of Michelangelo":

> I may say at once that I am no connoisseur in art, but simply a layman (*Laie*). I have often observed that the subject-matter of works of art has a stronger attraction for me than their formal and technical qualities, though to the artist their value lies first and foremost in these latter. I am unable rightly to appreciate many of the methods used and the effects obtained in art. I state this so as to secure the reader's indulgence for the attempt I propose to make here.
>
> Nevertheless, works of art do exercise a powerful effect on me, especially those of literature and sculpture, less often of painting. This has occasioned me, when I have been contemplating such things, to spend a long time before them trying to apprehend them in my own way, i.e. to explain to myself what their effect is due to. Wherever I cannot do this, as for instance with music, I am almost incapable of obtaining any pleasure. Some rationalistic, or perhaps analytic, turn of mind in me rebels against being moved by a thing without knowing why I am thus affected and what it is that affects me.

The paradox is that we can gain only a dim understanding of the most grandiose works of art; they overwhelm us without our being able to comprehend them.

> I am not sufficiently well-read to know whether this fact has already been remarked upon; possibly, indeed, some writer on aesthetics has discovered that this state of intellectual bewilderment is a necessary condition when a work of art is to achieve its greatest effects. It would be only with the greatest reluctance that I could bring myself to believe in any such necessity.
>
> I do not mean that connoisseurs and lovers of art find no words with which to praise such objects to us. They are eloquent enough, it seems to me. But usually in the presence of a great work of art each says something different from the other; and none of them says anything that solves the riddle (Rätsel) for the unpretending admirer. (13:211)

Freud's modesty in this text is part of a strategy. The very structure of the beginning of "Moses" invites us to read it as a work of art should be read,[12] for every text is tissue which masks at the same time that it reveals. It invites us also to distinguish in it, as in a dream, a manifest and a latent content. As in a dream, it is the minute details that arouse suspicion and provoke interpretation. Here, the relevant details are the tone of the text, the irony directed at the "true" connoisseurs, and Freud's denial of his ability to appreciate a work of art as such—a denial which marks an instance of repression and invites us to assign it the opposite meaning of the one declared. What he does subsequently in interpreting the statue of Moses down to the smallest details—which the many "connoisseurs" he refers to have not succeeded in doing—totally cancels the opening statements and justifies our way of reading this text as a riddle to be solved, one that might not be seen as such if certain details are neglected.

The riddle of this text figures in miniature the riddle constituted by every work of art, and is itself figured in miniature by the riddle that is openly presented here: who is speaking, and where is he speaking from? Indeed, the text on Moses is anonymous; it is as though the author were playing a guessing game by creating a verbal portrait of himself in order to elicit his name ("I am no connoisseur of art, but simply a layman," etc.). Here Freud seems to be imitating Morelli, the Italian art lover who wrote under the Russian pseudonym Ivan Lermolieff; for Freud claims to have been "greatly interested" to learn that an Italian doctor was hiding behind the Russian pseudonym (13:222). Morelli set out to distinguish copies from originals; that is, to attribute to the work with absolute certainty the name of its father. To do this, he proceeded by pointing out what seemed to be the most insignificant details of the painting, such as the way the fingernails and ear lobes were drawn—in short, everything that was considered to be rubbish (*Refuse*). But Freud only plays at being Morelli the better to denounce the ideology in which the latter is trapped; for to consider it essential to find the name of the author is to conceive of him as the father of his works, as a creator. Yet it is precisely this theological conception of art that Freud sets out to unmask. To tell the name is not to understand the work. Michelangelo is known to all as the author of the statue of Moses, yet the "intentions" of the artist in sculpting it, and the reasons why it moves us, are yet to be understood. The "intentions" can be communicated only by the work in the writing that is specific to it,[13] its formal structure. What Michelangelo himself would have to say about them is of little importance, because true intentions are not conscious. If one can imagine the life of the author from the work, as Freud does with Leonardo, one can conclude nothing about the work from the conscious life of the artist, of which the name is the symbol. Freud preserves the autonomy of the work as a text, but this is not incompatible with a method of generalized intertextuality. The text engenders its father, as Freud shows in more detail in his treatment of Jensen's *Gradiva*. The theological conception of art accepted the notion of an autonomous, conscious subject who was the father of his works, as God was of creation. By playing at being Morelli through his anonymity, Freud deconstructs the metaphysical conception of the subject: it is not he who is speaking, but the text (which does not mean that the text must be taken literally).

"The Moses of Michelangelo," too, therefore justifies the

distinction we have introduced between what Freud openly *says*, and what he in fact *does*. What he *does* is discernible through the structure of the text and the apparently trifling details. From this standpoint it is possible to do a better reading of the beginning of "Moses." The opposition between the connoisseurs of art and the mere laymen at first seems to function in favor of the former, since Freud humbly presents himself as a mere layman.[14] But at the end of the text, as in "The Uncanny," the "connoisseurs" are reduced to glib talkers caught up in subjective opinions, elevating their own fantasies about the works to the status of knowledge, yet unable to solve the riddle of the text in question. Freud's plea to them for lenient criticism should thus be interpreted ironically. What Freud means is that the art "connoisseur" criticizes without knowing what he is talking about, for he is talking about himself; only the psychoanalyst can disclose the "historical" truth, if not the "material" truth, of what he says.[15]

Thus a veritable reversal occurs between the beginning and the end of the text. Subsequently, Freud nonetheless seems to accord the connoisseur of art expertise regarding the qualities of form and technique, to which he claims to be indifferent since he is interested principally in the "content." It would appear then that the art connoisseur grasps the specificity of works of art better than the psychoanalyst, since to the artist "their value lies first and foremost in [their formal and technical qualities]." Likewise, "The Uncanny" attributes to aestheticians the task of understanding how the artist obtains different effects from the same material by varying the means of expression: "[The poet] is able to guide the current of our emotions, to dam it up in one direction and make it flow in another, and he often obtains a great variety of effects from the same material. All this is nothing new, and has doubtless long since been fully taken into account by students of aesthetics. We have drifted into this field of research half involuntarily" (17:251). Yet these loquacious specialists fail where Freud, a mere amateur, succeeds: "The science of aesthetics investigates the conditions under which things are felt as beautiful, but it has been unable to give any explanation of the nature and origin of beauty, and, as usually happens, lack of success is concealed beneath a flood of resounding and empty words. Psychoanalysis, unfortunately, has scarcely anything to say about beauty either" (*Civilization and Its Discontents*, 21:82–83).

To what can this failure be attributed, then, if not to the fact that traditional aesthetics is trapped in the metaphysical distinction between "form" and "content," and trapped as well in the separation of the "faculties"—intelligence and sensibility—as if it were possible to understand the "content" without the "form" or the "form" without the "content," even though the work of the artist is at the same time the "expression" of unconscious intentions; as if in order to enjoy art one absolutely must not understand it, even though intelligence itself is a form of enjoyment? In his analysis of the *Moses*, Freud brings together "form" and "content," affect and representation. Right after the introduction, he shows that the numerous interpretations of *Hamlet* failed because they did not account for the effect it produced. On the basis of a formal study which is attentive to the smallest details, he establishes the relations between the structure of the work—an expression of the unconscious ideas which he calls the "artist's intention"—and the effect it has upon the spectator. Running counter to the ideology of traditional aesthetics, he establishes a concatenation between affect and representation, power and meaning, the economic and the symbolic. "In my opinion, what grips us so powerfully can only be the artist's *intention*, in so far as he has succeeded in expressing it in his work and in getting us to understand it" ("The Moses of Michelangelo," 13:212). At the end of the text, he wonders whether Michelangelo succeeded at this perfect expression and writes that he was an "artist in whose works there is so much thought striving for expression" (p. 236). He adds that Michelangelo went further than any other artist in this direction, to the utmost limits of what art can express. If Freud, as interpreter, has given a fallacious interpretation, the artist must share the responsibility for it. The problem here is to know the limits of expressiveness in a given artist's work and in art in general.

But in establishing a relation of expressiveness between

"form" and "content," doesn't Freud himself remain imprisoned in the classical space of representation? Doesn't the concept of "expressiveness" belong to the sphere of metaphysics? Doesn't Freud denounce one aspect of it (the separation of "form" and "content," signifier and signified) only to adopt its opposite (the union of the two), and therefore remain caught in the same closure? Or rather, even though retaining the language of representation, doesn't he cancel the two opposites in order to introduce a completely original conception of the status of "form" and "content" in the work of art? I shall examine this question later; here, my aim is simply to propose a reading of the beginning of "Moses," justifying my general method, a symptomal reading of Freud's discourse on art.

Freud says next that he cannot enjoy a work when he does not understand the effect it has on him. In his *discourse*, he accounts for this on the basis of his rationalistic or analytic disposition. And indeed, the very task of the analytic cure is to be able to link a meaning to an affect which has lost its meaning or never had any to begin with. But this necessity of linking affect to representation is not characteristic of every turn of mind; without this link, affect is transformed into anxiety. The status of representation and affect respectively cannot be understood independently of each other, though their fates may be different. Thus one can read in this declaration the avowal of a conflictual relation between art and science. Is Freud a prisoner of the ideology that admits of a de jure opposition between art and science? Or is the opposition in question here merely one of two enemy brothers working toward the same goal, but competing with each other? If this is the case, traditional ideology's substitution of a de jure opposition for a de facto conflict must itself be interrogated.

THE ARTIST AS GREAT MAN AND HERO, SUBSTITUTE FOR, AND MURDERER OF THE FATHER

Indeed, Freud's oft-declared admiration for art and artists harbors a certain ambivalence and repeats the general public's admiration, all the better to denounce it. In many texts he acknowledges artists' superiority in being able to "know" man, sparing themselves the detour through work taken by the man of science. In 1884 he writes in a letter: "I think that general hostility reigns between artists and researchers immersed in the details of a scientific investigation. As we know, art gives the former a key which allows them to enter easily into women's hearts, whereas we scientists remain baffled by that strange lock and must wrack our brains in order to find the key that fits."

Theodor Reik is surprised by Freud's harshness regarding Dostoevsky's morality and denounces it.[16] In his response to Reik, Freud acknowledges his ambivalent feelings toward Dostoevsky: "You are right in suspecting that, in spite of my admiration for Dostoevsky's intensity and pre-eminence, I do not really like him. That is because my patience with pathological natures is exhausted in analysis. In art and life I am intolerant of them" (21:196).

This ambivalence, which reflects people's general attitude toward artists, indicates a certain repression and a displacement of interest from art to artists. Freud's numerous declarations regarding the limits of the "application" of psychoanalysis to art which, he insists, in no way diminishes the "grandeur," indeed the "saintliness" of the artist, have an essentially strategic significance. In his studies of Leonardo, Goethe, and Michelangelo, but also in the one of Moses, he maintains that these great minds, because of their love of knowledge, would have been delighted with the psychoanalytic treatment to which he subjects them. In making this claim he hopes to overcome the public's resistance, by inviting it to adopt the same attitude as its own idols. Thus the Preface to the Hebrew translation of the *Introductory Lectures on Psycho-Analysis* written in 1930 (15:11) says that Moses and the Prophets would surely have accepted his *Lectures* without resistance, and warns the Hebrews of today against renewed idolatry of the Golden Calf, which would go hand in hand with a rejection of psychoanalysis. If Freud safeguards the ideological image of the artist in his declarations, he does so the better to denounce it. The same is true of his repeated references to the "fascinating" character of psychoanalytic studies of art,[17] and to the disturbing effect works of art have on whomever receives them. These repetitions are intended to reveal that the interest taken in art is not purely "disinterested," and implies a relation to the repressed which Freud proposes to bring to light.

On the one hand, the work of art is one of the offshoots of what is repressed in the artist, and as such is symbolic and symptomatic. It can be deciphered from traces, minute details which indicate that the repression is not entirely successful; this failure is the only thing that opens a space of legibility in the work.[18] One of these traces is the effect of the work on other people: what is repressed by the artist and can be read in his work produces a powerful and enigmatic affect. What is true of art is true also of religion and psychotic delusions, namely that the constraint imposed by the logical mode of thought is no longer in force. Only some element "which returns from oblivion asserts itself with peculiar force, exercises an incomparably powerful influence on people in the mass" (*Moses and Monotheism*, 23.85). What is expressed in art must have undergone repression "before it is able to display such powerful effects on its return" (p. 101), which is to say that the work of art, like religion, implies the return of something universally repressed.[19]

On the other hand, the fact that the public's real interest in art lies not in art itself, but in the image it has of the artist as a "great man," is repressed. In light of this, it is easier to understand why the "application" of psychoanalysis to art meets with resistance. Thus even Freud, who destroys the artist as idol in practice, if not in what he says, cannot completely stifle a feeling of guilt, for to a certain extent, to "apply" psychoanalysis to art is to commit a murder; that is, to do away with the artist as a genius, or a great man. This murder comes in response to another one—the distortion of the repressed in its return, the traces of which are hard to cover up: "The distortion (*Entstellung*) of a text resembles a murder: the difficulty is not in perpetrating the deed, but in getting rid of its traces." (*Moses and Monotheism*, 23:43). During his first visits to San Pietro in Vincoli where Freud went often to study the *Moses*,[20] he tried to avoid the gaze of the prophet as if he himself were guilty, and his "Moses" seemed to him to be the product of an illegitimate love engendered somewhat clandestinely: "My relationship to this work is something like that to a love child. Every day for three lonely weeks in September of 1913 I stood in the church in front of the statue, studying it, measuring and drawing it until there dawned on me that understanding which in the essay I only dared to express anonymously. Not until much later did I legitimize this nonanalytical child."[21]

Thus Freud's anonymity in the "Moses" has an overdetermined meaning.[22] By remaining anonymous, Freud plays at being Morelli, inviting us to read his text as a riddle, and demystifying the theological conception of the autonomous subject who is father of his works. But his anonymity is also that of the criminal who conceals his name for fear of punishment. In this sense "The Moses of Michelangelo" foreshadows *Moses and Monotheism*. Just as the Jews killed Moses and repressed the murder, Freud, in his analysis of Michelangelo's statue, "kills" Michelangelo, thereby becoming, in a way, Moses himself, the destroyer of idols. Here then, what Freud says about Moses in *Moses and Monotheism* could be said of Michelangelo and all other artists: "To deprive a people of the man whom they take pride in as the greatest of their sons is not a thing to be gladly or carelessly undertaken, least of all by someone who is himself one of them. But we cannot allow any such reflection to induce us to put the truth aside in favour of what are supposed to be national interests" (23:7).[23] But the murder of Moses, more than any other, is bound to arouse a strong feeling of guilt, for Moses is the very paradigm of the father. In the first place, he is father of the Jews: "We must not forget that Moses was not only the political leader of the Jews settled in Egypt, but was also their law-giver and educator and forced them into the service of a new religion, which to this very day is known after him as the Mosaic one. . . . I venture to say this: it was one man, the man Moses, who created the Jews" (p. 18). But he is also the paradigm of the father in general. "Fate had brought the great deed and misdeed of primaeval days, the killing of the father, closer to the Jewish people by causing them to repeat it on the person of Moses, an outstanding father figure

(*Vatergestalt*)" (pp. 88–89). As lawgiver, Moses is a father, but he is also the interpreter of God, and thus a figure whose province is mediation. As such, he does not speak, but rather makes God's word intelligible by writing it down. Another trait attributed to Moses has a special claim to our interest. Moses is said to have been "slow of speech": "he must have suffered from an inhibition or disorder of speech" (p. 33).

As an interpreter and destroyer of idols, Freud identifies with Moses. But he takes his distance from him as well, for he substitutes for the Mosaic law the law of ἀνάγκη, necessity. It is therefore understandable that the "murder" of Moses provokes in him an acute feeling of guilt. But this feeling must nonetheless persist as Freud "applies" psychoanalysis to art and artists, since, each time he puts an end to the public's infatuation with an idol, he repeats the murder of the father. If Freud must proceed with great care when he speaks of art and the artist, it is because in their relationship to the artist men repeat an infantile mode of behavior. In "applying" psychoanalysis to art, Freud advocates the murder of the father and his substitutes. Clearly, the public worships the artist and all other "great men." Yet in *Moses and Monotheism*, where Freud tries to define the nature of the great man, he shows that no thinker, artist, technical expert, or great chess player is worthy of the name (p. 108). Success in a life of action is no more satisfactory as a criterion, as Freud shows by deliberately citing the examples of Goethe, Leonardo da Vinci, and Beethoven. The concept of the "great man" is vague, and connotes nothing more than the presence of numerous human capabilities in the individual so designated. The interest he arouses is due to the influence he has on other men, influence which is made possible only by their need to admire an authority, attracted as they are to all father substitutes.

The characteristics attributed to the "great man" are those of the father; thus the concept of the "great man" is a pragmatic one whose coherence lies in the uniformity of infantile psychic reactions. But the psychic overvaluation of the actual father is limited to a short space of time. Due to rivalry and disappointments, the child becomes detached from his parents and adopts a critical attitude toward the father. The child's "family romance," the source of all myth, divides the family in two, making one parent noble, the other humble—a development which marks a change in the child's affective relationship to his parents (pp. 12–13). And so the myth of the hero is born; he takes the father's place and always ends up killing him: "The hero . . . always rebels against his father and kills him in some shape or other" (p. 87). People's attitude toward artists repeats this ambivalence. The cult of the artist is ambiguous in that it consists in the worship of father and hero alike; the cult of the hero is always a form a self-worship, since the hero is the first ego ideal. This attitude is religious but also narcissistic in character, and repeats that of the child toward the father, and of the parents toward the child, to whom they attribute all the "gifts" and good fortune that they granted to themselves during the narcissistic period in infancy. (I develop this theme in chapter 3).

But if the artist is esteemed *like* a God he is nevertheless not God himself, but a substitute. The religion of the father and the cult of art correspond to distinct moments in human evolution, which in turn correspond to different stages in the evolution of the libido. The artistic phase belongs to the animistic phase and corresponds to the narcissistic stage, whereas the religious phase is tied to the stage at which the libido is directed toward objects, the stage of fixation on the parents.[24] Epic poetry and tragedy take the place of the totemic meal and repeat it differently, opening a space that is specific to art. The fact that the deified hero may have preceded the deification of the father in no way weakens the argument, for the deification of the hero foretells the return of the primeval father transformed into a god. In "Group Psychology and the Analysis of the Ego," Freud suggests that the chronological succession would be as follows: mother goddess, deified hero, and god the father.[25]

THE BIOGRAPHICAL ILLUSION

This religious and narcissistic attitude toward artists can be observed at all levels of cultural production. It explains for instance people's interest in biographies—a fact that emerges clearly when biographies are lacking, as in the case of Shakespeare. Biographies never provide any insight into the hero, but rather reveal the infantile attitude that the biographer shares with the reader, one of admiration and narcissistic identification.

Biographers idealize the hero while trying at the same time to reduce the distance separating them from him. Yet it is essential that distance be preserved: the artist and his work must remain "taboo" in a sense,[26] in order to avoid murder and maintain the theological illusion of art.

> Biographers are fixated on their heroes in a quite special way. In many cases they have chosen their hero as the subject of their studies because—for reasons of their personal emotional life—they have felt a special affection for him from the very first. They then devote their energies to a task of idealization, aimed at enrolling the great man among the class of their infantile models—at reviving in him, perhaps, the child's idea of his father. To gratify this wish they obliterate the individual features of their subject's physiognomy; they smooth over the traces of his life's struggles with internal and external resistances, and they tolerate in him no vestige of human weakness or imperfection. They thus present us with what is in fact a cold, strange, ideal figure, instead of a human being to whom we might feel ourselves distantly related. That they should do this is regrettable, for they thereby sacrifice truth to an illusion, and for the sake of their infantile phantasies abandon the opportunity of penetrating the most fascinating secrets of human nature. (*Leonardo*, 11:130)[27]

Freud lays equal emphasis, however, on biographers' desire to overcome distance: "The biographer's justification also contains a confession. It is true that the biographer does not want to depose his hero, but he does want to bring him nearer to us.... And it is unavoidable that if we learn more about a great man's life we shall also hear of occasions on which he has in fact done no better than we, has in fact come near to us as a human being" ("Address Delivered in the Goethe House at Frankfurt," 21:211–212). The double aim of biographers, to maintain and to overcome distance, is not a contradiction in Freud's discourse; it simply reflects the child's ambivalence toward his parents. The attitude of the biographer, like that of the art lover toward the artist, repeats the artist's attitude toward his father, which includes both admiration and the desire to kill. That is why, in the public eye, the artist is the image of father and hero alike. The ambiguous status Freud assigns him corresponds to the ambivalent attitudes of the artist and the public, who are both prisoners of their infantile prototype. In any event, to admire the hero is to continue to admire the father indirectly, for the hero acquires his status only through identification with the father and the desire to take his place. (I shall take up this problem again later.) The "murder" of the father by the artist is achieved by means of regression to the narcissistic stage.

Freud's unmasking of this dynamic, however, consists in showing that the theological attitude of worship toward the artist is simply the other side of narcissistic identification. Both the religious and the animistic phase must be surpassed by the scientific phase—that of adulthood—characterized by renunciation of the pleasure principle and subordination of object choice to reality.[28] Freud substitutes the search for the laws governing not only the pathological and the normal, but also the "sublime," for biographers' idealization of artists. The continuity between the "great man" and the reader is established not by means of identification, but because the behavior of both can be explained by the same psychic mechanisms. The psychoanalyst acts as a mediator between the artist and the public, between the father and the son, because the son cannot bear to look his father in the face any more than he can confront his own unconscious, just as primitive peoples cannot safely look at their chieftain.[29] The contribution of psychoanalysis to biography is to have shown that the artist is no more a great man or hero than we are. The "application" of psychoanalysis to art completely reverses the stance of traditional biographies. "Killing" the father means renouncing both the theological idealization and the narcissistic identification which prompts the subject's desire to be his own father. Yet it also means respecting the superego, which alone makes possible the renunciation of the pleasure principle.

A NEW ICONOCLAST

For Freud, then, the problem of art is linked to that of the father, that is, to the Oedipus complex. Art, like all cultural phenomena, is a reaction formation which stems from this complex (see note 9). The traditional ideology of art unmasked by Freud is both theological and narcissistic, and is ultimately founded on the oedipal relation; it is the victim of infantilism and of an incompletely resolved Oedipus complex. Freud's attitude toward the artist repeats the attitude toward the father: admiring overvaluation, a reluctance to "kill" him, then the end of these illusions and also of childhood. The reign of pleasure and illusion gives way to that of necessity, and likewise, a period of admiration for the artist is followed by the analysis of his works: the "sublime" obeys the same laws as the normal and the pathological. Behind the great man one discovers the child, or even the neurotic. What is more, it is not only artistic "creation" that constitutes a reaction to the Oedipus complex. For Freud, the oedipal moment always forms the thematic core of works of art as well, whether it presents itself to the reader as a paradigmatic model as in Sophocles' *Oedipus Rex*, or does so indirectly as a variation of, and difference from, a universal structure, as is the case with *Hamlet*, *The Brothers Karamazov*, *The Tales of Hoffman*, Jensen's *Gradiva*, and the works of Leonardo da Vinci.

In this light, it is clear why the "application" of psychoanalysis to art encountered such strong resistance despite Freud's cautious and modest declarations: art was the last bastion of narcissism. Psychoanalysis inflicted on man one of his three great narcissistic wounds by deconstructing the idea of the autonomous subject endowed with self-mastery and self-sufficiency, indeed a subject who is his own creator.[30] Narcissism, however, is essentially a death force, so to denounce it is to work in favor of Eros. Later we shall have to examine more closely the role played in art by Eros and the death impulses respectively, as well as the situation of art in the economy of life. (I study this problem in chapter 3.)

If Freud's texts are read, then, using the deciphering

method he himself taught us, distinguishing what he *says* from what he actually *does* in his discourse,[31] one realizes that despite language that still belongs to the closure of metaphysics, Freud is not a prisoner of his ideology. He does not, however, demystify ideology as Marx does, because for Freud the epistemological rupture necessarily involves a psychic break: one can break with ideology only by renouncing the wish to be one's own father. Knowledge of ideology is futile if it is not accompanied by instinctual renunciation[32]—the latter is at least a necessary, if not a sufficient, condition of the former. Instinctual renunciation alone makes it possible to adopt a scientific attitude and accept necessity. In support of this claim, let me cite this fine passage from the *New Introductory Lectures*:

> The strength of Marxism clearly lies, not in its view of history or the prophecies of the future that are based on it, but in its sagacious indication of the decisive influence which the economic circumstances of men have upon their intellectual, ethical, and artistic attitudes. A number of connections and implications were thus uncovered (*aufgedeckt*), which had previously been almost totally overlooked. But it cannot be assumed that economic motives are the only ones that determine the behaviour of human beings in society.... It is altogether incomprehensible how psychological factors can be overlooked where what is in question are the reactions of living human beings.... In an earlier enquiry I also pointed out the important claims made by the super-ego, which represents tradition and the ideals of the past and will for a time resist the incentives of a new economic situation. And finally we must not forget that the mass of human beings who are subjected to economic necessities also undergo the process of cultural development—of civilization as other people may say—which, though no doubt influenced by all the other factors, is certainly independent of them in its origin. (22:178–179)[33]

2

FASCINATION BY ART

Art as a Cognitive Model of Psychic Processes

At the time at which the Oedipus complex gives place
to the super-ego [the parents] are something quite magnificent; but later they lose much of this.
New Introductory Lectures, 31, 22:64

Repeating the attitude of every child toward the father, initially Freud seems, like the general public, to have boundless admiration for the artist. This fascination is motivated by the superiority of the artist's knowledge over science (as traditional psychology would have it). It is expressed in the letters to Fliess regarding the analysis of the works of Meyer, *Oedipus Rex*, and *Hamlet*,[1] and is repeated and further justified in *The Interpretation of Dreams* and *Delusions and Dreams in Jensen's 'Gradiva.'* In these works the knowledge of artists, and specifically of poets, is utilized by Freud as a counterproof of his first topic and, in particular, corroborates the discovery of the Oedipus complex.[2] The mythic paradigm of Oedipus and its corollary, Hamlet, guarantees the universality of the oedipal structure that Freud has just discovered through his self-analysis and through the analysis of dreams. But in order for these works to play this role, it must already be possible to interpret them psychoanalytically, for they convey the meaning sought only in their masking of it through distortion. Hence the circular character of Freud's demonstration, which necessarily refers us from the first moment to the second, when the work is subjected to the analytic method.

What is more, in *The Interpretation of Dreams* as well as in the essay on *Gradiva*, Freud always takes as his model for understanding unconscious processes—specifically dream processes—the procedures of works of art, whether literature or painting, perhaps without sufficiently highlighting the importance of these models. Between the *Traumdeutung* and the essay on *Gradiva*, *Jokes and Their Relation to the Unconscious* takes dreams as the analogical model for the techniques of jokes, at the same time that jokes serve as counterproof for the interpretation of dreams. *Jokes* leads to the second moment in Freud's procedure, which is begun in the truly pivotal essay on *Gradiva*.

ART AS THE MODEL FOR UNDERSTANDING THE PSYCHE

The Interpretation of Dreams
     The Work of Art and Typical Dreams. In *The Interpretation of Dreams*, the comparison with literary works intervenes when Freud broaches the analysis of typical dreams, which are characterized by their relation to a universal fantasy, linked to infantile wishes common to all men. The expression of these wishes is less disguised in these dreams than in others and therefore always engenders anxiety. Since these typical dreams have the same source in everyone, they have a universal meaning. The usual method of interpreting them by association is no longer sufficient, so to the genetic method there must be joined a method which could be called structural, and which is circular. The first method enables one to

attain to the singular; the second, to the universal. The principle that renders typical dreams intelligible is found in a postulated universal structure, for which Freud finds the archetypal models in certain literary works. The latter display this structure with practically no distortion, as a sort of basic type which allows one to grasp the variations, whose degree of distortion varies in proportion to the degree of repression, according to the principle of "the secular advance of repression" articulated in *Totem and Taboo*.[3]

The first example Freud gives is the dream of nudity and the embarrassment it engenders. It is marked by the contrast between the dreamer's shame and the spectators' indifference. Its ultimate explanation lies in the infantile wish to exhibit oneself. The counterproof, in Freud's view, is an Andersen tale, "The Emperor's New Clothes," treated in Fulda's *The Talisman*.

> We possess an interesting piece of evidence that the dream in the form in which it appears—partly distorted by wish-fulfilment—has not been rightly understood. For it has become the basis (*Grundlage*) of a fairy tale.... Hans Andersen's fairy tale tells us how two imposters weave the Emperor a costly garment which, they say, will be visible only to persons of virtue and loyalty. The Emperor walks out in this invisible garment, and all the spectators, intimidated by the fabric's power to act as a touchstone, pretend not to notice the Emperor's nakedness.
>
> This is just the situation in our dream.... The imposter is the dream and the Emperor is the dreamer himself; the moralizing purpose of the dream reveals an obscure knowledge of the fact that the latent dream-content is concerned with the forbidden wishes that have fallen victim to repression. (*The Interpretation of Dreams*, 4:243–244)

At the basis of this dream there is thus a memory (or a fantasy) from our childhood: "It is only in our childhood that we are seen in inadequate clothing both by members of our family and by strangers—nurses, maid-servants, and visitors; and it is only then that we feel no shame at our nakedness" (p. 244). In a note, Freud indicates that there is a naked child in the story as well. Since the joy of nakedness can be read in the myth of Adam and Eve also,

Freud concludes that paradise is nothing other than the sum of all the fantasies of our childhood. Freud's intertextual and circular method is initiated here. But if exhibitionism as a neurotic symptom, the typical dream, Andersen's tale, and religious myth all have as their ultimate foundation the same wishful fantasy, they are nonetheless not identical. Along with similarities, the structural method indicates differences; or rather, it is only in the differences that the unique and universal type can be read. The specificity of the different signifiers is respected, even if a single signified is postulated as an explanatory principle. All that is given is the different texts, and the infinite referral from one to the other, their mutual clarification of each other, proves the method's operational character. Yet in *The Interpretation of Dreams*, poetic works in particular are the models referred to, and only incidentally, it seems, is religious myth alluded to. But in his "Preface to the Third Edition of 1911," Freud indicates that later editions will have to lay more emphasis on the links between different psychic and cultural productions.

> I may even venture to prophesy in what other directions later editions of this book—if any should be needed—will differ from the present one. They will have on the one hand to afford closer contact with the copious material presented in poetry, in myths, in linguistic usage and in folklore; while on the other hand they will have to deal in greater detail than has here been possible with the relations of dreams to neuroses and mental diseases. (pp. xxvii–xxviii)

The relationship between these different productions, unsuspected up to this time, is due to the fact that the impressions of earliest childhood, whatever their content, tend to repeat themselves. Their ever-different reproduction is always the fulfillment of a wish.

Here Freud goes no further than to conclude that "there can be no doubt that the connections between our typical dreams and fairy tales and other poetic motifs (*Dichtungsstoffen*) are neither few nor accidental" (p. 246). The poet is an instrument for the transformation of dreams, the proof being that "he may follow the process in a reverse direction and so trace back the imaginative writing to a dream" (p. 246). Thus typical dreams can be understood through the model of folk tales, which can play this role because they are themselves reducible to dreams, of which they are only transformations. Freud's second counterproof in the analysis of typical dreams of exhibition is the legend of Ulysses and Nausicaä. One critic, Keller, says that Homer has evoked this situation from the deepest and most lasting essence of humanity. For Freud, this is indeed so, but this essence is not of a metaphysical nature: "The deepest and eternal essence of man, upon whose evocation in his hearers the poet is accustomed to rely, lies in those impulses of the mind which have their roots in a childhood that has since become prehistoric" (p. 247). The legend of Nausicaä is merely a "concrete expression" of a dream.

In the analysis of the second example of typical dreams, dreams of the death of parents, brothers, and sisters, Freud proceeds according to the same method. These dreams are founded on the infantile Oedipus complex. As a counterproof, Freud cites a very large number of archaic myths and legends whose theme is the unlimited power of the father. The conflict between father and son is the favorite theme of dramatists, and Freud remarks, with Aristotle, that this theme assures them success: "An author who, like Ibsen, brings the immemorial struggle between fathers and sons into prominence in his writings may be certain of producing his effect" (p. 257).

Then follows the exposition of Sophocles' *Oedipus Rex*, a paradigmatic model in which the Oedipus complex can be read almost without distortion.[4] For Freud, its universality is confirmed by the universal success of the play—a sign of the universal emotional effect which is the tragic effect, and which reveals "this universal and profound essence" he was speaking of previously.

> This discovery is confirmed by a legend that has come down to us from classical antiquity: a legend whose profound and universal power to move can be understood only if the hypothesis I have put forward in regard to the psychology of children has an equally universal validity.... The action of the play consists in nothing other than the process of revealing, with cunning delays and ever-mounting

> excitement—a process that can be likened to the work of a psycho-
> analysis—that Oedipus himself is the murderer. (pp. 261–262)

The other interpretations fail to account for this effect, in particular
the theological interpretation, which explains it by means of the
contrast between the all-powerful will of the gods and the vain
efforts of man pursued by misfortune. Apart from the fact that the
theological interpretation is susceptible to being deconstructed by
psychoanalysis, Freud shows that the theme invoked, chosen by
certain modern authors, leaves the spectator unmoved. Consequently if we modern men are still moved by Sophocles' tragedy,
it is due not to the contrast between fate and human will, but rather
to the nature of the material that serves to illustrate this contrast:
"There must be something which makes a voice within us ready to
recognize the compelling force of destiny in the *Oedipus*, while we
can dismiss as merely arbitrary such dispositions as are laid down
in [Grillparzer's] *Die Ahnfrau* or other modern tragedies of destiny"
(p. 262).

In the last analysis, if the destiny of Oedipus moves us it
is

> because it might have been ours—because the oracle laid the same
> curse upon us before our birth as upon him. It is the fate of all of
> us, perhaps, to direct our first sexual impulse towards our mother
> and our first hatred and our first murderous wish against our father.
> Our dreams convince us that that is so. King Oedipus, who slew his
> father Laïus and married his mother Jocasta, merely shows us the
> fulfilment of our own childhood wishes. (p. 262)

The end of the text closes the circle again: the text began
with evidence from antiquity, with the Oedipus legend confirming
the discovery of the Oedipus complex and making possible the
interpretation of typical dreams about the death of family members;
now, dreams confirm the universality of the Oedipus complex, just
as in the play itself a dream provides the key to Sophocles' tragedy.
In the last analysis, the dream is what makes possible the interpretation of tragedy: "The legend of Oedipus sprang from some
primaeval dream-material which had as its content the distressing

disturbance of a child's relation to his parents owing to the first stirrings of sexuality" (pp. 263 264). This is proved beyond the shadow of a doubt by the text of Sophocles' tragedy itself. Jocasta consoles Oedipus, who is troubled by the oracle, by reminding him of a dream that nearly all men have and which, she thinks, can have no significance:

> Many a man ere now in dreams hath lain
> With her who bare him. He hath least annoy
> Who with such omens troubleth not his mind.

Freud comments, "The story of Oedipus is the reaction of the imagination to these two typical dreams" (p. 264).[5]

Thus in Freud's work the meaning of dreams is founded on the tragedy and, in reciprocal and circular fashion, the meaning of the tragedy is founded on dreams.

A second counterproof comes next in the analysis of *Hamlet*, which repeats *Oedipus Rex* differently, the variation being due to the difference in the degree of repression from one epoch to another; so that Oedipus behaves like a psychotic, so to speak, and Hamlet like a hysterical neurotic. The comparative structural method and the associative genetic method are both necessary here.

> But the changed treatment of the same material reveals the whole difference in the mental life of these two widely separated epochs of civilization: the secular advance of repression in the emotional life of mankind. In the *Oedipus* the child's wishful phantasy that underlies it is brought into the open and realized as it would be in a dream. In *Hamlet* it remains repressed; and—just as in the case of a neurosis—we only learn of its existence from its inhibiting consequences. (p. 264)[6]

Artistic Procedures and Dream Processes. But in *The Interpretation of Dreams*, works of literature and art serve as models for understanding not only typical dreams, but also all of the primary processes at work in dreams. It is perhaps in this text, in which Freud is more interested in making dreams intelligible than in works of art, that he best helps us to think through what constitutes the specificity of art, especially that of painting and the figurative writing that is proper to it.

Indeed for Freud, dreams are less a language than a kind of figurative writing whose signs must be successively transferred into the language of the dream thoughts. In the section of "The Claims of Psycho-Analysis to Scientific Interest" titled "The Philological Interest of Psycho-Analysis," Freud writes:

> If we reflect that the means of representation in dreams are principally visual images and not words, we shall see that it is even more appropriate to compare dreams with a system of writing than with a language. In fact the interpretation of dreams is completely analogous to the decipherment of an ancient pictographic script such as Egyptian hieroglyphs. In both cases there are certain elements which are not intended to be interpreted (or read, as the case may be) but are only designed to serve as "determinatives," that is to establish the meaning of some other element. The ambiguity of various elements of dreams finds a parallel in these ancient systems of writing; and so too does the omission of various relations, which have in both cases to be supplied from the context. (13:177)[7]

It is of fundamental importance that the model for this writing be hieroglyphic or Chinese writing—in any case, nonphonetic writing. The grammar and logic of dreams are not those of consciousness, which, as Derrida has shown,[8] are linked to the *logos* and the *phōnē*. The logic of dreams is an archeo-logic that makes use of the primary processes that govern the unconscious system. As a writing before the language of reason, its best model turns out to be artistic writing, which is also irreducible to any other, and also obeys its own structural laws. There is a text proper to dreams, just as there is one proper to works of art, a text which is symbolic and symptomatic of a conflict of forces kept in balance by an invisible acupuncturist, comparable to the director in Antonin Artaud's "Theater of the Seraphim." [9] Psychic material, like artistic material—except when it is literary—does not speak. But it has specific laws of expression which are to be transcribed (perhaps an impossible task) into the language of consciousness. That is why the comparison with works of art is, to a certain extent, more effective than the one with archaic forms of writing.

For after all [these ancient languages and scripts] are fundamentally intended for communication, that is to say, they are always, by whatever method and with whatever assistance, meant to be understood. But precisely this characteristic is absent in dreams. A dream does not want to say anything to anyone. It is not a vehicle for communication; on the contrary, it is meant to remain ununderstood. . . . The one certain gain we have derived from our comparison is the discovery that these points of uncertainty which people have tried to use as objections to the soundness of our dream-interpretations are on the contrary regular characteristics of all primitive systems of expression. (*Introductory Lectures*, 15:232)

Works of art occupy an intermediate position between dreams and archaic writing. Like dreams, they do not speak and their final aim is not communication. Like dreams, they seek to conceal their meaning to a certain extent. But like writing, they must remain comprehensible, although the nature of the material they use must force them to invent their own system of expressiveness to produce the *signifiance* of their signifiers.[10]

Dreams have no means at their disposal for representing these logical relations between the dream-thoughts. . . . The incapacity of dreams to express these things must lie in the nature of the psychical material out of which dreams are made. The plastic arts of painting and sculpture labour, indeed, under a similar limitation as compared with poetry, which can make use of speech; and here once again the reason for their incapacity lies in the nature of the material which these two forms of art manipulate in their effort to express something. Before painting became acquainted with the laws of expression by which it is governed, it made attempts to get over this handicap. In ancient paintings small labels were hung from the mouths of the persons represented, containing in written characters the speeches which the artist despaired of representing pictorially. (*The Interpretation of Dreams*, 4:312)

This text makes possible a better understanding of what Freud means by "expressiveness" in art in "The Moses of Michelangelo," and why it is impossible to separate "form" from "content." Though Freud's terms may suggest that he is still a prisoner of the logic of representation, in fact he no longer is: like dreams, of which

it is the paradigm, art is governed by processes that have an expressiveness proper to it that engender a specific text which is not
the translation of a previous text; in dreams as in art there is but
one text, which conveys its meaning only through its distortion. The
true meaning, the "latent content," is given only in the manifest
content. As in the case of dreams, the expressiveness of art is never
complete, partially because of censorship, but above all because of
the nature of the material used. The text of art, like that of dreams,
"represents" in the sense of *Darstellung* more than of *Vorstellung*; that
is, in the sense of a figuration more than of a representation referring
to a presence and a signified external to it. Still, if dreams and art
are governed by their own laws of expressiveness, they are nonetheless not independent of the force invested in them, nor of the
force that censors them. It is no longer a matter of representation
at this point, however, but rather of a conflict of forces that are
structured by the texts of art and dreams alike.

Thus, in both dreams and art, logical relations are expressed by means of specific figurative procedures, and any variation
in the figuration transforms the meaning of the relations
established.

> Just as the art of painting eventually found a way of expressing (*zum
> Ausdruck zu bringen*) by means other than the floating labels at least
> the *intention* of the words of the personages represented— affection,
> threats, warnings, and so on—so too there is a possible means by
> which dreams can take account of some of the logical relations
> between their dream-thoughts, by making an appropriate modifica-
> tion in the method of figuration characteristic of dreams. (pp. 313–
> 314)

In the entire chapter on dream work and, in particular, the
section devoted to the work of figuration, it is remarkable that Freud
always takes painting or sculpture as a paradigm, revealing in that
very gesture the irony of the texts where he declares himself to be
a mere layman and attributes exclusively to professional aestheticians formal knowledge of the work and the appreciation of its
aesthetic value! Thus in order to explain, for example, the relation
between the somatic source of dreams and the representation in-

vested in them—dreams making use of somatic sources only when such sources are associated with a content representative of the dreams' psychic source—Freud compares the somatic sources to cheap materials that one uses whenever one needs to, whereas a precious material prescribes the way it is to be used. When an artist must work with a rare stone, its size, color, and markings determine the figuration, whereas when using a uniform and plentiful material he can give shape to what he previously imagined (p. 237).

Then too, the general structure of dreams is often compared to an architectural edifice. Freud compares one of his dreams to the facade of an Italian church that has no relation to the building behind it (p. 211). The relation between daydreams and the childhood memory is analogous to the one between a Roman palace in the baroque style and the ancient ruins it stands upon. The pavements and columns of the ancient edifices furnished the material for the modern palaces (5.492). This analogy should prevent the interpretation of dreams and art as translations of memories or fantasies: a new structure which has its own laws is erected upon an older one without ever replacing it completely, and using it as material to give birth to a perfectly original work.

Moreover, dream censorship and the distortions resulting from it are compared to the constraints placed on the poet and the political writer. Freud quotes Mephistopheles in Goethe's *Faust*: "Das Beste, was du wissen kannst,/Darfst du den Buben doch nicht sagen. [After all, the best of what you know/Cannot be told to boys.] The distortion of expression varies in proportion to one's vulnerability to censorship: one may have to avoid certain forms of attack, or be content with allusions, or disguise subversive revelations in an innocent form; "The stricter the censorship, the more far-reaching will be the disguise and the more ingenious too may be the means employed for putting the reader on the scent (*Spur*) of the true meaning" (4:142). Freud then compares the transposition of the dream of one of his women patients to the censorship of letters, which blackens out the passages that seem subversive. The censorship of letters "caviars" these passages, whereas dream censorship replaces them with an incomprehensible murmur.

There is, however, a great difference between these two

forms of censorship, for while it is automatic in dreams, in letters it is deliberate. By means of the analogy he advances, doesn't Freud seem to indicate that an unconscious censorship plays a role in letters as well? If deliberate censorship alone intervened in literary works, would they still be works of art? Yet Freud also indicates by this analogy that in art, the secondary processes of the preconscious-conscious system necessarily play a role, although the linkage of the work of the primary and secondary processes in the work of art poses a problem. In spite of these differences, the consequence of censorship is the same in both cases: transformation. The dream is a transformer of affects and a combinatory of representations that must take account of the possibilities of figurability.[11] The same is true for art, which transforms dreams by giving them concrete expressions and making them communicable.

> [The dream-work] does not think, calculate or judge in any way at all; it restricts itself to giving things a new form (*umzuformen*). It is exhaustively described by an enumeration of the conditions which it has to satisfy in producing its result. That product, the dream, has above all to evade the censorship, and with that end in view the dream-work makes use of a *displacement of psychical intensities* to the point of a transvaluation of all psychical values. The thoughts have to be reproduced exclusively or predominantly in the material of visual and acoustic memory-traces, and this necessity imposes upon the dream-work *considerations of figurability*. (5:507)[12]

Freud also finds in the procedures utilized by art a model for understanding the different processes used by dreams to evade censorship. Thus the process of condensation, which transforms psychical interconnections into vivid ideational content, has as its analogue the work of early sculptors who expressed by size the rank of the persons they represented.

> A king is represented twice or three times as large as his attendants or as his defeated enemies. A sculpture of Roman date would make use of subtler means for producing the same result. The figure of the Emperor would be placed in the middle, standing erect, and would be modelled with especial care, while his enemies would be prostrate at his feet; but he would no longer be a giant among dwarfs. The

bows with which inferiors greet their superiors among ourselves today are an echo of the same ancient principle of figuration. (5:596)

The formation of composite images—a particular kind of condensation, involving at least one element in common among several images and producing an image with vague contours, analogous to the image obtained by taking several photographs on the same plate—seems an unusual and bizarre procedure. Nevertheless,

> the counterparts to the construction of these composite figures are to be found in some creations of our imagination, which is ready to combine into a unity components of things that do not belong together in our experience—in the centaurs, for instance, and the fabulous beasts which appear in ancient mythology or in Böcklin's pictures. The "creative" imagination, indeed, is quite incapable of *inventing* anything; it can only combine components that are strange to one another. But the remarkable thing about the procedure of the dream-work consists of thoughts—a few of which may be objectionable and unacceptable, but which are correctly constructed and expressed. The dream-work puts these thoughts into another form, and it is a strange and incomprehensible fact that in making this translation (this rendering, as it were, into another script or language) these methods of merging or combining are brought into use. After all, a translation normally endeavors to preserve the distinctions made in the text and particularly to keep things that are similar separate. The dream-work, quite the contrary, tries to condense two different thoughts by seeking out (like a joke) an ambiguous word in which the two thoughts may come together. (*Introductory Lectures*, 15:172–173)

In *The Interpretation of Dreams*, Freud indicates that in both art and dreams, the psychical process at work is the same, but not the intention that presides over the formation. The fantastic creations of waking life are determined by the impression they are meant to make; composite dream images are dictated by a factor that is extraneous to their form: the common element in the dream thoughts. Still, dreams do not neglect the purely formal characteristics of figuration, so in this respect the paradigm of the work of art is even more appropriate than in other instances.

So it is, then, that Freud reflects on the expressiveness of certain formal characteristics: the differences in the sensory intensity of various images, like the differences in clarity of various parts of a dream or of entire dreams in relation to one another, correspond to differences in the work of condensation, and thus differences in the level of investment in the various representations: "The lack of clarity shown by the dream was a part of the material which instigated the dream: part of this material, that is, was represented in the *form* of the dream. *The form of a dream or the form in which it is dreamt is used with quite surprising frequency for representing* (Darstellung) *its concealed* (verdeckten) *subject matter"* (*The Interpretation of Dreams*, 4:332).[13]

The expression of one dream thought can even affect another's means of expression and dictate the choice of one expression over another. Poetic work is what serves as a model here.

> Any one thought, whose form of expression may happen to be fixed for other reasons, will operate in a determinant and selective manner on the possible forms of expression allotted to the other thoughts, and it may do so, perhaps, from the very start—as is the case in writing a poem. If a poem is to be written in rhymes, the second line of a couplet is limited by two conditions; it must express an appropriate meaning, and the expression of that meaning must rhyme with the first line. No doubt the best poem will be one in which we fail to notice the intention of finding a rhyme, and in which the two thoughts have, by mutual influence, chosen from the very start a verbal expression which will allow a rhyme to emerge with only slight subsequent adjustment. (5:340)

After Freud, Ferdinand de Saussure and Roman Jakobson also show that every poetic text is dictated by a pre-text which induces it. Says Jean Starobinski on the subject of Saussure's theory of hypograms:

> Thus the poetic message (which is a *fact of speech*) is not constituted only *with* words borrowed from the language, but also *upon* nouns or words given one by one: the poetic message then appears as the useless luxury of the hypogram. Thus, one arrives at this conclusion, implicit in all of Saussure's research, that the words in the work issue

directly from other words that precede them, and that *they are not directly chosen* by a shaping consciousness. The question being "What lies directly behind the line of poetry?" the answer is not the creative *subject*, but the inductive *word*. Not that Saussure goes so far as to obliterate the role of the artist's subjectivity; but it still seems to him that it can produce its text only after being traversed by a pre-text.[14]

As in art, considerations of figurability are fundamental; dream thought is unutilizable in its abstract form and must be put into pictorial language. Thus logical relationships are represented by relations of simultaneity: "Here [dreams] are acting like the painter who, in a picture of the School of Athens or of Parnassus, gathers into one group all the philosophers or all the poets. It is true that they were never in fact assembled in a single hall or on a single mountaintop; but they certainly form a group in the conceptual sense" (4:314).

In a general way, dreams repeat, in their figurative procedures, archaic modes of thought. Thus, in representing frequency by accumulation, dreams restore the primitive conception of the word. Today, the term "frequency" signifies repetition in time, whereas formerly it meant accumulation in space. The dream work thereby changes temporal relations into spatial relations.[15] This mode of thinking, as well as the use of symbols common to popular representations—folklore, myth, legends, sayings, proverbs, and the wordplay in fashion at a given time—authorizes us to characterize the writing of dreams, like that of art (to the extent that it plays the role of paradigm) as archeological writing. Although it is not meant to be understood, it is no more difficult for its readers to grasp than hieroglyphic writing. Like the latter, it must be deciphered, but resistance is encountered in the process. Indeed—and this is the fifth point of comparison—Freud resorts to the model of art once again to enable us to understand both his method and the resistance to it. In "On Psychotherapy," he distinguishes analytic technique from the method of hypnotic suggestion by means of the same contrast that Leonardo da Vinci uses to distinguish painting from sculpture: *per via di porre* and *per via di levare*, by adding something and by taking something away (7:260). The model that makes the resistance to dream interpretation intelligible is found in the inhibitions that the artist experiences when he tries to use reason to constrain his imagination. Freud cites a fine text by Schiller recommending to Koinez the free association of ideas.[16]

> The ground for your complaint seems to me to lie in the constraint imposed by your reason upon your imagination. I will make my idea more concrete by a simile. It seems a bad thing and detrimental to the creative work of the mind if Reason makes too close an examination of the ideas as they come pouring in—at the very gateway, as it were. Looked at in isolation, a thought may seem very trivial or very fantastic; but it may be made important by another thought that comes after it, and, in conjunction with other thoughts that may seem equally absurd, it may turn out to form a most effective link. Reason cannot form any opinion upon all this unless it retains the thought long enough to look at it in connection with the others. On the other hand, where there is a creative mind, Reason—so it seems to me—relaxes its watch upon the gates, and the ideas rush in pell-mell, and only then does it look them through and examine them in a mass. You critics, or whatever else you may call yourselves, are ashamed or frightened of the momentary and transient extravagances which are to be found in all truly creative minds and whose longer or shorter duration distinguishes the thinking artist from the dreamer. You complain of your unfruitfulness because you reject too soon and discriminate too severely.[17]

Thus, whether the issue is the source of dreams, their general structure and their relation to the dreamer's past, censorship, the primary processes that come into play in the dream work, the interpretation of dreams, or the resistance of the dreamer who receives the interpretations, the model chosen by Freud to render dreams comprehensible is always art. It is an analogical model only, for Freud is very careful to suggest the differences in intention and to recognize the deliberate use of certain procedures by art, whereas in dreams they are always used automatically. In art, the secondary processes always join the primary processes; art gives concrete expression to the narcissistic writing of dreams and makes it communicable. It can be said that art and dream are two dialects, different but not opposed,[18] for in spite of the differences, they have three points in common

First, art, like the dream, has its own expressive procedures, and considerations of figurability are fundamental; both are untranslatable into the language of reason. Each language has its own dream language, each dreamer has his own grammar, just as each artist has his own style. Unconscious thoughts are no more translated or even transcribed into the language of dream than into the language of art: there is no preexisting text, but rather a single text.[19] The text of the latent content is nothing but a set of traces that are discovered in the details of the manifest text or of the work of art, details which seem insignificant and inexpressive. The distortion of the text implies not the presence of a transformed originary text, but the absence of originary meaning which, as such, is a requirement for a substitute and for "supplementarity." The latter is originary and can be read in repetition and distortion. The text of the dream and of art alike, which come second insofar as they are substitutes, are originarily and originally second, and are irreducible to any other text. To suppose that the text of one system in the psychic apparatus can be transcribed into another is to shortchange the psychic economy. Psychic writing is a single energy system. The dream spares speech, which is itself treated like a thing, but one cannot change writing into speech.[20]

Second, the dream, like art, is a figurative enigma. The analogies Freud establishes between dreams and art, far from inviting us to remain at the level of the manifest meaning of dreams, suggest that we read works of art as dreams are read: Freud's predecessors would not have made the mistake of confusing a rebus with a descriptive drawing if they had suspected that the drawing itself can sometimes be an enigma.[21]

But finally, if art in turn is an enigma, it is because the primary processes must be at work in it not only deliberately but also unconsciously. If the former were true they would lose their character as primary processes. Is the artist aware of these processes or not? Is he a being worthy of so much admiration if the processes used are at work unconsciously? This would bring him close to the dreamer—and no longer just analogically—as well as to the neurotic, who is played with by his processes rather than being one who plays with them. The repeated paradigm of the work of art in the *Traumdeutung* invites us to pass to the second stage: analyzing the work of art in order to discover in it the same processes that are at work in dreams. It is in his essay on Jensen's *Gradiva* that the conversion is most clearly made: the work of art as theoretical model becomes in turn an object of investigation.

Gradiva

The Poet's Endopsychic Knowledge. In *Delusions and Dreams in Jensen's 'Gradiva,'* Freud openly displays admiration for writers and poets who, without putting forth any effort, possess surer knowledge of the morbid and normal psychic processes than psychiatry and traditional psychology. But little by little the polemical aim of the work is revealed: the novel supports psychoanalysis in imposing its new views of the psyche on the general public and on psychiatry. However, Freud is surprised at the "knowledge" of these novelists, and his investigation leads him to the second stage of the analysis. He realizes that the hero Norbert's dreams and delusions can all be interpreted in the same way as real dreams and delusions, and that the distance between the latter and fictional characters must be reduced. For this reason, Freud "applies" psychoanalysis to the heroes' behavior just as he would to patients, and then moves from the heroes to the author himself, whose complexes he tries to deduce. The work engenders its father, for the characters must be understood as the author's doubles, a projection of his fantasies and ideals. The writer, however, is unaware of this connection, just as he is unaware that he "truthfully" describes psychic processes. For instance, Jensen subtitled his work A *Fantasy*,[22] though the subtitle A *Psychiatric Study* would be more fitting. But the artist supposedly has more a divining intuition of psychic processes than a knowledge of them.

Thus, to cite only a few examples, the time during which the fictional couple in *Gradiva* is supposed to have been in love, two thousand years ago, is said by Jensen to correspond to the real and forgotten period of childhood, and the burial of Pompeii to repression. Indeed, Freud himself often uses the burial of ancient cities under new cities as an image for this process.[23] In the *Gradiva* essay, he pays homage to the keen insight of the novelist who is said to have sensed the resemblance between an episode in individual psychic life and a historical event isolated from the history of humanity. Jensen is also supposed to have guessed that neurotic symptoms and dreams were compromises. Most turns of phrase in the novel seem to be mixtures of archeological terms currently in use (the hero is an archeologist) and repressed erotic aspirations. But to grant Jensen's novel "scientific" status, the psychoanalytic method must already be applied in reading it: the text does not literally state the meaning Freud gives it. Here we come upon the circle of interpretation once again: Jensen's work corroborates psychoanalytic discoveries on the condition that their truth already be granted and that they be "applied" to the work—which is to say that the author plays out the knowledge without possessing it, and because of that he makes a work of art. It is no surprise, then, that he called his work a "fantasy" and needs a psychoanalytic interpretation to tell its meaning.

By following Freud's text closely, we shall see how his admiration for the artist's "knowledge" gradually subsides in the course of the interpretation of Jensen's novel. He begins by affirming the superiority of the poet over the man of science: "Poets are valuable allies and their evidence is to be prized highly, for they are apt to know a whole host of things between heaven and earth of which our philosophy has not yet let us dream. In their knowledge of the mind they are far in advance of us everyday people, for they draw upon sources which we have not yet opened up for science" (p. 8). To anyone who might object that the author's point of view is always subjective, Freud responds by adding to the genetic method the comparative structural method, which makes it possible to read the universal through the play of variations: "The second method would seem to be far the more effective and perhaps the only justifiable one, for it frees us at once from the difficulties involved in adopting the artificial concept of 'writers' as a class. On investigation this class falls apart into individual writers of the most various worth—among them some whom we are accustomed to honor as the deepest observers of the human mind" (p. 9).

Later on, Freud recognizes the superiority of the knowledge of painters over that of science, and claims that an etching by Félicien Rops, for example, better than any rational explanation, suggests the process of repression. The artist has illustrated

> the typical case of repression in the life of saints and penitents. An ascetic monk has fled, no doubt from the temptations of the world, to the image of the crucified Saviour. And now, the cross sinks down like a shadow, and in its place, radiant, there rises instead the image of a voluptuous, naked woman, in the same crucified attitude. Other artists with less psychological insight have, in similar representations of temptation, shown Sin, insolent and triumphant, in some position alongside of the Saviour on the cross. Only Rops has placed Sin in the very place of the Saviour on the cross. He seems to have known that, when what has been repressed returns, it emerges from the repressing force itself. (p. 35)

Then, Freud elevates Jensen's "fantasy" to the status of a psychiatric study.

> My readers will no doubt have been puzzled to notice that so far I have treated Norbert Hanold and Zoe Bertgang, in all their mental manifestations and activities, as if they were real people and not the author's creations, as if the author's mind were an absolutely transparent medium and not a refractive or obscuring one. And my procedure must seem all the more puzzling since the author has expressly renounced the portrayal of reality by calling his story a "phantasy." We have found, however, that all his descriptions are so faithfully copied from reality that we should not object if *Gradiva* were described, not as a phantasy but as a psychiatric study. (p. 41)

However, though two points seem unconvincing and arbitrary, knowledge of the author's sources makes it possible to account for them on the basis of psychic laws. Everything in the work is explicable and conforms to reality: "The author has presented us with a perfectly correct psychiatric study, on which we may measure our understanding of the workings of the mind" (p. 43). Nevertheless, Freud seems surprised by this "knowledge": "It is strange enough that the author should have done this!" (p. 43).

To consider the work of a novelist as a study in psychiatry, to judge it from the point of view of truth—doesn't this eliminate the specificity of the work of art and ensnare one in the traditional logic of the sign? Shouldn't one leave it to science (here, to psychiatry) to do its own studies? Freud partially responds to these objections. To believe in the specificity of art and in the value of "a pure aesthetics" is to fall victim to the division of the human faculties and to be a prisoner of language. Traditional psychiatry, which claims to be scientific, knows less of man than the novelist, and conversely, knowledge does no harm to beauty, for the poet's knowledge is not spoken directly as such.

> The truth is that no true poet has ever obeyed this injunction. The description (Schilderung) of the human mind is indeed the domain which is most his own; he has from time immemorial been the precursor of science, and so too of scientific psychology. . . . Thus the poet cannot evade the psychiatrist nor the psychiatrist the poet, and the poetic treatment of a psychiatric theme can turn out correct without any sacrifice of its beauty" (p. 44).[24]

Hence the mediation of psychoanalysis is necessary to disclose the knowledge behind beauty—a truth which is figured in Jensen's novel. The relation between the two characters Norbert and Zoe plays out the one that exists between the artist and the psychoanalyst. Of course, Norbert is not presented as an artist, but as an archeologist. Yet he is sick, and it is while admiring the statuette of Gradiva that he begins to have delusions. The archeological investigation serves as a counterinvestment to his erotic desires, which are indirectly discharged in the fantasies conjured up about a work of art. That Zoe plays the role of the psychoanalyst is openly stated by Freud at the beginning of chapter 4: "The emergence of Zoe as a physician . . . arouses a new interest in us" (p. 87).

If we accept this reading within the reading, we can say that the artist, like Norbert, plays out the unconscious processes without understanding them and that the psychoanalyst alone, like Zoe, can interpret them. There are not two texts—an unconscious text and a conscious text—but a single one which is a compromise, and which is understood in different ways by Norbert and Zoe. Norbert, like the artist, has an endopsychic perception of the psychic processes, especially of repression. He has a dim, symbolic intuition of the meaning of the burial of Pompeii, whereas it is clearly understood by Zoe. Freud underlines the frequency with which the novelist puts into the mouths of his heroes phrases filled with double entendre. While Norbert's speeches have, for him, only the meaning perceived by consciousness, Zoe perceives their unconscious meaning as well. She, on the other hand, uses ambiguous language deliberately: the first meaning is adapted to Norbert's delusion, whereas the second goes beyond it and translates delusion into the language of unconscious truth. Indeed, mind and art have triumphed in being able to put delusion and truth into the same formula. The predominance of ambiguous language in *Gradiva* is not accidental. It is an extension of the double determination of the symptoms insofar as this language itself constitutes a symptom and results from compromise between the conscious and the unconscious. Moreover, the method of cure used by Zoe is the same as that of the psychoanalyst: she brings amorous transference into play. Norbert, the archeologist, is doomed by the death drive without Zoe, whose name means "life": like psychoanalysis, she works in the service of Eros.

From this study of Jensen's *Gradiva*, we can draw a certain number of conclusions. First, the artist has knowledge superior to that of traditional psychology and psychiatry:

> In short, let us ask whether the poet's conception of the genesis of a delusion can hold its own before the judgement of science. And here we must give what will perhaps be an unexpected answer. In fact, the situation is quite the reverse: it is science that cannot hold its own before the achievement of the author. Science allows a gulf to yawn between the hereditary and constitutional preconditions of a delusion and its creations, which seem to emerge ready-made—a gulf which we find that our author has filled. Science does not as

yet suspect the importance of repression, it does not recognize that in order to explain the world of psychopathological phenomena the unconscious is absolutely essential, it does not look for the basis of delusions in psychical conflict, and it does not regard their symptoms as compromises. (p. 53)

Second, the novelist confirms the results of psychoanalysis. But third, rather than asking, like the psychoanalyst, what the motivations are for the repression of Norbert's erotic desires, the novelist merely describes his behavior perfectly. In this respect, the novelist does not do scientific work; he does not seek to explain. Thus, despite his repeated signs of admiration for the artist's knowledge, Freud ends up wondering how the poet could have acquired the same knowledge as the physician, or at least could have been able to behave *as if* he knew the same things (p. 55). It is a question not so much of knowledge as of acting as though one had knowledge. Elsewhere Freud speaks of it as "endopsychic perception." But what does that mean, and what is the truth value of such knowledge? This perception is the privilege of poets, primitive peoples, certain mental patients, and the superstitious. It is never manifested directly, but only indirectly, projected into works of art, myths, and paranoid delusions; it is always manifested in distorted fashion and is displaced from the inside outward. Thus this obscure recognition "of course has nothing of the character of a recognition" (*The Psychopathology of Everyday Life*, 6:258, n. 2).

It is therefore not surprising that the poet knows without knowing and that he cannot locate the place of truth in his discourse. Endopsychic perception is a shadowy perception: what is projected into the external world is witness to what has been obliterated from consciousness, as in paranoia, where repressed relationships are projected outside.

In this disorder . . . repression is effected not by means of amnesia but by a severance of causal connections brought about by a withdrawal of affect. These repressed connections appear to persist in some kind of shadowy form (which I have elsewhere compared to an endopsychic perception), and they are thus transferred, by a process of projection, into the external world, where they bear witness to what has been effaced from consciousness. ("Notes Upon a Case of Obsessional Neurosis," 10:231–232)

The same process comes into play in primitive man during the animistic phase.

> We are thus prepared to find that primitive man transposed the structural conditions of his own mind [in a footnote Freud adds, "which he was aware of by what is known as endopsychic perception"] into the external world; and we may attempt to reverse the process and put back into the human mind what animism teaches as to the nature of things. (*Totem and Taboo*, 13:91)[25]

Generally speaking, the mythological view of the world "*is nothing but psychology projected into the external world*" (*The Psychopathology of Everyday Life*, 6:258).

The superstitious person performs the same displacement: "*Because* the superstitious person knows nothing of the motivation of his own chance actions, and *because* the fact of this motivation presses for a place in his field of recognition, he is forced to allocate it, by displacement, to the external world" (p. 258).

Finally, in "Creative Writers and Daydreaming" (1908), Freud shows that the poet borrows his materials from the popular treasure-house of myths, legends, and folk tales, and that "myths, for instance, are distorted vestiges of the wishful phantasies of whole nations, the *secular dreams* of youthful humanity" (9:152).

It is true that in this text Freud takes as examples works of no great originality and authors devoid of pretension. As for the others, we can say that they project into their works their own fantasies, which must nonetheless have a basis in universal truth in order to interest the reader. Whether it be the obscure knowledge of the paranoiac, that of the primitive man in the animistic phase, or that of the superstitious person and the poet, united, in spite of their difference, by a single narcissistic structure, Freud proposes to transform that knowledge into a science; that is, into metapsychological knowledge.

By the end of his analysis, Freud's admiration for the poet's knowledge is thus strongly attenuated, for the poet is the plaything of knowledge—this is what is called inspiration—more than its possessor. Whereas ideologies fashion illusions into "truth," the poet presents truth as illusion, and is himself under an illusion. The only respect in which the poet is superior to other people is that he is more introverted, which allows him to tune in to repressed relations.

Finally, we can draw another important conclusion from the study of *Gradiva*; namely, that the text of art is a compromise which can be understood in its obvious, literal meaning or in its unconscious meaning, depending on whether or not one "applies" the analytic method, which starts with details neglected by all other methods of reading. Indeed, the postulate of this reading is that the smallest detail has its significance: "Our author . . . as we have long since realized, never introduces a single idle or unintentional feature into his story" (*Delusions and Dreams*, 9:68). That the author himself may be ignorant of this purpose should be no surprise, since he writes without recognizing his own knowledge. When Jensen was asked if he was acquainted with the interpretation of the dreams in *Gradiva* given by Freud,[26] he answered in the negative, and ill-humoredly, saying that his fantasy alone had created *Gradiva* and had taken pleasure in it. When Freud later did his study of Stefan Zweig's "Four-and-Twenty Hours in a Woman's Life," the author no more recognized his own intentions in the proposed interpretation than had Jensen. Freud did not conclude from this disagreement that he had made a mistake, nor that he had projected his own ideas into the work, thereby giving it a tendentious interpretation; for the author's declared intentions are of little importance. One must rely on the text which alone speaks "truthfully": its meaning is to be found in it and should not be looked for outside, even though it is not independent of the writer's psyche. But what must the psyche itself be, if not a text, in order to be "represented" by a text? How are the text of the work and the text of life connected with one another? Is it not the text of the work alone that structures the life of the writer into a text, by structuring his fantasies? However this may be, Freud, in his studies of both Jensen and Stefan Zweig, gives his interpretation on the basis of the novelist's words alone:

"[We have] given the story almost entirely in the author's own words," he says (*Delusions and Dreams*, 9:43). At the conclusion of the *Gradiva* essay, he writes:

> Our opinion is that the author need have known nothing of these rules and purposes, so that he could disavow them in good faith, but that nevertheless we have not discovered anything in his work that is not already in it. We probably draw from the same source and work upon the same object, each of us by another method. And the agreement of our results seems to guarantee the fact that we have both worked correctly. Our procedure consists in the conscious observation of abnormal mental processes in other people so as to be able to elicit and announce their laws. The author no doubt proceeds differently. He directs his attention to the unconscious in his own mind, he listens to its possible developments and lends them artistic expression instead of suppressing them by conscious criticism. Thus he experiences from himself what we learn from others—the laws which the activities of this unconscious must obey. But he need not state these laws, nor even be clearly aware of them; as a result of the tolerance of his intelligence, they are incorporated within his creations. We discover these laws by analysing his writings, just as we find them from cases of real illness; but the conclusion seems inescapable that either both of us, the writer and the doctor, have misunderstood the unconscious in the same way, or we have both understood it correctly. (p. 92)

Regarding "Four-and-Twenty Hours in a Woman's Life," Freud opposes the avowed intentions of the artist to what his text says: "This little masterpiece ostensibly sets out only to show what an irresponsible creature woman is, and to what excesses, surprising even to herself, an unexpected experience may drive her. But the story tells far more than this. If it is subjected to an analytical interpretation, it will be found to represent . . . something quite different" ("Dostoevsky and Parricide," 21:191). The declared intentions are only a facade given to the story by the author to veil the analytic signification. The text is thus tissue that hides, or masks, its meaning: only certain details hidden in the woof of the material provide the thread that makes it possible to discover (*aufdecken*) the secret of the text: "It is characteristic of the nature of artistic creation that the author, who is a personal friend of mine, was able to assure me, when I asked him, that the interpretation which I put to him had been completely strange to his knowledge and intention, although some of the details woven into the narrative seemed expressly designed to give a clue to the hidden traces of it" (p. 192).

This true meaning is here said to be related to a male fantasy: every man's desire to be initiated into sexual life by his mother in order to fight against masturbation. For Freud "such an interpretation is so extremely obvious that it cannot be resisted" (pp. 191–192).

Thus, if one must go from the declared intention to the text itself, the latter cannot say something other and something more than what the author says about it unless it is subjected to an analytic interpretation. Freud's return to the text is not a return to its literal sense, which he himself rejects. Rather, he invites us, starting from the text itself, to find its "true" meaning—the only one that makes it possible to attribute meaning to everything that is literally said in the text; once the interpretation is complete, nothing should remain enigmatic. This true meaning exists nowhere but in the text and is read in the gaps in the text that it fills in.

Thus *Delusions and Dreams in Jensen's 'Gradiva'* is a pivotal text in which Freud moves from an admiring attitude toward artists to a certain disillusionment. The work of art, once a paradigmatic model confirming psychoanalytic knowledge, acquires a different status, itself becoming an object of investigation. The artist does not really know what he is saying and says more than he thinks he says, which is why Plato was already banishing poets, among others, from his ideal city. Inspiration is a form of delusion, and the poet has no control over the truth or nontruth of his discourse. For inspiration, a concept belonging to the theological ideology of art, Freud substitutes the working concept of the primary process. The artist is closer to the neurotic, the primitive man, and the child than to the "great man"; and as Freud says later in his study of Leonardo, every great man has something childish about him. The work of art which had served, up to this point, as a counterproof to psychoanalytic discoveries must itself be subjected to interpretation. Only in this way can the counterproof be founded—though this will be a circular and therefore hypothetical foundation.

Freud's later recapitulative texts clearly confirm that *Delusions and Dreams in Jensen's 'Gradiva'* is a pivotal work. For instance, in the "Appendix to the Second Edition" of the *Gradiva* essay (1912), Freud writes:

> In the five years that have passed since this study was completed, psycho-analytic research has summoned up the courage to approach the creations of imaginitive writers with yet another purpose in view. It no longer merely seeks in them for confirmations of the findings it has made from unpoetic, neurotic human beings; it also demands to know the material of impressions and memories from which the author has built the work, and the methods and processes by which he has converted this material into a work of art. (9:94)

Similarly, in "An Autobiographical Study," he claims: "I was able to show from a short story by W. Jensen called *Gradiva*, which has no particular merit in itself, that invented dreams can be interpreted in the same way as real ones and that the unconscious mechanisms familiar to us in the 'dream-work' are thus also operative in the processes of imaginative writing" (20:65). And finally, in "On the History of the Psycho-Analytic Movement": "Another path led from the investigation of dreams to the analysis of works of imagination and ultimately to the analysis of their creators—writers and artists themselves. At an early stage it was discovered that dreams invented by writers will often yield to analysis in the same way as genuine ones (*Gradiva*)" (14:36).[27]

Beginning with the *Gradiva* essay, then, there is a change in outlook. The work of art serves knowledge less than it becomes an object of knowledge. Though poets' descriptions can serve to illustrate knowledge, they cannot take its place. To think they can would be to forget the role disguise necessarily plays in art and to forget its aim to seduce, to procure for the public certain affective ends. Which is to say that art is subject to the pleasure principle, whereas science tries to renounce it.

Up till now we have left it to the writer to depict for us the "necessary conditions for loving" which govern people's choice of an object, and the way in which they bring the demands of their imagination into harmony with reality. The writer can indeed draw on certain qualities which fit him to carry out such a task: above all, on a sensitivity that enables him to perceive the hidden impulses in the minds of other people, and the courage to let his own unconscious speak. But there is one circumstance which lessens the evidential value of what he has to say. Writers are under the necessity to produce intellectual and aesthetic pleasure, as well as certain emotional effects. For this reason they cannot reproduce the stuff of reality unchanged, but must isolate portions of it, remove disturbing associations, tone down the whole and fill in what is missing.... Moreover they can show only slight interest in the origin and development of the mental states which they portray in their complete form. In consequence it becomes inevitable that science should concern herself with the same materials whose treatment by artists has given enjoyment to mankind for thousands of years, though her touch must be clumsier and the yield of pleasure less. These observations will, it may be hoped, serve to justify us in extending a strictly scientific treatment to the field of human love. Science is, after all, the most complete renunciation of the pleasure principle of which our mental activity is capable. ("A Special Type of Object Choice Made by Men," 11:165)

3

FREUD'S METHOD OF READING

The Work of Art as a Text to Decipher

*Looking at her, one could not help thinking of the poet's
words: "Her mask reveals a hidden sense."
Studies on Hysteria, 2:139*

THE DREAM AS THE PARADIGM OF THE WORK OF ART

The first stage of Freud's procedure made possible the confirmation of dream analysis by means of art works—literary symbolism could corroborate the symbolism of dreams. In the second
stage, dream interpretation makes it possible to uncover the primal
foundations underlying the motifs of art works and the secular
transformations of repression. The method of interpreting works of
art is borrowed from the interpretation of dreams. It has the same
aim of discovering the archaic beneath what appears to be new,
and makes possible the understanding of themes borrowed from
individual or collective memory. But what is original and primal is

always also originary and essential: the raw material is sexual and is constituted by the oedipal structure. Thus Freud's method is always at once genetic and structural; it takes account of both repetition and difference. The change in perspective between the first stage and the second is very clear if we compare The Interpretation of Dreams with "Revision of the Theory of Dreams" (Lecture 29 of the New Introductory Lectures) dating from 1932. If Freud writes in this lecture that the manifest content of dreams is reminiscent of the motifs of certain literary works by virtue of the situations and images it depicts, he does so in order to make dream interpretation the model for understanding artistic motifs, and not the reverse, as in the Traumdeutung.[1]

> Our work of interpretation uncovers (aufdecken), so to speak, the raw material (Rohstoff), which must often enough be described as sexual in the widest sense, but has found the most varied application in later adaptations. Derivations of this kind are apt to bring down on us the wrath of all non-analytically schooled workers, as though we were seeking to deny or undervalue everything that was later erected on the original basis. Nevertheless, such discoveries are instructive and interesting. The same is true of tracing back the origin of particular themes in plastic art, as, for instance, when M. J. Eisler (1919), following indications in his patients' dreams, gave an analytic interpretation of the youth playing with a little boy represented in the Hermes of Praxiteles. And lastly I cannot resist pointing out how often light is thrown by the interpretation of dreams on mythological themes in particular. Thus, for instance, the legend of the Labyrinth can be recognized as a representation of anal birth: the twisting paths are the bowels and Ariadne's thread is the umbilical cord. (22:25)

THE TEXT AS SYMPTOM

The primal matter of art works is covered over by later edifices that hide it and is transformed beyond recognition—exactly as in dreams, neurotic symptoms, or any other psychic production. This explains why the work of art is an enigma or a riddle to be deciphered, and why Freud terms his method one of discovery (*Auf-deckung*) or of unmasking (*Entlarvtung*).[2] Only the latter makes it possible to perceive the enigma as such. For what is an enigma? It is not an extraordinary and rare phenomenon, but only seems so to anyone who fails to pay attention to certain details, or assumes that they can be insignificant. But for Freud, for whom the cardinal rule in the interpretation of dreams and all other psychic and cultural productions is not to neglect a single detail,[3] the enigma is apparently everywhere: "These are the most difficult problems that are set to us, but their difficulty does not lie in any insufficiency of observations; what present us with these riddles (*Rätsel*) are actually the commonest and most familiar (*vertrautesten*) of phenomena" (*New Introductory Lectures*, 22:81).

The enigma is everywhere, because the meaning that is always postulated is always absent in its plenitude. It is given only in distorted form through a chain of signifiers which are always already substitutive. Every text is lacunary, full of holes—the holes that it covers with its tissue in order to hide them. Yet the tissue that masks reveals at the same time by perfectly adopting the contours of what it veils. Continuity bespeaks discontinuity, just as meaning does the lack of meaning. And conversely, discontinuity—disruption of meaning in the details—bespeaks meaning and a deeper continuity. It is in its very veiling that the text displays what it is hiding,[4] which is to be found nowhere as a present meaning. The "text-as-tissue" is also a form of protection against what is given only in its distortion, and in the means of its distortion—protection against censored desire and the possible punishment of castration. Every text is the product of conflicting forces. The result of a compromise, it "speaks" simultaneously desire, transgression, and possible punishment; in particular, it speaks the desire for incest and its prohibition, which are the very foundation of culture. The text is a compromise between Eros and the death drive as well, for every disruption of meaning implies that the death drive is at work in the shadows, while every link implies the work of Eros. If it is true that the distortion of a text is comparable to a murder, every text bears the traces of it. The tissue of the text hides these traces in giving them away, or gives them away in hiding them. What Freud writes of bungled actions in *The Psychopathology of Everyday Life*, he might have written of any text: "The substitute names (*Ersatz-namen*) no longer strike me as so entirely unjustified as they did before the matter was elucidated: by a sort of compromise they remind me just as much of what I wanted to forget as of what I wanted to remember; and they show me that my intention to forget something was neither a complete success nor a complete failure" (6:4). And later on: "I am very often faced with the task of discovering, from the patient's apparently casual utterances and associations, a thought-content which is at pains to remain concealed but which cannot nevertheless avoid unintentionally betraying its existence in a whole variety of ways" (6:80).

The "enigmatic" character of all psychic productions thus stems from their lacunary character, which is in turn a result of castrating censorship. The text is given only in its difference, its deferral, its alteration, its transformation, as the variant of a type which is never present—an originary substitute, a translation devoid of an original text. The cutting done by censorship is linked to originary repression. If the latter must play a role in the text of language and of art, it is because for the unconscious, a link—even a verbal one—is the same thing as physical contact, as is clearly seen in obsessional neurosis and in the prohibitions of primitive peoples. But in every society the incest taboo, insofar as it forbids certain types of contact, is at the basis of all prohibition in discourse. In *Totem and Taboo* Freud writes, "The prohibition does not merely apply to immediate physical contact but has an extent as wide as metaphorical use of the phrase 'to come in contact with'. Anything that directs the patient's thoughts to the forbidden object, anything that brings him into intellectual contact with it, is just as much prohibited as direct physical contact" (13:27). And farther on: "It is further to be noticed that the two principles of association—similarity and continuity—are both included in the more comprehensive concept of 'contact.' Association by contiguity is contact in the literal sense; association by similarity is contact in the metaphorical sense" (p. 85).

If the enigma of the text is linked to a disruption, an originary repression, a castration, and the prohibition against contact, one can say that it refers to the enigma par excellence: femininity.

"Throughout history people have knocked their heads against the riddle of the nature of femininity," Freud remarks in the *New Introductory Lecture* titled "Femininity" (22:113). Woman is enigmatic because she lacks a penis. Freud reminds us that it is she who invented weaving (*weben*) in order to veil her nudity; that is, to hide the fact that she has nothing to hide: to cover over a hole (*verdecken*; p. 132).[5] In Freud's view, the spider (*Spinne*) that weaves is a symbol of the phallic mother (p. 24). Indeed the text is such a symbol only because it is tissue that hides, clothing that conceals, through fear of castration. That is why one could not choose a better paradigm of the dream than the Andersen tale "The Emperor's New Clothes." The dream, like the work of art, is tissue; like an imposter, it covers the latent content with a costly and invisible garment (the manifest content). But only the "good and loyal subjects" (the psychoanalysts) see nudity without being afraid; that is, only they are able to do the unmasking, to point to the holes under the clothing without being afraid of castration.

In "The Rat Man," Freud compares his patient's imaginative creation in dreams to an epic poem (I shall come back to this comparison) in which the sexual desires toward the mother and sister, as well as the premature death of the latter, were connected to the father's punishment of the little hero; he remarks, "It was impossible to unravel this tissue of phantasy thread by thread (*Es gelang nicht, dieses Gewebe, von Phantasiem hüllengen Faden für Faden abzuspinnen)*" (10:207, n. 1). But if woman is an enigma it is because man exists, and because in man and woman alike there is a refusal of femininity;[6] what is enigmatic is originary bisexuality. In the *New Introductory Lecture* "Femininity," Freud writes: "Some portion of what we men call 'the enigma of women' may perhaps be derived from this expression of bisexuality in women's lives" (22:131). Freud, who like Oedipus is a solver of riddles, discovers that the fundamental riddle is that of man, but only insofar as there is femininity, femininity which is refused. The very riddle of life is asked by children in the form of the question "Where do babies come from?"—a riddle which the masculine sex reduces to "the enigma of women."

Every text is a compromise between desire and its prohibition, between Eros and the death drive, and thus also between the masculine and the feminine. One might well ask whether to some extent in certain of Freud's texts, Eros is not assimilated to the masculine and the death drive to the feminine.[7] (If so, Artaud's thought would be very close to Freud's.) The task of one who solves riddles, designated in German by the word *abspinnen*, is the reverse of the spider's: it involves unraveling the threads that cover desire and separate it from its direct expression, reestablishing contact, reintroducing continuity into the chain of the text. The point is to unveil, uncover, unmask, *abspinnen, aufdecken, entlarvten*, what was covered over and woven, *verdeckt* and *gewebt*.

"Interpreting a dream implies assigning a 'meaning' to it— that is, replacing it by something which fits into the chain of our mental acts as a link having a validity and importance equal to the rest," Freud writes (*The Interpretation of Dreams*, 4:96). To lay the text bare is not to find another text behind it. Rather, it means going in search of the collective or individual past whose traces remain in the text itself. What connection is there between the past and its traces? What kind of existence does the past have outside of its traces? What connection is there between the text of art and the other texts dealing with the past? If the work of art is nothing more than a distortion of the past, is it a true "creation"?

MEMORY AND FANTASY

Indeed, Freud shows that both the individual and the collective past are constituted phantasmally by an individual or a people, rather than recovered. He begins by demonstrating this in regard to screen memories (*Deckerinnerung*, a memory that covers over). In chapter 4 of *The Psychopathology of Everyday Life*, "Childhood Memories and Screen Memories," Freud reminds us that his starting point was a strange observation: a person's earliest childhood memories usually have to do with indifferent things of secondary importance, whereas there is no trace (*Spur*) of the important affective impressions of the period (6:43ff.). One might suppose therefore that the criterion of selection in childhood memory is different from that of adult memory. But analytic therapy proves that this hypothesis is unnecessary: "The indifferent memories of childhood owe their existence to a process of displacement (*Verschiebungvorgang*)." They are substitutes (*Ersatz*) for important affective impressions whose direct reproduction meets with resistance. Since the indifferent memories are preserved only because of their association with other repressed memories, "they have some claim to be called 'screen memories'."

The displacement effected by the screen memory can be carried out in two different temporal directions. The screen memory may belong to the earliest years of childhood, while the repressed memory it represents is part of a later period, which is an instance of *retrogressive* displacement (*rückgreifende oder rucklängige*). Or, as is more frequently the case, the displacement works in the other direction, so that an indifferent impression belonging to a later period functions as a screen memory for the repressed memory. The latter is an anticipatory screen memory, or one that has been *displaced forward* (*vorgreifende oder vorgeschoben*). The key memory is behind the screen memory. And finally, there is a third possibility: the screen memory may be contemporary with the impression that it covers over. Generally speaking, screen memories function as counterinvestments intended to maintain repression.

But what is true of screen memories can be extended to include all childhood memories. Analytic examination reveals that there is no guarantee of their accuracy. Most are falsified, incomplete, or have undergone spatial or temporal displacement, but not because of faulty memory. The distortions are due to the intervention of a bias—powerful psychic forces shape and orient our way of evoking the past, just as they render our childhood years incomprehensible. One can only conclude therefore that "in the so-called earliest childhood memories we possess not the genuine memory-trace but a later revision of it, a revision which may have been subjected to the influences of a variety of later psychical forces. Thus the 'childhood memories' of individuals come in general to acquire the significance of 'screen memories'" (6:48).

At this point, can childhood memories be distinguished from fantasies? Freud compares his own childhood memories with scenes elaborated in plastic form, analogous to theatrical performances (*Darstellungen auf der Bühne*). The essay "Screen Memories," which precedes *The Psychopathology of Everyday Life*, compares the construction of childhood memories to that of works of fiction, showing that the process involves projecting several fantasies onto one another (3:315). The fantasies are unconscious because they have a sexual content which can only find expression through allusion and disguise in a scene from childhood: "Every suppressed phantasy of this kind tends to slip away into a childhood scene," a scene privileged by the "innocence" attached to it (3:318). Hysterics proceed in the same manner, with the same motives.

Does memory then differ from fantasy at all, if it is itself a composite product of fantasy? What does in fact distinguish memory is the memory trace whose content provides the fantasy with a point of contact which meets it halfway, so to speak. The remaining content of the fantasy is reworked in such a way as to find other points of contact with the childhood scene, which is transformed in the process. There is thus a sort of mutual transformation of the past by the fantasy and the fantasy by the past, arising from certain memory traces which serve as points of contact between the two.

"The phantasy does not coincide completely with the childhood scene" (3:319), Freud remarks. The childhood memory is thus the result of a complicated process, analogous to the one at work in the formation of hysterical symptoms. We should note that hysteria appears to Freud as the caricature of a work of art.[8] What memories, hysteria, and works of art have in common is that they are phantasmal constructions from memory traces, and have a plastic or theatrical form. All three put the past into play while distorting it. By virtue of this relation to the memory trace, none of the three is really an invention. Their falsity stems from displacement, condensation, substitution, and the combinations made; the processes are the same as those that enter into the elaboration of dreams. The falsifications serve the ends of repression and replace the painful and unpleasant impressions. The important thing is that the falsified memory alone is conscious: "the raw material of memory-traces out of which it was forged remains unknown to us in its original form." Properly speaking, we have no memories *from* childhood.

> It may indeed be questioned whether we have any memories at all *from* our childhood: memories *relating to* our childhood may be all that we possess. Our childhood memories show us our earliest years not as they were but as they appeared at the later periods when the memories were aroused. In these periods of arousal, the childhood memories did not, as people are accustomed to say, *emerge*; they were *formed* at that time. And a number of motives, with no concern for historical accuracy, had a part in forming them, as well as in the selection of the memories themselves. (3:322)[9]

Since fantasies themselves are produced from material acquired from one source or another, they can barely be distinguished from memories.[10] Thus in the writing of *Leonardo da Vinci and a Memory of His Childhood*, Freud actually constructs one of the painter's fantasies, as he says in a letter to Pfister dated March 6, 1910: "I am in the process of editing for this same collection a study of Leonardo da Vinci based on the only childhood fantasy that the man unwittingly left us." And in the *Leonardo* study: "The scene with the vulture would not be a memory of Leonardo's but a phantasy, which he formed at a later date and transposed to his childhood" (11:82). Thus Havelock Ellis' remark regarding the reality or nonreality of the vulture itself in no way weakens Freud's argument: "[Havelock Ellis] objects that this memory of Leonardo's may very well have had a basis of reality, since children's memories often reach very much further back than is commonly supposed; the large bird in question need not of course have been a vulture. This is a point which I will gladly concede" (11:82).

In memories, therefore, the past appears only in distorted form. The meaning of the experience is always given after the fact. Scenes from the past act in deferred fashion (*nachträglich*). At the moment at which a child lives an impression, he does not understand it. He grasps it only when it is relived, at which point he fantasizes the memory, whose meaning can be grasped only in the course of analysis. There are thus three moments: that of lived experience, the moment at which the memory-fantasy is formed, and the one at which it is interpreted.[11]

This after-the-fact temporality runs counter to the linear representation of time in consciousness; Freud's conception of "memories" no longer has anything to do with the logic of representation. Memories are originary substitutive formations that supplement the lack of meaning in past experience. Memory is always already a matter of imagination, just as meaning, rather than being given in the present, is constructed after the fact.

What is true of the individual past is true also of the collective past. The childhood memories of individuals are remarkably analogous to those of whole peoples as they are figured in myths and legends.[12] The historical memory of nations constructs a history in an after-the-fact temporality, based on real events and with a pragmatic aim. All that remains of the actual past is an obscure tradition preserved in legends, which poets—especially epic poets—take hold of. The condition of possibility of an epic poem is the existence of a period of ancient history which must have seemed important, grandiose, and almost always heroic just after it ended, but which is so remote in time that knowledge of it is available "merely" through an obscure and incomplete tradition. If the epic as a literary genre has disappeared over the centuries, it is because history took the place of tradition. The taste for ages past, like the taste for the individual past, stems from dissatisfaction with the present and nostalgia for a fantasized golden age. People "are probably still under the spell of their childhood, which is reflected to them (*gespiegelt*) by their not impartial memory as a time of uninterrupted bliss" (*Moses and Monotheism*, 23:71). The epic poem uses imagination to fill the gaps in the incomplete and vague memories which make up tradition. It thereby shapes the image of the age it wants to reproduce according to its present intentions: "One might almost say that the vaguer a tradition has become the more serviceable it becomes for a poet" (p. 71).

In our time, even the most heroic deeds could not inspire an epic. Indeed, Freud recalls that Alexander complained of not being able to find a Homer to sing his praises. Since for epic poets the ideal of objective truth was lacking, a contrast was possible between the written and the oral tradition; to a certain extent the latter escaped distorting tendencies. The oral tradition is at once the complement to and the reverse of the written account. Nevertheless, the oral tradition can end up being smothered by writing and totally forgotten, so when it returns it does so all the more powerfully.[13] It is understandable, then, that Freud compared the Rat Man's imaginative creations with the formation of an epic poem (10:206–207, n. 1). The neurotic and the poet alike remodel the past using complicated processes intended to efface misfortune or unspeakable acts by means of fantasy. In the patient being treated, the problem is to erase the memory of autoerotic activity by raising the remaining traces of it to the level of object love, just as the historian illuminates the past in light of the present. The fact that most people fantasize the same childhood scenes can be explained by the uniformity of the tendencies contained in the Oedipus complex, which is the nucleus of the neuroses, and by the consistency with which modifying influences later appear. If one accepts the view that this complex itself refers to the real murder of a "primal father," the analogy between the childhood memories of the individual and those of whole peoples is even more appropriate.

Generally speaking, the period of ancient history, which is always grandiose and more or less forgotten by the the people to whom it belongs, corresponds to the prehistory of the child; the obscure and incomplete tradition transmitted through legend corresponds to the memory-fantasy; the later historical period which puts an end to the epic, to the time of analytic interpretation; and repressed oral tradition, to infantile amnesia.

Thus the protohistory of individuals and peoples alike is a phantasmal reconstruction from traces, traces which are insufficient for the constitution of an objective history. The gaps are filled by the fantasies in which desire is invested. Just as history as a science puts an end to epic poetry, so too does the psychoanalyst put an end to phantasmal accounts, and construct the history of the individual.

INTERPRETATION AND CONSTRUCTION

The method of interpreting works of art, modeled on that of interpreting dreams, consists in retrieving individual and collective archaic experience through its distortions. How is such a method possible if the archaic as such is nowhere in existence, that is, if no vestiges of the past remain, but only subsequent elaborations of these vestiges? Since the raw material of memory traces is unknown in its original form, solving the riddle of psychic productions consists neither in digging up the past as if it existed anywhere but in its traces, nor in finding its prefabricated meaning in the unconscious. The riddle is thus a false one, because meaning is nowhere to be found. Solving the riddle, therefore, consists not in retrieving an original full meaning that never existed, but in sorting out the distortions, distinguishing the originary substitutive formations from the later ones. Even what appears to be most primal, however, has already undergone considerable development and distortion. For instance, totemism in the pure state is nonexistent, for it is to be found only "in various stages of decay and disintegration or in the process of transition" (*Totem and Taboo*, 13:4, n. 2). In the same way the "primitive man," insofar as he is understood to be a "natural" man, is a mythic concept like that of the golden age in which there are supposedly no prohibitions against incest and eating taboo foods (pp. 102–103, n. 1). These myths are like "wishful phantasies that are projected onto the past" ("The Taboo of Virginity," 11:200). Indeed, nature as uninhibited spontaneity is a myth, since the original is always already cultural, just as the representative and the substitutive are originary. The "primal" can therefore only be postulated and constituted; "the determination of the original state of things thus invariably remains a matter of construction" (*Totem and Taboo*, 13:103, n. 1).

Since the primal exists nowhere as such but only as the product of a mythic fantasy or of a theoretical construction, what is the difference between these two products? The first does not present itself for what it is but as truth, whereas the second recognizes itself to be a construction and is the product of an elaborate method which is conscious of its own limits. That is why the analytic discovery of the text, which is a construction, arouses resistance in those who prefer to cling to the phantasmal and illusory belief in an original state, a nature without culture, a pure presence and a pure signified.

In what then does the analytic method of interpetation, or solving of riddles, consist, and what are its declared limits? The general method is the one used in the interpretation of dreams, where Freud establishes the same relation between the screen memory and lived experience as between the manifest content of a dream and its latent content.[14] A dream's manifest content is not a transcription or a translation of its latent content, but rather a very specific type of writing. Similarly, memory is a construction of the meaning of lived experience from traces, which are all that remain of the past and which tend to be obliterated themselves by censorship; they can therefore be read only in their effacement in substitutive formations. The traces are clues that put one on the track of the repressed: "If you were a detective engaged in tracing a murder, would you expect to find that the murderer had left his photograph behind at the place of the crime, with his address attached? or would you not necessarily have to be satisfied with comparatively slight and obscure traces of the person you were in search of? So do not let us underestimate small indications; by their help we may succeed in getting on the track of something bigger" (*Introductory Lectures*, 15:27).

The less intent one is on preserving the memory of the past, the greater the number of substitutive formations in which the traces can be indirectly read—formations which play the role of a counterinvestment. However, the starting point for the return of the repressed is precisely that which at once blocks it out and indirectly reveals it.[15] It is therefore difficult to erase all the traces, because their very effacement reveals them in inverted form; and yet, since they stand in relation to a prohibition and the desire to transgress it, man attempts to conceal them just as he himself would try to to escape punishment. Indeed, for the unconscious and for primitive societies alike, the trace and the name are equally taboo. So, for example, a son-in-law will not set foot on the beach once his mother-in-law has traversed it until the tide has washed away the trace of her footsteps, since they are to speak to each other only at a distance and may not pronounce each other's names;[17] to wash away the traces is to efface her name and her person. And conversely, it is possible to reconstitute an identity only from traces.

The importance of the theme of the trace in Freud's work has been strikingly elucidated by Jacques Derrida, who shows the relation between the trace and the reconstitution, after the fact, of the meaning of experience: "The impression has left behind a laborious trace which has never been *perceived*, whose meaning has never been lived in the present, i.e., has never been lived consciously."[17] That is why the best model Freud ever found for the psychic apparatus is that of the mystic writing pad which takes account of both the durable nature of the traces and the ongoing receptivity of the apparatus to new impressions. It is interesting to note that the celluloid cover that represents the Pcs. system (pre-conscious-conscious), whose function is to protect against excitation, is called the *Deckblatt* ["cover sheet"] in German, for the layer that receives the excitations forms no durable trace; the foundations of memory are produced in other systems of supplementarity.[18] The writing engraved on the wax tablet supplements the apperception of the perception, permitting a retrospective reading of its meaning. Only the repetition of the impression in its trace, and its effacement at the moment of its appearance, enable one to read the meaning of the experience. The condition of possibility of its legibility is the contact between the two layers but also the breach between them, that is, continuity and discontinuity, Eros and the death drive, desire and castration. Psychic writing is an originary writing implying the effacement of a simple origin and a system of relations between different conflictual instances.[19] The trace is what remains of what has been repressed and denied, modified and removed from its context. It is not always easy to recognize it, because it repeats the repressed in distorted form. And as Freud shows in *Moses and Monotheism*, the term *Entstellung* means not only "changed in its appearance" but also "displaced" (*verschieben*), which is why interpretation is required (23:43). The latter proceeds from traces in order to construct the meaning of experience.

In *The Interpretation of Dreams*, Freud contrasts his method with others used up to that point. On the one hand, he opposes it to symbolic interpretation, which considers the dream content as a single entity and substitutes for it an analogous intelligible content. It is the fate of most artificial dreams created by poets to be interpreted in this way, though it is worth noting that Freud does not use this method to interpret the dreams of Jensen's heroes. On the other hand, he distinguishes his method from that of deciphering or decoding, which treats the dream like a kind of cryptography in which each sign can be translated by another sign having a known meaning, in accordance with a fixed key. The interpretation in this case does not bear on the dream as a whole but on each one of its elements, as if the dream were a conglomerate, each fragment of which should be assessed separately. But Freud's method is closer to the second than to the first:

> Thus the method of dream interpretation which I practise already differs in this important respect from the popular, historic, and legendary method of interpretation by means of symbolism and approximates to the second or "decoding" method. Like the latter, it employs interpretation *en détail* and not *en masse*; like the latter, it regards dreams from the very first as being of a composite character, as being conglomerates of psychical formations. (4:104)

The Freudian method differs from the decoding method, however, in that the "code" in question is not proper to dreams alone but is characteristic of all unconscious representations. It is to be found in folklore, popular myths, legends, figures of speech, proverbs, and literature, which are but so many dialects of the unconscious. Freud deciphers them using the same code and es-tablishes a circular system of reference among them. Moreover, collective symbolism plays only a secondary role in dreams, the essential thing being the code invented by each individual dreamer. Thus there is no "Book of Dreams" containing master keys to meaning.[20]

> The same unconscious processes, which are at work everywhere, arise from a single method. The psycho-analytic method of investigation can accordingly be applied equally to the explanation of normal psychical phenomena, and has made it possible to discover the close relationship between pathological psychical products and normal structures such as dreams, the small blunders of everyday life, and such valuable phenomena as jokes, myths and imaginative works. ("On Psycho-Analysis," 12:210)

The analysis of details, however, constitutes but one step in the method. Details are the traces or indications to be interpreted in order to construct the meaning of past experience—fragments to be gathered and fitted together like the pieces of a puzzle. The text "Constructions in Analysis," which distinguishes interpretation from construction, deals with the interpretation of a pathological case and has as its goal the retrieval, or construction, of forgotten memories.[21] The material available to the analyst is an aggregate of distorted fragments which constitute the traces of the past. They are found in dreams, in ideas the patient suddenly has in the course of free association, in the offshoots of repressed affects and the reactions against these feelings, and finally in the signs indicating the repetition of affects inside and outside the analytic situation. Using this raw material (*Rohstoff*), the analyst must fashion the "text" of the patient's history, which has only a fragmentary and disparate existence, either in symbolic or economic form. Whereas the patient must *remember* the repressed, the psychoanalyst must "guess," or more accurately, construct, what has been forgotten from the clues it has left behind. Freud then moves from the metaphor of material to be fashioned to that of archeological construction. The words "raw material" are replaced by "debris." The advantage of the second metaphor is that it stresses the necessity of reaching an archaic originary nucleus covered by several successive layers. The work of construction implies that of deconstructing later structures which have functioned as counterinvestments of the repressed. The architectural metaphor also highlights the fact that we are no longer dealing with linear temporality, but rather with overlapping periods of time.

> [The analyst's] work of construction, or, if it is preferred, of reconstruction, resembles to a great extent an archaeologist's excavation of some dwelling-place that has been destroyed and buried or of some ancient edifice. The two processes are in fact identical, except that the analyst works under better conditions and has more material at his command to assist him, since what he is dealing with is not something destroyed but something that is still alive—and perhaps for another reason as well. But just as the archaeologist builds up the walls of the building from the foundations that have remained standing [the return of the repressed], determines the number and position of the columns from depressions in the floor [the lacunae, the gaps in discourse] and reconstructs the mural decorations and paintings from the remains found in the debris, so does the analyst proceed when he draws his inferences from the fragments of memories, from the associations and from the behaviour of the subject of the analysis. Both of them have an undisputed right to reconstruct by means of supplementing (*Ergänzung*) and combining (*Zusammenfügung*) the surviving remains (23:259).[22]

Moreover, the archeologist and the psychoanalyst have the same difficulties. For instance, just as the former must determine the approximate age of his find, so must the latter locate temporally the psychic formations he uncovers; and the fact that an object is found at a given level does not mean that it is contemporaneous with it, for it could have been placed there as the result of a later disturbance. But the psychoanalyst has an advantage. In archeology, important fragments are lost forever and cannot be joined to the pieces at hand which means that archeological reconstructions are merely plausible. But the psychic object whose prehistory is to be reconstructed is quite a different matter: "All of the essentials are preserved, even things that seem completely forgotten are present somehow and somewhere, and have merely been buried and made inaccessible to the subject. Indeed, it may, as we know, be doubted whether any psychical structure can really be the victim of total destruction" (p. 260). Another difference is that the psychical object is more complex than the archeological object. And finally, whereas reconstruction marks the end of the archeologist's work, it is but a preliminary step for the analyst;[23] every construction is merely tentative, since new material requires a new construction and the rectification of previous errors. For this reason construction remains the best term for representing analytic technique, since interpretation is pertinent only to details.

> If, in accounts (*Darstellungen*) of analytic technique, so little is said about "constructions," that is because "interpretations" (*Deutung*) and their effects are spoken of instead. But I think that "construction" is by far the more appropriate description. "Interpretation" applies to something that one does to some single element of the material, such as an association or a parapraxis. But it is a "construction" when one lays before the subject of the analysis a piece of his early history that he has forgotten (p. 261).

If the archeological construction merely acquires a certain degree of plausibility, what is the truth value of the analytic construction? Does the indestructibility of the psychical object guarantee the truth of analytic discourse? What proof does the analyst have of the truth of his constructions? The past, though persistant, is given only in its traces and their effacement. Since its meaning exists only insofar as it is phantasmally reconstructed by the patient, he can never "remember" it, strictly speaking. And though all the essentials are preserved, the repressed always returns differently, for it never merely repeats the identical. The fact that the patient accepts an analytic construction, saying that he seems always to have known what it discloses, does not mean that he recognizes an always already present truth, but merely the link between material he has denied up to that point and the object of an earlier repression. In any case, his acceptance or denial of a construction's value proves neither its truth nor its falsehood; both responses can result from psychic resistances. Because recognition can imply misrecognition and bad faith, the analyst can merely construct a plausible historical truth. Verification of the construction is a practical rather than a theoretical matter, for "truth" in this situation can be known only through its effects on the patient and especially on his dreams, dreaming being a kind of remembering.

> These scenes from infancy are not reproduced during the treatment as recollections, they are products of construction.... [They] are as a rule not reproduced as recollections, but have to be divined—constructed—gradually and laboriously from an aggregate of indications.... I am not of the opinion, however, that such scenes must necessarily be phantasies because they do not reappear in the shape of recollections. It seems to me absolutely equivalent to a recollection if the memories are replaced ... by dreams, the analysis of which reproduce every portion of its content in an indefatigable variety of new shapes. Indeed, dreaming is another kind of remembering, though one that is subject to the conditions that rule at night and to the laws of dream formation. It is this recurrence in dreams that I regard as the explanation of the fact that the patients themselves gradually acquire a profound conviction of the reality of these primal scenes. ("From the History of an Infantile Neurosis," 17:50–51)

But the dream can be considered as a memory only in light of the psychoanalytic construction, which is itself based on the dream. This circular relation dooms interpretation to remain hypothetical and renders its "truths" problematic. Because only the results obtained can attest the value of interpretation, Freud compares his own constructions to psychotic delusions: "Just as our construction is only effective because it recovers a fragment of lost experience, so the delusion owes its convincing power to the element of historic truth which it inserts in the place of rejected reality ("Constructions in Analysis," 23:268).

Thus, since one is referred from construction to construction, from version to version, and from interpretation to interpretation without a nonexistent originary text ever being reached, analysis is necessarily "interminable." And yet since it must be ended, even if only provisionally, termination is justified by the possibility the constructions offer of adding all the various fragments together to form a meaningful whole, thereby filling all the gaps. In this connection Freud advances the metaphor of the puzzle, which appears several times in "The Aetiology of Hysteria" (1896), "Remarks Upon the Theory and Practice of Dream-Interpretation' (1923), and *Moses and Monotheism* (1938). Thus regarding the reality of the infantile scenes described by hysterics, he says in the earliest of these texts:

> But another and stronger proof of this is furnished by the relationship of the infantile scenes to the content of the whole of the rest of the case history. It is exactly like putting together a child's picture-puzzle: after many attempts, we become absolutely certain in the end which piece belongs in the empty gap; for only that one piece fills out the picture and at the same time allows its irregular edges to be fitted into the edges of the other pieces in such a manner as to leave no free space and to entail no overlapping. In the same way, the contents of the infantile scenes turn out to be indispensable supplements to the associative and logical framework of the neurosis, whose insertion makes its course of development for the first time evident, or even, as we might often say, self-evident. (3:205)

When the same metaphor is taken up in the 1923 "Remarks," Freud relies on it once again to establish the certainty of the construction (19:116). But in *Moses and Monotheism*, Freud expresses skepticism in this regard, saying that the fact that all the fragments fit together like the pieces of a puzzle testifies only to the construction's high probability: "Not even the most tempting probability is a protection against error; even if all the parts of a problem seem to fit together like the pieces of a jigsaw puzzle, one must reflect that what is probable is not necessarily the truth and that the truth is not always probable" (23:17).

What is the reason for this change of opinion? Is it because Freud is dealing here with "applied" analysis rather than the analysis of patients? All the reservations he expresses in this text suggest that this is the case, for he could furnish no objective proof of his demonstration; the conclusions drawn from the hypothesis that Moses was an Egyptian were based merely on psychic probabilities. Indeed, he hesitated to publish his essay precisely because he does not want to be classed with the scholastics and Talmudists "who delight in exhibiting their ingenuity, without regard to how remote from reality their thesis may be" (23:17). Still, he makes up his mind to have the piece published because the psychological method goes farther than the existing "objective" methods used by historians, who depend on a Biblical text which has been falsified by censorship. Psychoanalysis takes account of the transformation of legends by repression, and can establish order by making intelligible apparent disorder. The analytic method allows for better interpretation and produces the best results.

> I know myself that my structure has its weak spots, but it has its strong points too. On the whole my predominant impression is that it is worth while to pursue the work in the direction it has taken The Biblical narrative that we have before us contains precious and, indeed, invaluable historical data, which, however, have been distorted by the influence of powerful tendentious purposes and embellished by the products of poetic invention. In the course of our efforts so far, we have been able to detect one of these distorting purposes. That discovery points our further path. We must uncover (aufdecken) other similar tendentious purposes. If we find means of recognizing the distortions produced by those purposes, we shall bring to light fresh fragments of the true state of things lying behind them. (23:41–42)

But if the comparison of the construction to the jigsaw puzzle now attests merely its probability rather than its certainty, it is not only because analysis is being "applied" to a field outside pathology, for even here this method is the best, all things considered. Rather, its limited power results from the fact that the criterion of truth in play here is the logical criterion of coherence: the whole must fit together like the pieces of a puzzle. This criterion is pertinent, however, only to conscious psychic phenomena, not to the unconscious. Scientific method, which is necessarily rational, cannot help but adopt this criterion, but psychic reality obeys a different logic. Thus the construction is necessarily hypothetical, for "what is probable is not necessarily the truth."

Nevertheless, when "applied" to phenomena other than dreams or pathology, and particularly when applied to art, which is what interests us here, the analytic method can be termed hypothetical for other reasons as well. In a text or a work of art, the fragments of the past are given once and for all and are essentially symbolic in character; no analytic relation obtains which would make possible a repetition of affects through transference. What is more, neither the heroes nor the author of a work free associate in the analyst's presence. And finally, the analyst's construction cannot be confirmed by the effects produced on the author, either because he is dead, or because he reacts to the construction put forth by denying or rejecting it. Under these circumstances, which may well lead one to question the legitimacy of applying analysis to art, Freud's precautions in this regard are quite understandable.

His answer, as was the case in *Moses and Monotheism*, is that the analytic method is in any case more useful and produces better results than any other method—especially that of professional aestheticians! Moreover, though it is true that the text does not "react" to an analysis and that the author is not changed by it, the public, by contrast, has a significant affective response that can play the role of the patient's emotional fragments and that proves that the work is an offshoot of the repressed. The associations are made on the one hand by Freud, which is why his texts on art often seem to be written in a confused fashion, but in fact obey a profound logic. On the other hand, free association is played out by the context of the work, as well as by the other works of the author. Finally and most importantly, the work of art, unlike the dream or the neurotic symptom—and this is what fundamentally distinguishes it from them—is a cultural production. Since the author's unique past is at play in the work and must have the power to move all men, it is never prescribed as such, for here the idiosyncratic must at the same time be the most typical. In this connection Freud has shown that in the analysis of "typical" dreams the associative, or genetic, method was inadequate and had to be complemented by a structural method. The latter can thus offset the shortcomings of the genetic method in the analysis of art works as well. Because of these shortcomings, however, as Freud himself says concerning his analysis of Leonardo da Vinci, the analytic interpretation of a work of art is only a "psychoanalytic novel," or even a "delusion" (*Leonardo*, 11:134).

THE WORK OF ART AND FANTASY

Once Freud has explained his method in detail, what link does he establish between a work of art and an artist's past—a unique past which constitutes a variant of universal archaic experience? Can what Freud said of the epic poem be generalized to include all works of art? Can the relation between memory and fantasy be transposed onto the one between fantasy and the work of art? We have seen that the childhood memory, a phantasmal construction, was not the translation or pictorial representation of a preexisting reality, but rather a substitutive formation supplementing the lack of meaning in lived experience and therefore an originary supplement, the only text constitutive of the past as such. This being so, does the work of art translate memory-fantasies, or is it too a completely original return of the repressed? Is it a substitute for memory, a kind of completely original memory; that is, a text which, far from translating fantasy, makes possible the structuring and constituting of fantasy after the fact?

Indeed, art functions as a specific memory which makes possible the reconstruction of the author's fantasies. The fantasy is an account of the author's history after the fact that can be given through using the analytic method, which uncovers the way in which this history has been structured symbolically in a work of art. Here one must read Freud's texts carefully. For though the texts dealing with the relations between traces of the past and fantasies pose no problem, it sometimes seems that the texts treating the relations between fantasy and the work of art posit an expressive link between the two. A cursory reading reveals three successive moments in the artist's life: the moment of lived experience in early childhood to which no meaning is attached; that of the memory-fantasy which makes the former intelligible; and the point at which the work of art translates or expresses this fantasy. If this reading were correct, Freud would indeed be elaborating a psychogenesis of art which obliterates the specificity of his object. In "Creative Writers and Daydreaming," (literally, "The Poet and His Imagination")[24] for instance, he does seem to suggest that poetic creation derives either from universal archaic material—distorted vestiges of the wishful fantasies of all peoples, which are always linked to children's sexual theories[25]— or from an individual's unique fantasy material. At the end of his essay, he acknowledges that he has spoken more about fantasy than poetry: "You will say that, although I have put the creative writer first in the title of my paper, I have told you far less about him than about phantasies. . . . All I have been able to do is to throw out some encouragements and suggestions which, starting from the study of phantasies, lead on to the problem of the writer's choice of his literary material" (9:152).

This derivation must not be understood, however, as a translation or an "expression," because even in a case where the poet finds symbolic material already available, he must rework it: "Even here, the writer keeps a certain amount of independence, which can express itself in the choice of material and in changes in it which are often quite extensive" (p. 152). This holds true all the more in cases where the material being reworked is the author's own.[26] Artistic elaboration is analogous to the elaboration performed by the dream work; the manifest content does not translate the latent content, but is rather the result of a specific type of figurative writing from which alone the text of the latent content can be constituted. Moreover, if Freud emphasizes the importance of childhood memory in the poet's life, it is because poetry is, like daydreaming, "a continuation of, and substitute for, what was once the play of childhood" (p. 152). As Freud shows in his well-known analysis of the *fort-da* game in *Beyond the Pleasure Principle*, the child's game is not the reproduction or repetition of a fantasy (in this case, the fantasy of the mother's presence and absence), but rather a symbolic invention that allows the child to master this absence through an affective discharge (18:14–17). This discharge might have taken a different form—sobbing or shrieking, for example—for another child who found himself in different circumstances. Indeed, to understand this child's play with the spool, one must take account not only of the differential relation between *o* and *a*, but of the way the entire game is staged.[27] It is particularly significant that the child has an excellent relationship with his parents. His symbolic invention makes possible the structuring of his fantasy regarding the mother's presence and absence. The fantasy does not predate the game, for if it did, the child might not have needed to play it. The only element that is repeated is the affective impression—here, a painful one—which, through its very repetition, brings the subject indirect pleasure and also procures for him the more direct pleasure afforded by the discharge of affect and the symbolic mastery over absence.

The same is true for the artist who repeats his childhood play ever-differently. The artist discharges an affect in the course of the creative process and masters it in the work itself. In this connection, Freud and Breuer write that "Goethe did not feel he had dealt with an experience till he had discharged it in creative artistic activity. This was in his case the preformed reflex belonging to affects, and so long as it had not been carried out the distressing increase in his excitation persisted" (2:207).

Once it is created, the work makes possible constitution of one or several fantasies after the fact. If the memory-fantasy is not a repetition of the past but an originary substitute, neither is the work of art a translation of the fantasy; rather, it substitutes for it at the same time that it makes possible its constitution after the fact. The work of art is thus the substitute for a substitute. There are therefore not three moments but two: a past event, affective in character; and the discharge in an art work. The intermediary stage of the fantasy is unconscious, the fantasy being always already presented and distorted in the very play of the work. The unconscious fantasy presumed to be at the source of the work of art is itself a postulate of the analytic method, which infers the fantasy from its reading of the work. As such, it is nothing more than a construction after the fact. In art, as we saw in our consideration of *Gradiva*, the artist's fantasies are put into play before they are understood. Thus for Freud, the relation between fantasy and the work of art is not one of expressiveness, in the sense that term has in the traditional logic of the sign. In his treatment of both fantasy and the work of art, Freud introduces no dissymmetry; neither phenomenon is said to "go back" to an originary signifier. So in what he actually *does*, Freud is not caught in the closure of classical representation, although his language is indeed equivocal in this respect. When he writes in the *Introductory Lectures* that "the creative imagination" is incapable of invention and is satisfied to assemble disparate elements, one might think that the work of art, which is satisfied to combine and distort preexisting fantasies, merely "expresses" them. The concepts "derivation" and "source" might also confuse the reader, since they seem to establish a relation of mechanical causality between the work and the artist's past or the collective past. If this were the case, however, the imagination would scarcely be "creative."

Now, though it is true that the work of art bears the traces of the past, these traces are not to be found anywhere else. In other words, the work does not translate memory in distorted form, but rather constitutes it phantasmally; it is an original memory, the substitute for infantile psychic memory. For anyone who has perfect knowledge of his own history, it would seem that the work of art is neither possible nor necessary, even if the work is consciously fantasized. It is an originary inscription, but one that is always already a symbolic substitute. One can state that for Freud, every representation substitutes for an originary absence of meaning, for one is always referred from substitute to substitute without ever coming back to an originary signified, the latter being merely fantasized by desire. Representation, as *Vorstellung*, is originary. But since Freud's language is suspect in this regard, let us consider once again what Freud *does* in order better to understand what he *says*.

The analysis in *Leonardo da Vinci and a Memory of His Childhood* provides an exemplary case.[28] The *Mona Lisa*'s smile is a translation neither of the smile of Leonardo's model, nor of his mother's real smile, nor of Leonardo's fantasy of his mother's smile. To grasp its meaning one must, paradoxically, refer to the smiles in other paintings by Leonardo or in other works of art, such as Verrochio's figures, or archaic Greek statues. In this way we can see that the Mona Lisa's smile, more than any other, makes us aware of the universal fantasy of the mother's smile as an expression of both tenderness and sensuality—a smile that everyone longs for because it has never existed. "The mother's smile" as such is an artistic invention that makes possible the constitution of individual fantasies. That is why the "Leonardesque smile" is both characteristic of that artist's style and a norm for other painters; it is a kind of type of which the smiles in other works of art can be read as variants. Thus the Mona Lisa's smile is an original inscription, a symbolic substitute for the meaning of an experience in Leonardo's childhood. Yet the model, Mona Lisa, had to smile in order for the work to be possible. For that smile is what allows the return of the repressed, which is tied to Leonardo's relation to his mother in childhood. Moreover, it is this link to the repressed that explains Leonardo's fascination with his model; the seduction was possible only because every perception is preinvested by desire.

Indeed, the reality of the perception is guaranteed only by the artist's attention and his heightened investment of that perception. As Freud says, the return of the repressed is possible only if three conditions are fulfilled: the force of the counterinvestment must be weakened either by morbid processes affecting the ego, or by a redistribution of energy, as happens for example in sleep; the instinctual drives linked to the repressed must be strengthened, as in puberty; and events in the present must produce impressions so similar to the repressed material that they awaken it. In Moses and Monotheism Freud writes, "In the last case the recent experience is reinforced by the latent energy of the repressed, and the repressed comes into operation behind the recent experience and with its help" (23:95). In every case, the repressed material presents itself in distorted form both because resistance has been only partially overcome, and because the material has been modified by recent events.

These conditions seem to have been fulfilled in Leonardo's encounter with Mona Lisa, an encounter that repeats and transforms his affective relationship with his mother, and prompts the sketching of forgotten memory traces in a work of art. Indeed, he meets Mona Lisa at the age of fifty, when there is a resurgence of libido in all men. In Leonardo this altered the play of affects and brought about a redistribution of the energy devoted to science and art. The reawakening of sexuality stimulated creation and lifted the inhibition that had been attached to it.[29] The spectator's fascination with the smile in Leonardo's paintings, like Leonardo's fascination with his model's smile, is explained by the same originary fantasy of the mother's smile. This smile is always already lost, known only later through the very existence of its lack and through the satisfaction brought by the hallucination, the dream, the fantasy, or the work of art. The lack is ever seeking substitutive expressions from which the universal fantasy is structured.

Leonardo's other paintings are all related to the *Mona Lisa*. Together they form a chain of substitutive signifiers which all refer to the same signified—the mother's smile—which exists only in its inscription in the painter's works. All can be read as identical yet differentially related. Freud explains in the following terms why he moves from the study of Mona Lisa's portrait to that of the painting of St. Anne, which he finds "hardly less beautiful."

> It would best agree with our expectations if it was the intensity of Leonardo's preoccupation with the features of Mona Lisa which stimulated him to create the composition of St. Anne out of his phantasy. For if the Gioconda's smile called up in his mind the memory of his mother, it is easy to understand how it drove him at once to create a glorification of motherhood, and to give back (*wiederzugeben*) to his mother the smile he had found in the noble lady. (11:111–112)

The term "to give back" is obviously very ambiguous here, and seems to imply that the mother initially possessed the smile. However, the context makes it clear that "to give back" means to give for the second time in a work of art, the *St. Anne*. For St. Anne is but another symbolic substitute for the mother. The "gift" is as unconscious as the memory of his mother sparked by the sight of Mona Lisa. What must be understood is that the production of the first work was the occasion for a return of the repressed, which allowed Leonardo to express clearly the fantasies of his childhood history. That is why the second painting was necessary: it repeats the smile of the first, but with a difference that is symptomatic of the lifting of repression performed by the *Mona Lisa*. "But although the smile that plays on the lips of the two women is unmistakably the same as that in the picture of Mona Lisa, it has lost its uncanny (*unheimliche*) and enigmatic (*rätselhaften*) character; what it expresses is inward feeling and quiet blissfulness" (p. 112).

Now the enigmatic and uncanny quality of the smile indicates the return of the repressed; indeed in this context the two terms are equivalent. These qualities are not inherent in certain works of art, as is thought by professional aestheticians who neglect them, but rather are characteristic of all art (see my argument above). A work which depicts the enigma par excellence, however, the mother, is that much more enigmatic. yet the uncanniness of the first painting disappears in the second, in which the smile conveys only "quiet blissfulness." That is why the second painting is closer to Leonardo's "historical truth" than the first; it displays the specific form of the fantasy whose structuring took place in the first painting. The composition of the painting of St. Anne, so different from the composition of other painters' treatments of the same theme, is explained by Leonardo's life. Hans Fries, Holbein the Elder, and Girolamo dai Libri seat Anne near Mary and place the child between them. Jacob Cornelisz depicts St. Anne as though in a Trinity. Leonardo's Mary, however, is seated on her mother's knees, leaning forward and reaching her arms out toward the child who is playing roughly with a lamb. The grandmother is looking at Mary and Jesus with a happy smile. Freud remarks, "Only Leonardo could have painted it, just as only he could have created the phantasy of the vulture. The picture contains the synthesis of the history of his childhood: its *details* are to be explained by reference to the most personal impressions in Leonardo's life" (p. 112; my emphasis).

What is important here is that the impressions in the artist's life have been postulated from the composition of his painting, for it is only after analyzing the St. Anne that Freud writes that "his father's mother, Donna Lucia . . . —so we will assume—was no less tender to him than grandmothers usually are" (p. 113). The synthesis of his childhood history does not precede its disguised production in a work of art. There is another striking detail in this painting about which the art critics have argued without being able to account for it satisfactorily, and which is all the more significant since it differs from traditional representations of the theme; that is, the fact that the grandmother is pictured as a young woman. Since Leonardo had had, so to speak, two mothers, he gave two mothers to Jesus. The peculiarity of the position of the two women, like the peculiarity of the grandmother's age, expresses the peculiarity of the life of Leonardo, who was raised by his mother and by his step-mother, who was younger than the mother. The St. Anne is analogous to the composite formations in dreams: "By combining this fact about his childhood with the one mentioned above (the presence of his mother and grandmother) and by his condensing them into a composite unity, the design of 'St. Anne with Two Others' took shape for him" (p. 113).

St. Anne's "blissful smile" is the product of repression, because it marks the artist's denial of his mother's suffering and masks the jealousy she felt when she was forced to give up her son to her rival, just as she had previously given up her husband to her. Just as unconsciously as does the dream, the artist uses the primary processes of combination, condensation, and transformation. The smile in the St. Anne indeed refers back to the same smile as the one in the Mona Lisa, but reveals more clearly, because of its relation to Mary's smile and to Leonardo's repression, that the mother's smile never existed. Though the St. Anne can be understood only in connection with Leonardo's life, it does not translate his life, but is rather a figurative production which is just as original as the manifest content of a dream. One could even say that it is from this painting that the artist could become aware of his fantasy identifying with each other the two women who raised him. In a footnote added to the Leonardo essay in 1919, Freud remarks that it is difficult to trace the outline of the figures of Anne and Mary because they are like badly condensed figures in a dream. Thus what appears to be a technical defect in composition, and causes the painting to be considered "less beautiful" than the *Mona Lisa*, is justified by its hidden meaning, decipherable only by means of analysis: the two mothers in Leonardo's childhood have fused in his mind into a single form.

In a 1923 footnote, Freud compares the *St. Anne* in the Louvre to the celebrated London cartoon, where the same material is used to form a different composition. The forms of the two mothers have fused even more completely, and it is difficult to discern the contours of each. Critics have even said that there appear to be two heads emerging from a single body. The date of the cartoon is not known, and Freud mentions in this regard the disagreement among critics who place it variously before the painting and after it. In Freud's view it could only have preceded the painting, for in the London cartoon, the fantasy of unity is expressed almost as in a dream. The painting on the other hand is closer to the material truth, marking an advance in the lifting of repression and a greater acceptance of the reality of the separation of the two women. One can also see in the painting a kind of counterinvestment of the cartoon's meaning, as if Leonardo's anxiety about his own fantasy had made him want to conceal it in his later work. In the same way, during analytic treatment a gain in awareness may have certain repercussions, such as a renewed outbreak of symptoms. Freud leans toward the first hypothesis, suggesting that between the cartoon and the painting, Leonardo went from a kind of childhood memory, essentially phantasmal in character, to adult memory as it is constituted in the course of analytic treatment. The cartoon corresponds to the time of fantasy, the painting to that of interpretation.

> It would fit in excellently with our arguments if the cartoon were to be much the earlier work. It is also not hard to imagine how the picture in the Louvre arose out of the cartoon, while the reverse course of events would make no sense. If we take the composition

shown in the cartoon as our starting point, we can see how Leonardo may have felt the need to undo the dream-like fusion of the two women—a fusion corresponding to his childhood memory—and to separate the two heads in space (p. 115n).

Leonardo's procedure, which consists in dissociation by displacement, resembles that of the dream, where a particular formal expression of one of the dream thoughts can organize the formal structure of the dream as a whole. Likewise in the painting, a single modification results in the transformation of the entire composition. The fact that the Virgin is forced to lean in order to hold back the infant Jesus who is escaping from her arms is a mere rationalization analogous to secondary revision in dreams.[30]

The smiles of St. John the Baptist and Bacchus are variants of the same type (p. 117). These pictures breathe a mystical air into whose secret one dares not penetrate. Nevertheless, Freud tries to establish their relationship to the other works of Leonardo. In his last paintings, the smiles of these androgynous young men, effeminate in their form and fragility, express a great achievement of happiness. Without being ashamed, they nonetheless seem to want to keep the source of this happiness secret, for it arises from a forbidden, homosexual love; "It is possible that in these figures Leonardo has denied the unhappiness of his erotic life and has triumphed over it in his art, by representing the wishes of the boy, infatuated with his mother, as fulfilled in this blissful union of the male and female natures" (pp. 117–118).

Thus in his last works, Leonardo constructed the meaning of his erotic history. Repression is lifted as far as possible but nonetheless remains, as we see from the transformation of affect, the mysteriousness of the smile, and the disguising of homosexuality, which does not explicitly present itself as such. Moreover, Freud suggests that through art, Leonardo was able to triumph over the unhappiness of his erotic life, and that without it, he would have been neurotic. Art frees the artist from his fantasies, just as "artistic creation" circumvents neurosis and takes the place of psychoanalytic treatment. However, it must be said that the treatment has been played out without being understood. Only the analytic method, taking the work of art as its starting point, can reconstruct the artist's fantasies and their meaning. In this light it is clear why Freud could not accept Pfister's interpretation—wrongly attributed to Freud—according to which the outline of a vulture was discernable in the folds of St. Anne's drapery.[31] Pfister, who was a great admirer of Rorschach,[32] views the work as a picture-puzzle or a projective test; thus to his mind, Leonardo's fantasy of the vulture was projected directly into the work. Freud's note on the subject is full of humor. Despite the interest he acknowledges in Pfister's remark, he appeals to the reader to verify its validity, taking care not to do so himself. In his interpretation, Pfister seems to forget that there is no projection without distortion, and that his case may actually be weakened by the fact that the vulture is so clearly visible in all its details, with its tail pointed straight at the child's mouth, as in Leonardo's fantasy.

The work of art is not the projection of a fantasy, but, on the contrary, a substitute which makes possible its structuring after the fact, allowing the artist to free himself from it. The art work is the originary inscription of the analytic method, what Freud in "Dostoevsky and Parricide" calls "a confession of its author," but only for those who know how to read it.[33]

GENESIS AND STRUCTURE

Because the fantasy does not precede the work but rather is constituted from it, an artist can and must produce several works, each one "expressing" his fantasies more and more clearly. Freud thus advances a principle for dating the works of a particular artist as a function of the degree of repression. Apparently the relation between the various works is the same as the one between the various dreams one has in a single night; a night's dreams form a single entity. They can signify the same thing, or express the same impulses using different means. Often the first dream is the more distorted, while the following one is bolder and more distinct. In order to establish the relationship between dreams it is important to distinguish between those that have a unified form and those that are broken up into fragments, which correspond to isolated nodes of the dreamer's latent dream thought, or to opposing currents in his psychic life. The relation between a long dream—the main dream—and a shorter dream that precedes it is like the relation between a fulfillment and its condition. Often, two dreams that follow each other in succession produce together, in two stages, the fulfillment of a wish; sometimes one of the dreams represents the fulfillment of a wish, while the other represents its punishment.[34] Freud seems to have used this model to link Leonardo's works to one another. It is interesting to note that Freud's conclusions regarding dreams and works of art alike are based exclusively on a formal study: greater or lesser clarity, more or less condensation, their continuous or discontinuous character—these structural features of a text, considered in comparison to those of other texts, give its meaning or confirm its meaning.

Thus, in his textual analysis of Jensen's *Gradiva*, Freud shores up his study by examining other works by the author. *The Red Umbrella* is reminiscent of *Gradiva* by virtue of several motifs, including the white flowers of death, the forgotten object, significant animals, the identity of the central problem, and the same setting. The third story, *The Gothic House*, does not display the same similarities in the manifest content, but is close to the others in its latent content. So it is that Jensen collected the three works and gave them a common title, *Sovereign Powers*. Here, Freud uses the structural method to find the common fantasy—the type—underlying the variations in the manifest content of the works, a fantasy that acquires a structure in the works themselves. In Jensen, the three tales share the common theme of love which develops out of the intimate, almost fraternal bond of childhood friendship—a theme which is linked to the fantasy of the sister as lover. Jensen's last novel, *Strangers Among Men*, is more explicit in this regard. On the basis of this structural study, it is possible to advance some hypotheses concerning the sources of the author's "inspiration," and to construct his childhood fantasies; it is the text that engenders its father. Freud concludes hypothetically that Jensen must have been attached to a little girl during his childhood, specifically to his sister. He even goes so far as to suppose that she had a serious physical defect, such as a club foot, which Jensen transformed into a graceful gait in *Gradiva*. Jensen confirmed that his first passion had been for a little girl he grew up with, who died of tuberculosis at the age of eighteen. Much later, he fell in love with another girl who reminded him of her, and who died suddenly.

Hypothetically, then, Freud links heroes' fantasies to authors' fantasies. In his essay on Dostoevsky, he deduces from the choice of characters, who are always violent, murderous, and egotistical, the sadistic personality of Dostoevsky himself, although in his real life—perhaps precisely because of his creativity—Dostoevsky's sadistic impulses may have been usually directed against himself and have found an outlet in masochism and feelings of guilt. Still, there remained some sadistic traits in his personality which were manifested in his irritability, his intolerance, and the way he treated his readers. Similarly, Dostoevsky's homosexual tendencies are confirmed by the author's remarkable insight into this type of relation in many of his novels. In *The Interpretation of Dreams*, after his comparative structural study of *Hamlet* and *Oedipus Rex*, Freud concludes from Hamlet's aversion toward Ophelia that Shakespeare himself was developing an increasing aversion to sexuality,

> the same distaste which was destined to take possession of the poet's mind more and more during the years that followed, and which reached its extreme expression in *Timon of Athens*. For it can of course only be the poet's own mind which confronts us in Hamlet. I observe in a book on Shakespeare by Georg Brandes (1896) a statement that *Hamlet* was written immediately after the death of Shakespeare's father (in 1601), that is, under the immediate impact of his bereavement and, as we may well assume, while his childhood feelings about his father had been freshly revived. It is known, too, that Shakespeare's own son who died at an early age bore the name of "Hamnet," which is identical with "Hamlet." Just as *Hamlet* deals with the relation of a son to his parents, so *Macbeth* (written at approximately the same period) is concerned with the subject of childlessness. But just as all neurotic symptoms, and for that matter, dreams, are capable of being "over-interpreted" and indeed need to be, if they are to be fully understood, so all genuinely creative writings are the product of more than a single motive and more than a single

impulse in the poet's mind, and are open to more than a single interpretation. In what I have written I have only attempted to interpret the deepest layer of impulses in the mind of the poet. (4:265–266)[35]

Thus, though the works of an author and the relationship between them cannot be understood from the author's life, the study of the works nonetheless makes it possible to deduce hypothetically some features of his life. Conversely, when the author's life is known, it can confirm the study of his work. The date of the works is tied to certain events in the author's life, not because these events are expressed in the work, but because they made possible a return of the repressed. For instance, the death of Shakespeare's father facilitates the return of childish death wishes, and the awakening of a certain affect which is discharged and transformed in the process of creation. Thus in a letter to Fliess Freud says, concerning the analysis of a work by Conrad F. Meyer, that it is necessary to know the order of publication of the works to be able to interpret them.[36] In another letter, he writes that one can better understand Flaubert's *The Temptation of St. Anthony* if one remembers that the author was epileptic and was himself subject to hallucinations.[37] Generally speaking, the life of the artist makes it possible to understand the (unconscious) choice of material and themes, and the specificity of his heroes' fantasies. In this respect, the work is a confession, a sort of involuntary and unsuspected memoir produced by its author. Dostoevsky, by attributing his own illness, epilepsy, to most of his criminal heroes, proceeds as though he were seeking to confess that he himself had committed parricide.[38] The author's narcissistic identification with his heroes makes of the latter his doubles.

It is thus possible to go from the work to the artist and from the artist to the work, with the second stage serving as the counterproof to the first. But it is not the "content" of the work alone that puts the author's past into play in this manner. The form and the "style" do so as well, which is why it is futile to attempt a stylistic study independent of the themes—not because the ideas are inseparable from the language that expresses them, as every writer is aware, but because in the last analysis what determines the choice of composition or images or ways of writing is unconscious. We saw that this was the case with Leonardo, whose very technique was determined by a sort of inhibition in his creativity, which stemmed from unconscious feelings of guilt toward his father. That is how Freud explains why the *Last Supper* was never completed.

> Leonardo could not become reconciled to fresco painting, which demands rapid work while the ground is still moist, and this was the reason why he chose oil colours, the drying of which permitted him to protract the completion of the painting to suit his mood and leisure. . . . The miscarriage of a similar technical experiment appears to have caused the destruction of *The Battle of Anghiari*, the painting which, in competition with Michelangelo, he began to paint some time afterwards. (*Leonardo*, 11:68)

The incompleteness of his works was thus tied to his character traits, what appeared complete in the public's eyes never was, from his point of view: "While it [the *Mona Lisa*] was being painted it was considered to be the highest that art could achieve, but it is certain that Leonardo himself was not satisfied with it, declaring it to be incomplete, and did not deliver it to the person who had commissioned it" (p. 109).

Generally speaking, it is possible to explain an author's style in the same way as slips of the tongue. "A clear and unambiguous manner of writing shows us that here the author is at one with himself; where we find a forced and involved expression . . . we may recognize the intervention of an insufficiently worked-out, complicating thought, or we may hear the stifled voice of the author's self-criticism" (6:101). And later:

> The subtler determinants, too, of the expression of one's thoughts in speaking or writing deserve careful attention. We believe that in general we are free to choose what words we shall use for clothing our thoughts or what images for disguising them. Closer observation shows that other considerations determine this choice, and that behind the form in which the thought is expressed a glimpse may be had of a deeper meaning—often one that is not intended. The images and turns of phrase to which a person is particularly given

> are rarely without significance when one is forming a judgement of him; and others often turn out to be allusions to a theme which is being kept in the background at the time, but which has powerfully affected the speaker (pp. 215–216).

It is thus possible to develop a psychogenesis of the artist on the basis of the work which, like the biography of the author, allows for a better understanding of the work, and especially of the details that seem to be the least significant. Such an approach makes it possible, too, to relate the works to one another. When the author's biography is unknown, however, the work only authorizes us to "imagine" the author's fantasies, and all that can be written is a psychoanalytic "novel," which can be verified by means of the structural method comparing the various works of the author. The works of an author can also be related to those of another author, or to the works of an artist in another artistic discipline, or even to other cultural or psychic productions; for in order to be structured in a work of art, the fantasies of an artist must be typical, that is, linked to universal fantasies of which they are but a variation. This explains the otherwise odd fact that Freud's essay devoted to the study of Dostoevsky ends with the analysis of a work by Stefan Zweig, "Four-and-Twenty Hours in a Woman's Life." The situation of Stefan Zweig's hero, a gambler whose inhibition is lifted each time he loses at gambling, is analogous to Dostoevsky's, whose inhibited creativity stems from a feeling of guilt brought on by childhood masturbation.

Thus, in his analyses, Freud always uses two methods which complement each other and serve as counterproofs to each other: a *genetic method* that confirms the meaning of a work by means of the artist's biography, or constitutes the history and personality of the artist from his characters or works of plastic art; and a *structural method* that makes possible the comparison of various works, which in turn reveals the common fantasy that provides the key to them. This twofold method authorizes the dating of the various works in relation to the gradual lifting of repression. It also makes it possible to lay the foundation for a history of art, and to relate the works of different authors that have the same theme. But underlying this history is the principle of the secular advance of repression. The method invites a reading of the works as so many variations of a universal fantasy. Beyond the differences lies a postulated structural resemblance which renders them intelligible as the eternal, ever-different return of the same. That is why Freud compares Sophocles' *Oedipus Rex* with Shakespeare's *Hamlet* in a number of his writings. The most interesting essay in this regard is the one on Dostoevsky, where a comparison with *The Brothers Karamazov* figures as well. Freud remarks that it is no accident that the three literary masterpieces of all time, *Oedipus*, *Hamlet*, and *The Brothers Karamazov* treat the same subject, parricide, and that in all three the motive for the murder is sexual rivalry over a woman.

In the Sophoclean tragedy, which is the most remote in time, the repression is minimal, so that the play serves as the archetype for understanding the other works and is a paradigm for the human condition. The hero himself is the murderer. Yet even here disguise and softening effects are at work, for the spectator, who has no analytic preparation, would not be able to tolerate the intention to commit parricide. Thus the hero carries out the murder unwittingly, so to speak, just as he commits incest without knowing it. As he says in *The Interpretation of Dreams*, Freud himself translates into conscious terms what must remain unconscious in the hero's mind. The hero therefore commits the murder without wanting to, and under the influence of a woman. He cannot win possession of the queen, his mother, however, until he has repeated his crime against the monster who symbolizes the father. Finally, after his guilt has been made conscious, he does not try to excuse himself for his action by appealing to the expedient of fate. His crime is recognized and he punishes himself for it, as if he had been fully conscious of it at the time it was committed, which is psychologically correct, albeit apparently irrational.

In *Hamlet*, the presentation is much more indirect. The hero does not commit parricide himself, which is why the motives of sexual rivalry are less disguised. The hero's "Oedipus complex" is legible only in the reflected light of the effect on him of another's crime: he cannot bring himself to avenge his father. The feeling of guilt that paralyzes him is displaced onto his awareness of his inability to do his duty.

In *The Brothers Karamazov*, the murder is also committed by someone other than the hero, but by someone who has the same relationship to the father as he, for both are his sons. The motive of sexual rivalry is openly acknowledged. The brother of the hero is the murderer, and Dostoevsky attributes to him his own illness, epilepsy.

Thus in these three works, the oedipal structure appears in several variations due to differences in time, biographical differences between the authors, and variations in repression. There is thus an unquestionable link between the murder of the father in *The Brothers Karamozov* and the fate of Dostoevsky's own father, just as there is a relation between Shakespeare's life and Hamlet's personality.

The same method is at work in Freud's comparison of Michelangelo's *Moses* with the *Moses* of twelfth-century artist Nicholas of Verdun. This comparison plays the role of counterproof and serves to validate Freud's construction. Here again we see the different repetition of the same theme of Moses. The method is said to make possible a sort of a priori classification of all possible types of Moses, or at least to leave room for intermediary expressions that would fall between the Moses of Michelangelo and that of Nicholas of Verdun. In a postscript to "The Moses of Michelangelo," Freud writes:

> A glance at the accompanying illustration will show the main difference between the two compositions, which are separated from each other by an interval of more than three centuries. The Moses of the Lorraine artist is holding the Tables by their top edge with his left hand, resting them on his knee. If we were to transfer them to the other side of his body and put them under his right arm we should have established the preliminary posture of Michelangelo's Moses. If my view of the thrusting of the hand into the beard is right, then the Moses of the year 1180 shows us an instant during his storm of feeling, whilst the statue in S. Pietro in Vincoli depicts the calm when the storm is over. In my opinion this new piece of evidence

increases the probability that the interpretation which I attempted in 1914 was a correct one. Perhaps some connoisseur of art will be able to bridge the gulf in time between the Moses of Nicholas of Verdun and the Moses of the Master of the Italian Renaissance by telling us where examples of representations of Moses belonging to the intervening period are to be found. (13:237–238)

The circumlocutions Freud uses here to talk about the two artists are not stylistic devices, but rather point up the reason for the differences in treatment of a single theme by different artists belonging to different times and societies. But what is the meaning of the "single theme," here, the theme of Moses? Is Moses a reality, or a type? Do the two artists refer to a single figure, Moses? This figure is known only through the Bible which, as Freud tried to prove in *Moses and Monotheism*, already presents a falsified version of history, as is evident from the contradictions in the text and the different versions given of the same event—falsifications resulting from sexual repression. An originary text that would yield the real figure of Moses is nowhere in existence—which is to say that the "theme" of Moses exists only in its type, and that the latter varies as a function of the ways it is read. There is no text preceding the interpretation; rather, the reading constitutes the text as such. That is why the "theme" of Moses, like the "theme" of Oedipus, exists only in its variations, differing versions in which the varying degrees of repression in authors and ages can be read. Michelangelo's version of "Moses" condenses the two different versions of the event given in the Bible, whereas Nicholas of Verdun's articulates only the first. One never arrives at an original text, to which the various versions can be referred in order to evaluate their greater or lesser "faithfulness." The criterion determining the value of a work is not "truth" conceived as correspondence to a reality outside the work. And yet Freud establishes a hierarchy between the two works, for Michelangelo's better symbolizes the figure of the Father, the lawgiver. It expresses the highest ideal that man can attain and that is required of him; namely, instinctual renunciation. Though it is possible to imagine intermediate types of Moses, between the one who yields to his passions and the one who, after the storm, is completely calm, it is difficult to imagine a Moses who could go further in the domination of passion than the Moses of Michelangelo. So it is once again in relation to differences in repression, and thus in the moral or cultural demands upon various authors and ages, that Freud conceives his history of art.

One could do the same type of analysis of Hebbel's *Judith*, which Freud examines in "The Taboo of Virginity" (11:207–208).[39] The theme of Judith does not refer back to a figure that preexists the possible versions of it. The Biblical text itself is a version falsified by repression, since there was a desire to hide the sexual significance of the story. Hebbel's *Judith* is thus an interpretation, a kind of writing that structures a theme in its variation. Yet though it is a version devoid of an original text, it can nonetheless be said that, like Michelangelo's Moses, it is psychically "truer" than the Biblical version. The artist's text is "truer" because it merely puts his fantasies into play without claiming to tell the truth, and in this way tells more than the author himself wants to tell, as we saw with regard to *Gradiva*. What is "true" is said by means of an illusion, while the Bible, which claims to tell the truth, is more repressed and offers more secondary rationalizations. The text that seems to be more veiled is in fact the clearer one.[40] Thus in Hebbel's version, Judith adopts a patriotic motive to hide the sexual significance of her act: the decapitation of Holofernes is the symbolic substitute for castration. Hebbel must have intentionally sexualized the patriotic story in the Apocrypha of the *Old Testament* in which, upon her return, Judith is able to boast that she has not been deflowered, and there is no mention of her strange wedding night. Freud remarks, "But probably, with the fine perception of a poet, he sensed the ancient motive, which had been lost in the tendentious narrative, and has merely restored its earlier content to the material" (p. 207). Hebbel himself is unaware, however, of his "true intentions." Jadger points out that the motives acknowledged by the poet to justify his alteration of the material are artificial and seem to aim at justifying from the outside something of which the poet himself was unconscious. In the last analysis, the changes Hebbel makes in the Biblical text stem from his own parental complex, which caused him to side with the woman in the battle of the sexes. In the same way, Michelangelo had internal psychic motives for adopting an independent stance in regard to the Biblical text. Artists were not forbidden to depart from the Biblical texts, and they did so frequently.

In a painting, Parmigiano depicts Moses seated at the top of a mountain, casting the Tables on the ground, despite the Bible's indication that "he broke them at the foot of the mountain." Now Freud is careful to point out that for the men of the Renaissance, criticism of Biblical texts was not tolerated, so the special freedom accorded artists is significant; it seems to be an insidious way of simultaneously revealing and concealing the censorship at work in every text and every kind of writing. Artistic licence is intended to further "efface" the psychic truth of art: art is merely a matter of the imagination. Its license thus effaces its seriousness. But if art is taken to be a game and presents itself as such, it is to conceal all the better its spirit of seriousness. Society takes the artist to be the father of his creation, and the artist, wishing to believe himself the father of his works, wants to be his own father. Society therefore grants full license to the artist to show that he is subject to no external constraints, that he is free and fully his own master, that like God, he is self-sufficient. "Artistic license" is thus part of the ideological system of art: it satisfies the theological illusion, and is prey to the artificial separation of play and seriousness, the imaginary and the real. It is a denial of art's psychic truth, and the sign of resistance to psychoanalysis.

Thus in the *New Introductory Lectures*, after showing that man can only choose between destroying himself and destroying others, Freud writes, "A sad disclosure indeed for the moralist! But the moralist will console himself for a long time to come with the improbability of our speculations. A queer instinct, indeed, directed to the destruction of its own organic home! Poets, it is true, talk of such things; but poets are irresponsible people and enjoy the privilege of poetic license" (22:105–106). In *The Introductory Lectures*, speaking of the wish for the death of one's parents and its denial, he writes: "And, incidentally, this disavowal applies only to real life.

Narrative and dramatic works of the imagination may freely make play with the themes that arise from a disturbance of this ideal" (15:206). And finally, in *Civilization and Its Discontents*: "A great imaginitive writer may permit himself to give expression—jokingly, at all events—to psychological truths that are severely proscribed" (21:110). The three examples I have chosen intimate, then, that all texts are constituted by a reading that adopts a particular perspective, and that ideology alone, in normally ascribing to texts an absolute external referent, makes an artistic text pass for a work of "pure" imagination. But if from another point of view there are nothing but variations with no type to which they can be referred, how is it possible to grasp the resemblances, and how can one explain the fact that the works of a given period can continue to produce affective responses long afterward? The answer is that the individual fantasy of an artist is a variation of a universal fantasy and is for that very reason typical. The proof Freud offers is that the same themes and fantasies can be found in other cultural productions such as myths, religions, and folklore, or in psychic productions such as dreams or neurotic symptoms.

Freud's structural method not only relates the various works of a single author or works of different authors having the same "theme," but also, as its third function, relates all psychic productions to each other, and through their variations finds the universal fantasy that is structured in them.

Thus the parental fantasy of Hebbel's that is played out in *Judith* repeats the collective fantasy concerning the taboo of virginity. Freud discovers its presence in other works of art: in Anzengruber's *The Virgin's Venom*, where it is treated in the comic mode; in a short story by Schnitzler; in the dream of one of his patients; in the rites of certain primitive societies or in Roman society; and in certain medieval costumes or certain superstitions.

We have seen that Freud related the smile in various works by Leonardo to the smile in the paintings of his master, Verrochio, and more paradoxically, to the smile of archaic Greek statues; through the variations, the universal fantasy of the "mother's smile" can be constructed. In the same way, Leonardo's fantasy of the vulture finds its analogues in the vulture in hieroglyphic forms of writing and in Egyptian religions; it is referred to paintings representing the Virgin and Child, and at last finds its key in infantile sexual "theories" concerning the mother's lack of a penis.

The essay "The Theme of the Three Caskets" (12:291 ff.) compares the theme of *The Merchant of Venice* with that of *King Lear*, "Cinderella," and the myths of the three graces and the three fates, showing that in each case the third object—directly or indirectly a figure for a woman—symbolizes death.

Similarly, Hoffmann's "The Sandman," analyzed in "The Uncanny," can only be understood from the model of the typical dream and the myth; the key to it is provided by the universal childhood fantasy of castration. The specificity of the form it takes in Hoffmann's tale and the choice of this theme can be explained by the childhood of the author, who was the child of an unhappily married couple. When he was three years old, his father left the family and never came back, so the storyteller's relation to his father was always one of the painful aspects of his affective life.

Thus Freud always follows the same procedure, using the free association of ideas, which gives his writings a disorderly appearance. In fact, however, the disorder functions to reestablish "primitive ordering," that is, to construct the archaic primitive foundation of the work underlying the distortions of the manifest text. What mediates the passage from the manifest to the latent content is always the symbolism of typical dreams and the primary processes at work in them—condensation, displacement, and conversion into the opposite. Dream symbolism makes it possible to constitute the structure of the fantasy shared by the various psychic and cultural productions to which the interpretive method has referred, in circular fashion.[41] Thus concerning "The Sandman," Freud writes in "The Uncanny" that if one contents oneself with the manifest content, one's view "does not account adequately for the substitutive relation between the eye and the male organ which is seen to exist in dreams and myths and phantasies; nor can it dispel the impression that the threat of being castrated in especial excites a peculiarly violent and obscure emotion, and that this emotion is what first gives the idea of losing other organs its intense colouring" (17:231).

In the last analysis, what justifies the use of this method involving infinite referral and circular interpretation is that it works the best: without it, many details would have no meaning. We saw earlier that the basic postulate of Freud's method was that everything was meaningful, even if everything was not intended to be understood and sometimes aimed not to be. That is why Freud writes, "Elements in the story like these, and many others, seem arbitrary and meaningless so long as we deny all connection between fears about the eye and castration; but they become intelligible as soon as we replace the Sand-Man by the dreaded father at whose hands castration is expected" (p. 232).

Finally, the analysis always ends with the substitution of the genetic method for the structural one, in order to justify the difference within the repetition. Neither stage of the procedure can be eliminated, because they complete each other: using only the genetic method, the artist's individual fantasy can only be "fantasized," whereas using the structural method alone, the universal fantasy is constructed, but the justification for its uniqueness in a particular work is lost. Yet the universal is given only in the unique and the original. The best writers are not those who deliberately adopt universal themes which they treat stereotypically, for that is an indication of the limits of their art and it is on that basis that they are easily parodied. Freud cites an example from Dickens in which the depiction of pristine young girls clearly distinguishes between vice and virtue. This portrayal is contrasted with *David Copperfield*, which is a masterpiece because character in that work is individualized, and the characters who do wrong are nonetheless not hateful.[43] If the structural method refers us from version to version in circular fashion, so that each version serves as the counterproof of the others, it is because they are all variations of a postulated type—the Oedipus complex—which renders them intelligible in their very diversity. In *The Incest Motif*, Otto Rank shows how often poets choose the motif of incest, and points to the transformations, modifications, and softening of this material throughout world literature, especially in dramatic works. By means of this work, the artist structures his own fantasies relating to the Oedipus complex and thereby frees himself from them. In his Preface to Theodor Reik's *Ritual: Psycho-Analytic Studies*, Freud remarks,

> Otto Rank, in a large volume on the incest complex (1912), has produced evidence of the surprising fact that the choice of subject-matter, especially for dramatic works, is principally determined by the ambit of what psycho-analysis has termed the "Oedipus complex." By working it over with the greatest variety of modifications, distortions and disguises, the dramatist seeks to deal with his own most personal relations to this emotional theme. (17:261)[44]

The Oedipus complex is also the nucleus of the neuroses and is the basis of religion. It is this "eternal humanity," present in its very absence—that is, in its distortion—that explains the effect works of art have on enthusiasts, and that fundamentally motivates Freud's search I have already shown that the problem of art overlaps with the problem of the father. In "An Autobiographical Study," Freud writes:

> What psycho-analysis was able to do was to take the interrelations between the impressions of the artist's life, his chance experiences, and his works, and from them to construct his [mental] constitution and the instinctual impulses at work in it—that is to say, that part of him which he shared with all men. With this aim in view, for instance, I made Leonardo da Vinci the subject of a study... which is based on a single memory of childhood related by him. (20.65)[45]

Resistance to the "application" of psychoanalysis to art and the denial that accompanies the unveiling of the works' meaning stem from the aversion men feel toward their own infantile incestuous desires, which have subsequently been completely repressed. But the universal oedipal structure is given only in its substitutive distortion, and this originarily. Is this structure a principle of understanding constructed by analytic science to explain the variations, or is it a reality? Freud, who sees this structure repeated everywhere in its very differences, tries to ground its historical truth

in a material truth, the murder of the primal father.[46] The ontogenetic
structure supposedly refers to a phylogenetic event. But this ground-
ing rests on a myth, the myth of the primal horde. If the structure
can be explained by genesis, the latter is still mythic, and its meaning is still structural. Which means that there is no simple origin,
that the origin is both plural and conflictual. The psychic apparatus
with its three agencies always already exists, just as the death drive
always already inhibits Eros; in order for the brothers to have re-
pented of the primal murder, the superego had to have been already
in existence. But the psychic apparatus is itself a model for understanding the psyche. The oedipal structure is a construction of
science, an anhypothetical hypothesis.

DISTORTION, REPETITION, INTERPRETATION

We can draw a certain number of conclusions from Freud's method
of reading. First, Freud's conception of truth is a new one, despite
the fact that in certain respects it remains imprisoned in the logic
of representation and of the sign: truth is given only in its distortions
and is constructed from those distortions. There is no originary text
that the others supposedly translate; rather, one is always referred
from one text to another, one version to another, produced by the
differential play of a single universal fantasy that is structured in
that play. Nevertheless, an anhypothetical referent remains: the
oedipal structure. The chain of signifiers refers to a signified that
is always absent, postulated from its originary substitutes. It is this
referral that still ties Freud to the traditional ideology of representation. And yet Freud opposes the ideological conception of art as
an imitation of reality and a reflection of the author, a conception
which presupposes truth to mean correspondence to reality and
the identity of oneself to oneself. The work of art, on the contrary,
makes it possible for the nonunified and absent self to be structured,
to constitute its identity. The work of art is not external to the
"psychic reality" that it "represents," and so cannot imitate it. The
fantasy that it "expresses" is a construction after the fact.

When Freud says that Leonardo da Vinci put his science in the service of art conceived as imitation, he does not assume responsibility for this Leonardesque notion, but on the contrary denounces it as an element in the ideology of the Renaissance where the space of representation, in Michel Foucault's sense of the term, prevailed. He unmasks this notion as a secondary rationalization of Leonardo's, intended to hide the relation that existed between his art and his erotic desires. Norbert, the hero of Jensen's *Gradiva*, uses the same rationalization.

And indeed, even when for the first time [these products of his phantasy] gave rise to an incitement to action—when the archaeologist, obsessed by the problem of whether this posture of the feet corresponded to reality, began to make observations from life in order to examine the feet of contemporary women and girls—even this action was screened by conscious scientific motives, as though all his interest in the sculpture of Gradiva had sprung from the soil of his professional concern with archaeology. The women and girls in the street, whom he chose as the subjects of his investigation, must, of course, have taken another, crudely erotic view of his behaviour, and we cannot but think them right. We ourselves can be in no doubt that Hanold was as much in ignorance of the motives of his researches as he was of the origin of his phantasies about Gradiva....
The scientific motivation might be said to serve as a pretext for the unconscious erotic one, and science had put itself completely at the service of the delusion. It should not be forgotten, however, that the unconscious determinants could not effect anything that did not simultaneously satisfy the conscious, scientific ones. (9:50–52)

Because "truth" is given only in a distortion, there is a multiplicity of texts that repeat it differently, and their enigmatic character calls for an interpretation. André Green shows very well what the relation is between distortion, repetition, and interpretation: "Destined to let itself be deciphered by interpretation and to wander in distortion, truth repeats itself relentlessly in order to be recognized and hide itself indefinitely"; and later on: "The signifier, even as it relentlessly announces itself, distorts itself and eludes any unequivocal, global, and definitive grasp."[47]

Second, every text is a riddle which leaves us to guess the identity of its author by putting this identity into play and constituting it. The text refers to the text of life, that is, to life as a text, a chain of originary substitutes. Psychic life must itself be a text, for it to constitute itself in the text of the work. The text of art *is* the very text of life, which is why there is no need to rely on authors' "declared intentions" in order to decipher the riddle and understand what the authors mean. By saying less, the text says much more. This conception of a text that signifies without its author deconstructs the theological conception of art and bespeaks the death of the author—that is, of the father—as a self-sufficient creator. It is possible to accept this conception only by "killing" one's father oneself, and by understanding that the life of the individual is inscribed in the difference of life, in its necessity and in the chance at work in its play. It is not the result of the all-powerful will of the father, nor is it grounded by any finality. The second stage of Freud's reflection thus puts an end to admiration for the great man the artist is taken to be.

Third, the riddle of the text more or less effaces its origins as a function of collective and individual repression. The processes of repression, like those of censorship, vary with the times. Censorship can soften, weaken, disguise, and delete.[48] These variations express transformations in the relations of force; that is, the concept of the tissue-text cannot be thought without establishing an indissoluble link between force and meaning, affect and representation, the combinatory of the symbolic and the transformations of the economic. It is perhaps in this link that Freud's greatest originality lies. It is because for him there is no text of art without repression, and thus without intervention of the secondary processes that erect formations which play the role of counterinvestments, that Freud is against the surrealist conception, and has difficulty understanding certain views on modern art. In a letter to Stefan Zweig he writes of Salvidor Dali,

> For until then I was inclined to look upon surrealists, who have apparently chosen me for their patron saint, as absolute (let us say 95 per cent, like alcohol) cranks. The young Spaniard, however, with his candid fanatical eyes and his undeniable technical mastery, has

made me reconsider my opinion. It would in fact be very interesting to investigate analytically how a picture like this came to be painted. From the critical point of view it could still be maintained that the notion of art defies expansion as long as the quantitative proportion of unconscious material and preconscious treatment does not remain within definite limits. In any case these are serious psychological problems.[49]

This indissoluble link between force and meaning is revealed also in Freud's very original conception of the symbol. His conception implies neither a relation of complementarity with what it symbolizes, nor a relation of expressiveness. Rather the symbol is in a relation of substitutive violence with it, revealing it and masking it at the same time. The affective response we make to an indifferent substitutive representation can only be explained by its link with what it is the substitute for. The symbol is inscribed in a process of substitution referring to the chain of substitutes in life, to the absence of originary sexual pleasure [jouissance] and presence, which are always already fantasized. If the different substitutes can be displaced and replaced by each other, it is because the desires are in concatenation with each other.[50]

It is thus necessary now to study art from a metapsychological, or more specifically, an economic point of view, and to situate art within the economy of life.[51]

4

ART IN THE ECONOMY OF LIFE
The Metapsychological Point of View

It all seems to be a question of economy. In Hamlet's
words: "Thrift, thrift, Horatio!"
Jokes and Their Relation to the Unconscious, 8:42

AESTHETIC PLEASURE

To consider art only as a text to decipher is to forget that the text is itself a compromise between conflicting forces; it is to forget that representation and affect are indissociable. If it is true that the work of art is analogous to the dream, if like the dream, it plays out its author's fantasies, it too is a writing of desire. But unlike the dream, the dialect of art must be comprehensible and communicable, for art, as a form of cultural production, has a social function. That is, from the topical point of view, the unconscious processes of condensation, displacement, and figurative elaboration must be completely mastered by the preconscious or conscious processes; and from the dynamic and economic point of view, the artist's desires are not the only ones in play, since those of the art lover and the society in which he lives are involved as well. Freud's method, from this point of view, always consists in starting from the affective response produced by the work in the art lover, then working back to the affect initially experienced by the artist, and inquiring into the means that were capable of producing transformations of affect in the artist and in the art lover. These means arise from a symbolic combinatory which the artist has mastered. Art, a kind of symbolic game, makes economic play possible through the transformation of affect.

> Kindly nature has given the artist the ability to express his most secret mental impulses, which are hidden even from himself, by means of the works that he creates; and these works have a powerful effect on others who are strangers to the artist, and who are themselves unaware of the source of their emotion.... Yet if one considers the profound transformations through which an impression in an artist's life has to pass before it is allowed to make its contribution to a work of art, one will be bound to keep any claim to certainty in one's demonstration within very modest limits. (Leonardo, 11:107)

Freud's starting point is thus always the effect felt before a work of art, as we saw with regard to Michelangelo's *Moses*, Sophocles' *Oedipus Rex*, and Leonardo's works.[1] In *Jokes and Their Relation to the Unconscious*, Freud tries to explain the *amusing effect* of jokes, and finds two factors: the use of a special technique, and a tendency inherent in the joke. The technique involves condensation or displacement, or the establishment of unexpected links between disparate ideas, or the indirect presentation of ideas by means of allusion, analogies, and the utilization of illogical associations. The tendency has an aggressive or erotic origin. The dream processes are at work here but have been mastered, since they are used voluntarily.[2] The tendencies imply that jokes are always addressed to a third party who may in fact be present or absent, for no discourse is possible without the presence of the other, even if it be only in the form of absence; that is, without the presence at least of the unconscious—that of the author and of the public.

"Psychopathic Characters on the Stage" (7:305–310)[3] examines the means used by dramatists to move the public.[4] The
paradox here is that painful events are a source of great enjoyment.
Even when the pleasure in art is masochistic, the pleasure principle
is still the great beneficiary. Thus tragic pleasure can be of no help
in hypothesizing a tendency located beyond the pleasure principle,
which is independent of it and perhaps more primal—the death
drive.[5]

From the point of view of affect, what is proper to art is
its consistent transformation of painful affects into happy ones. For
instance, Leonardo da Vinci gives his mother (in *St. Anne*) the happy
smile she lacked in real life and, in his last works, paints young
men who seem happy to have satisfied a desire of a homosexual
nature, unlike what had happened in his real erotic life. "Art allowed
him to overcome the unhappiness of his life by transfiguring it into
happiness." The work of art procures a yield of pleasure, in one
form or another. The aim of an aesthetics oriented by the economic
point of view, which Freud attempts to found, would be precisely
to see by what point of transformation of affects art manages to
serve pleasure, regardless of the contents of its representations.

> The artistic play and imitation carried out by adults, which, unlike
> children's, are aimed at an audience, do not spare the spectators
> (for instance, in tragedy) the most painful experiences and can yet
> be felt by them as highly enjoyable. This is convincing proof that,
> even under the dominance of the pleasure principle, there are ways
> and means enough of making what is in itself unpleasurable into a
> subject to be recollected and worked over in the mind. The consid-
> eration of these cases and situations, which have a yield of pleasure
> as their final outcome, should be undertaken by some system of
> aesthetics with an economic approach to its subject-matter. (*Beyond
> the Pleasure Principle*, 18:17)

The pleasure that art brings must not be understood by
reference to what is experienced by consciousness, for in certain
cases and to a certain extent, consciousness can feel horror and
anxiety before the spectacle of tragedies or certain paintings; the

same is true in these instances as in nightmares, that is, a wish is nonetheless fulfilled. The notion of pleasure must be considered from a metapsychological point of view. If we experience horror in seeing *Oedipus Rex*, it is because one of our repressed infantile wishes is being represented on the stage; we feel horror because we are now adults and must keep this wish repressed. But we experience pleasure because the wish is disguised and because we are happy to be transported by art into the childhood situation, which is always imagined to be idyllic. The disguise of desire makes possible a saving of energy that serves as a counterinvestment, as well as the lifting of inhibition, discharge, and, at the level of consciousness, tragic pleasure. The same is true in every case: in order for there to be aesthetic pleasure, there must be a certain repression of desire, and thus a certain displacement or, generally speaking, a certain distortion at the level of the symbolic combinatory, a transformation in the linking of affect and representation; but there must also be a lifting of inhibition. In the observer there must be both recognition and lack of recognition. What makes possible the lifting of inhibition thanks to the saving on the energy of investment is the artist's formal work. Once again, the distinction between form and content appears completely meaningless; the lifting of inhibition is possible only by a diversion of the ego's attention, which plays the role of a counterinvestment. The "form," which apparently has no relation to the tendency that is to be invested in it, is intended to divert attention and, consequently, to allow for discharge.

To consider aesthetic pleasure in this way, from an economic point of view, is a new approach that stands opposed to traditional philosophical conceptions, which make of it a pleasure of the highest order, one that is totally disinterested: pleasure procured by beauty. In *Jokes*, Freud reminds us of Fischer's position: "This enjoyment, this kind of representation, is the purely aesthetic one, which lies only in itself, which has its aim only in itself and which fulfills none of the other aims of life" (8:95).[6] But, says Freud, it is very doubtful that we can undertake anything with no intention in view! What is this celebrated aesthetic feeling which, qualitatively speaking, seems to be specific and superior to the others?

In *Civilization and Its Discontents*, Freud describes it as mildly intoxicating, as giving a milder, finer, and higher satisfaction than any of the impulses in their crude and primary state. And yet beauty is of no apparent use and is not a cultural necessity, which is of course why professional aestheticians have made of aesthetic feeling a disinterested feeling and have not been able to account for its specific quality. As for Freud, he hopes to be able to characterize it in metapsychological terms. He begins by showing that art is not the only thing that procures this feeling: man feels joy each time that beauty is presented to his senses and to his judgment. The beauty of forms and gestures, the beauty of natural objects and landscapes, of artistic and even scientific creations, should not be distinguished in terms of the pleasurable effect they produce; the division ordinarily established between the various forms of beauty is ideological and symptomatic of repression, which is not at all surprising, for beauty derives from the sexual realm: the love of beauty is a case of inhibition in the aim of the sexual impulse.[7] As we shall see later, what essentially characterizes the structure of the artist is his capacity for sublimation. The latter allows this "introvert not far removed from neurosis" to escape his condition (as was the case with Leonardo or Goethe), or, when he is neurotic, to find refuge as was the case with Dostoevsky; for neurosis depends essentially on the fate of affect, much more than on that of representation.[8] Finally, beauty and seductiveness are originally attributed to the sexual object; it is the beauty of the body that is sexually exciting. It procures fore-pleasure, lifting inhibition and making possible the search for end-pleasure at the genital level. "The concept of 'beautiful' has its roots in sexual excitation and . . . its original meaning was 'sexually stimulating'" (*Three Essays on the Theory of Sexuality*, 7:156, n. 2). The counterproof—which is paradoxical, to say the least—is the ugliness of the genitals: "This is related to the fact that we never regard the genitals themselves, which produce the strongest sexual excitation, as really 'beautiful'" (p. 156, n. 2).

The quality of beauty is thus tied to secondary sexual characteristics, the ones that give only fore-pleasure.

But what relationship is there in art between fore-pleasure and end-pleasure? Beauty, here again, plays the role of the "incentive bonus" and makes possible the discharge of repressed dispositions. A small pleasure here releases a greater one whose source had been repressed. The incentive bonus is a fore-pleasure that is grafted onto a situation in which a chance for pleasure was thwarted: "with the assistance of the offer of a small amount of pleasure, a much greater one, which would otherwise have been hard to achieve, has been gained" (*Jokes*, 8:137).

Freud applies to the joke, then to artistic productions and many other realms, Fechner's "principle of aesthetic assistance or intensification" (p. 135).[9] This is the principle of an increase in pleasure resulting from the convergence of determinants of pleasure from different sources.

> If determinants of pleasure that in themselves produce little effect converge without mutual contradiction, there results a greater, and often a much greater, outcome of pleasure than corresponds to the pleasure-value of the separate determinants—a greater pleasure than could be explained as the sum of the separate effects. Indeed, a convergence of this kind can even lead to a positive resultant of pleasure and the threshold of pleasure may be crossed, where the separate factors are too weak to do so: though they must, in comparison with others, show a perceptible advantage in enjoyableness. (p. 135)[10]

Freud points to the problem of the resultant and its algebraic sign in cases where the determinants of pleasure conflict with those of unpleasure, for instance when an urge to release pleasure is repressed by an antagonistic force. "Tendentious jokes" fall into this category, as does art, in which the artist's work— beautiful form—is needed to divert the attention of the ego, a force antagonistic to pleasure, thereby making possible the lifting of inhibition and discharge. This principle of Fechner's is confirmed more by artistic productions than by jokes. It is also a factor in dreams, in which, at the moment when the force of the ego's counterinvestment is lifted, unconscious motions reinforce the preconscious investment with the desire that infuses mnesic images.

Aesthetic pleasure is thus a "composite" pleasure in which it is difficult to determine the part played by the different factors that make it up and contribute to its general effect; but though they derive from different sources, neither of the two types of pleasure is, properly speaking, "disinterested."

Fore-pleasure, which is linked to the system Pcs. as a source, has the eye as its erogenous zone in the plastic arts. It is the eye the transmits the special quality of excitation which produces the feeling of beauty; in itself, this stimulus is a determinant of pleasure. Moreover, the work of the artist essentially puts the primary processes into operation, the procedures of childhood; when addressed to adults, this work results in a saving of energy expended in investment which, in order to procure pleasure, must be capable of being discharged without being relocated elsewhere. It must not be reinvested in work or in the effort to pay attention. Aesthetic form makes possible a diversion of attention and thus also the release being sought.

This first saving makes possible the second pleasure which is, properly speaking, *sexual*, due to the lifting of repression.

Art's cathartic function resides in this liberation of the repressed; because of it, sources of pleasure which seemed to be barred find access to consciousness and, added to the fore-pleasure which is the precondition for them, constitute the very unique feeling of aesthetic pleasure.

We can describe the purpose |of art| in rather more detail by saying that it is a question of opening up sources of pleasure or enjoyment in our emotional life, just as, in the case of intellectual activity, joking or fun open up similar sources, many of which that activity had made inaccessible.... The prime factor is unquestionably the process of getting rid of one's own emotions ... and the consequent enjoyment corresponds on the one hand to the relief produced by a thorough discharge and on the other hand, no doubt, to an accompanying sexual excitation; for the latter, as we may suppose, appears as a by-product whenever an affect is aroused, and gives people the sense, which they so much desire, of a raising of the potential of their psychical state. ("Psychopathic Characters," 7:305ff.)

In *Jokes*, Freud studies very closely the various procedures that allow for a saving on the expenditure of energy and discharge. The difference between jokes, the comic, and humor arises from a difference between three types of saving; the first is due to a lifting of inhibition, the second to an economy in the movement of representations, and the third to an economy in affect:[11] "The pleasure in jokes has seemed to us to arise from an economy in expenditure upon inhibition, the pleasure in the comic from an economy in expenditure upon representation (upon investment), and the pleasure in humour from an economy in expenditure upon feeling (*Gefuhlsaufwand*)" (8:236).

The procedures used are the unconscious primary processes—the ones at work in dreams, and those with which our psychic apparatus functioned during our childhood. If we take jokes as the model for artistic activity as Freud authorizes us to do, we can say that aesthetic pleasure arises not from the satisfaction of a vital need, but from the play of our own psychic activity, which is a continuation of childhood play. "If we do not require our mental apparatus at the moment for supplying one of our indispensable satisfactions, we allow it itself to work in the direction of pleasure and we seek to derive pleasure from its own activity. I suspect that this is in general the condition that governs all aesthetic representation, but I understand too little of aesthetics to try to enlarge on this statement" (pp. 95–96).

ART AND PLAY

The artist, by means of the play of unconscious psychic processes, the play of affects in the process of transformation, and that of representations in the combinatory, tries to repeat what the child does in his play before reason and judgment come to impose constraints. That "revered" man, the artist, is at bottom only a child who gives other people the joy of being able to find their way back to the paradise of childhood. The notion of "play" does not, however, imply that art is a frivolous activity. Play is opposed not to seriousness, but to reality, when it grants a kind of hallucinatory satisfaction, as in dreams and hallucinatory psychosis. Thanks to jokes or art, people can retrieve the good humor that has been lost in the course of cultural progress. Art, then, is a substitute for child's play.

> In all three modes of working of our mental apparatus the pleasure is derived from an economy. All three are agreed in representing methods of regaining from mental activity a pleasure which has in fact been lost through the development of that activity. For the euphoria which we endeavor to reach by these means is nothing other than the mood of a period of life in which we were accustomed to deal with our psychical work in general with a small expenditure of energy—the mood of our childhood, when we were ignorant of the comic, when we were incapable of jokes and when we had no need of humour to make us feel happy in our life. (p. 236)

But like all substitutes, it repeats ever-differently. The play of the primary psychic processes has here been mastered by the preconscious system—the primary process as such has no artistic value. In playing with language, the child had already experienced a functional pleasure linked to the acquisition of mastery over words. It is in play that the child acquires mastery over the primary processes. But in addition to this mastery, the artist has mastered completely original means of "expression." Moreover, it is only because the unconscious processes are dominated by formal structures governed by the preconscious system that the fantasies in the artist's daydreams can become communicable. Gombrich goes so far as to say that "the envelope determines the content," and that "the code engenders the message."[12] This implies that the artist plays with forms and selects, among the preconscious processes, the structures which, in relation to his psyche and its conflicts, are perceived as the most significant. It is his art that informs his psyche, and not his psyche that comes to light in his art. Leonardo's many drawings constitute "so many surprisingly diverse variations on each of the motifs found in his paintings . . . revealing a wealth of possibilities which often leave him indecisive." This interpretation, which draws out the consequences that Freud himself did not draw out, namely the necessity for mastery over the primary processes in art—this interpretation, then, though it overemphasizes, perhaps, the predominance of "form" over "content," at least has the advantage of showing that Freud was not interested in the signified alone, since he subordinated the message to the code. In this respect Freud is not far removed from the formalism of the time, or not far from Klee's theories in any case.[13]

For the artist, play is a salutory procedure, whereas for art lovers it is a source of pleasure, since they do not redirect into work the affect liberated by the lifting of inhibition.

IDENTIFICATION

In order for pleasure to be generated in the spectator, several conditions must be met. The artist's fantasies must be disguised and objectified by formal work which, through the beauty it creates, charms by diverting attention, and makes possible the lifting of inhibition and the renewed enjoyment of repressed fantasies.

> When a poet presents his play to us or tells us what we are inclined to take to be his personal day-dreams, we experience a great pleasure, and one which probably arises from the confluence of many sources. How the poet accomplishes this is his innermost secret; the essential *ars poetica* lies in the technique of overcoming the feeling of repulsion in us which is undoubtedly connected with the barriers that rise between each single ego and the others. We can guess two of the methods used by this technique. The poet softens the character of his egoistic day-dreams by altering and disguising it, and he bribes us by the purely formal—that is, aesthetic—yield of pleasure which he offers us in the presentation of his phantasies. We give the name of an *incentive bonus*, or *fore-pleasure*, to a yield of pleasure such as this, which is offered to us so as to make possible the release of still greater pleasure arising from deeper psychical sources. In my opinion, all the aesthetic pleasure which a poet affords us has the character

of a fore-pleasure of this kind, and our actual enjoyment of an imaginative work proceeds from a liberation of tensions in our minds. It may even be that not a little of this effect is due to the poet's enabling us thenceforward to enjoy our own day-dreams without self-reproach or shame. ("Creative Writers and Daydreaming," 9:153)

It is also necessary that the art lover not have to struggle against too much suffering, for in that case all the energy saved would be immediately reutilized, and the discharge could not occur. Finally, and most importantly, it must be possible to make an identification. "Psychopathic Characters on the Stage" studies the themes or situations that an author must choose in order for identification to come into play. In tragedy, the suffering represented must not itself cause suffering; it must be able to compensate for the sympathy that arises with certain satisfactions. Here, pleasure derives from the masochistic satisfaction of seeing a human being subjected to divine power, or the pleasure can be direct when the character lays claim to his greatness in spite of his destiny, as in the case of Prometheus. Physical suffering is particularly intolerable on the stage. A character who is physically ill cannot be a hero on the stage, unless some physical particularity of his illness makes a psychic activity possible, as is the case with Philoctetes.

As regards moral suffering, the event must involve a conflict and include an effort of will. This condition is fulfilled in tragedies of rebellion, where the rebel struggles against divinity, in social tragedies, where the hero struggles against the social order, and in tragedies where there is a conflict between two heroes. In psychological dramas, the struggle that causes suffering is within the hero's psyche itself, where various aspirations are in conflict. They must end in instinctual renunciation.

These different possibilities can be combined as well, for a social conflict can be the cause, for example, of an internal conflict. The psychological drama turns into a psychopathological drama when the conflict is between conscious impulses and repressed, unconscious ones. Here, the precondition for enjoyment is that the spectator himself be a neurotic, for "it is only such people who can derive pleasure instead of simple aversion from the revelation and the more or less conscious recognition of a repressed impulse" ("Psychopathic Characters," 7:308–309). For the other spectators, such a revelation can only result in the reinforcement of repression and not in liberation and discharge.

Still, resistance comes to light even in the neurotic; how, then, can the success of a play like *Hamlet* be explained, since its hero behaves like a hysterical neurotic? First, the hero is not ill at the beginning of the play but only becomes sick in the course of the action. Moreover, the impulse that is repressed here is equally repressed by everyone; we can therefore recognize ourselves in the hero, for we are subject to the same conflicts as he. Nevertheless the repressed impulse, though clearly recognizable, must never be named directly. In this way, the spectator's attention is diverted so that, instead of setting great store by what happens, he is gripped by his emotions: "A certain amount of resistance is no doubt saved in this way, just as, in an analytic treatment, we find derivatives of the repressed material reaching consciousness, owing to a lower resistance, while the repressed material itself is unable to do so. After all, the conflict in *Hamlet* is so effectively concealed that it was left to me to unearth it" (pp. 309–310).

Freud concludes his text by stressing that the most important precondition of enjoyment is the diversion of attention. The limits placed on representation of psychopathic characters on the stage are the neurotic instability of the public on the one hand, and the dramatist's skill in avoiding resistances and providing fore-pleasure on the other.

Thus in order for identification to take place, there must be both recognition and lack of recognition. In identifying with the hero, the spectator simultaneously loses and recovers his self, recognizing his past which, up to that point, had been obscure, but at the same time suffering a blow to the ego, whose failure to recognize itself is unveiled.

> Here is one in whom these primaeval wishes of our childhood have been fulfilled, and we shrink back from him with the whole force of the repression by which those wishes have since that time been held

down within us. The poet, as he unveils the past and brings to light the guilt of Oedipus, is at the same time compelling us to recognize our own inner minds, in which these same impulses, though suppressed, are still to be found. [The play] strikes as a warning at ... our pride, at us who since our childhood have grown so wise and so mighty in our own eyes. Like Oedipus, we live in ignorance of these wishes, repugnant to morality, which have been forced upon us by Nature, and after their revelation we may all of us well seek to close our eyes to the scenes of our childhood. (*The Interpretation of Dreams*, 4:262–263)

Identification is what produces the cathartic effect, for to participate intensely in an emotion represented on the stage is to expend the corresponding energies and liquidate them. Emotional expenditure is all the more important in so far as it is linked to a return of the repressed: "It is worth especially stressing the fact that each portion which returns from the past asserts itself with peculiar force" (*Moses and Monotheism*, 23:85).

Thanks to identification, we can be the heroes that we are not in real life. The spectator feels like a poor wretch to whom nothing important can ever happen, and who has often been forced to lower his ambitions and accept a mediocre life. He longs to feel, act, and arrange things according to his desires, in short, to be a hero. "And the playwright and actor enable him to do this by allowing him to identify himself with a hero. They spare him something, too" ("Psychopathic Characters," 7:305). The spectator knows that such heroic conduct would be impossible without suffering or great risk which would perhaps cancel out his pleasure. He also knows that he has only one life and risks losing it just struggling against adversity. His enjoyment at the theater is thus based on illusion: by identifying with the hero who is acting and suffering on the stage, he knows that it is only a play that cannot threaten his security; he can therefore allow himself to play at being a great man and give in to his repressed impulses without hesitation. Since identification with a number of heroes also allows him to have several lives, literature and theater compensate for his mortality. Life is a game of chance, in which it is impossible to take back one's moves, just as art is a game that engages one in ever-different repetition.

> It is an inevitable result of all this that we should seek in the world of fiction, in literature and in the theatre compensation for what has been lost in life. There we still find people who know how to die—who, indeed, even manage to kill someone else. There alone too the condition can be fulfilled which makes it possible for us to reconcile ourselves with death: namely, that behind all the vicissitudes of life we should still be able to preserve a life intact. For it is really too sad that in life it should be as it is in chess, where one false move may force us to resign the game, but with the difference that we can start no second game, no return-match. In the realm of fiction we find the plurality of lives which we need. We die with the hero with whom we have identified ourselves; yet we survive him, and are ready to die again just as safely with another hero. ("Thoughts for the Times on War and Death," 14:291)

For both the spectator and the creative writer, heroes are thus like *doubles* in the various ways Freud defines this term in "The Uncanny," at once projections of the ego and the ego ideal.[15] Just as in nocturnal dreams or daydreams, whatever characters may be portrayed in them, "His Majesty the Ego" is always the one in question: "The hero of the day-dreams is always the subject himself, either directly or by an obvious identification with someone else" (*Introductory Lectures*, 15:99). These doubles are what constitute the true being of the artist and his identity, for the fact that he has to double himself, repeat himself, implies a nonpresence to oneself, an originary dissatisfaction, death immanent in life, and the absence of any simple and full origin. That is why, apart from the fore-pleasure stemming from the "incentive bonus" offered by the beauty of the work of art, and apart from the pleasure that arises from the lifting of inhibition, art brings both the artist and the public a narcissistic pleasure which is analogous to the pleasure given by dreams, with the difference that it can be universal thanks to identification. Thus in U*n oeil en trop*, André Green can rightly call art a "transnarcissistic object."

In a letter to his wife Freud explains in these terms the pleasure we take in reading *Don Quixote*:

> Don't you find it very touching to read how a great person, himself an idealist, makes fun of his ideals? Before we were so fortunate as to apprehend the deep truths in our love we were all noble knights passing through the world caught in a dream, misinterpreting the simplest things, magnifying commonplaces into something noble and rare, and thereby cutting a sad figure. Therefore we men always read with respect about what we once were and in part still remain.[16]

Leonardo da Vinci and a Memory of His Childhood shows how the strangely beautiful figure of the *Mona Lisa*, her at once fascinating and enigmatic smile, "has produced the most powerful and confusing effect on *whoever looks at it*" (11:107; my emphasis). The universal fantasy of the mother's smile, which is played out in the work, makes communication possible in the unconscious of all humanity. It is precisely the "profound and eternal essence of humanity" that the artist expects to awaken in his audience.

THE NARCISSISM OF ART

This relation between art and narcissism is fundamental. Indeed, the narcissistic structure seems to me to be the key to artistic activity, since it characterizes the psyche of both the artist and the art lover. The term "narcissism" is a mythic concept Freud borrows from a legend, and this is no accident, since the legend speaks the truth of the psyche without reflecting on it as such. And it is no accident either that the concept of narcissism appears for the first time in Freud's work a few months before his essay on Leonardo.[17] In that essay he writes, regarding Leonardo's homosexuality, "He finds the objects of his love along the path of *narcissism*, as we say; for Narcissus, according to the Greek legend, was a youth who preferred his own reflection (*Spiegelbild*) to everything else and who was changed into the lovely flower of that name" (11:100).[18]

The narcissism of art, analogous to that of dreams, is characterized by centrifugal identification which works by projecting the psychic processes onto the outside; in the art lover, centripetal identification is in play as well. In the first case the subject identifies the other with his own person, whereas in the second, he identifies his own person with someone else.

On dreams, Freud writes:

> Thus we know that dreams are completely egoistic and that the person who plays the chief parts in their scenes is always to be recognized as the dreamer. This is now easily to be accounted for by the narcissism of the state of sleep. Narcissism and egoism, indeed, coincide; the word 'narcissism,' is only intended to emphasize the fact that egoism is a libidinal phenomenon as well; or, to put it another way, narcissism may be described as the libidinal complement of egoism. ("A Metapsychological Supplement to the Theory of Dreams," 14:223)

The dream itself is a production intended to defend the ego from any disturbance, making it possible for the sleeper to continue sleeping by externalizing an internal process that was bothering him: "The internal demand which was striving to occupy him has been replaced by an external experience, whose demand has been disposed of." There is, so to speak, an essential link between projection and narcissism. "We will, however, defer the full treatment of projection till we come to analyze the narcissistic disorder in which this mechanism plays the most striking part" (p. 224).

The work of art, too, is a projection which puts an end to internal disturbance and, like the dream, makes possible the hallucinatory satisfaction of a wish. In this respect it is akin to paranoid hallucinatory psychosis as well. The narcissistic person, who is inclined toward self-sufficiency, will seek most of his satisfaction in internal mental processes, through the mere play of his psychic activity, as in art. Which is to say that the narcissism of art is not only a *secondary* narcissism linked to centrifugal or centripetal indentification, but also a *primary* narcissism linked to the belief in the omnipotence of ideas and the search for self-sufficiency. In this respect it is reminiscent of the infantile narcissism of animistic primitive peoples,[19] and is comparable to magic. It is, in short, the vestige of primitive animism in today's society. The vulgar expression "the magic of art" should be taken literally in this context, whereas "art for art's sake" is an ideological formula intended to veil the narcissistic relation that ties man to art. Indeed, in primitive societies magical procedures are based on imitation: when people want rain, they themselves play at being the rain; when they want to kill an enemy, they stab his effigy; they ensure the fertility of the soil by openly performing human sexual relations. Similarly, the "double" is endowed with powers which rest on the belief in the omnipotence of the ego, and the satisfaction of a wish is obtained by means of a kind of motor hallucination.

> This kind of representation of a satisfied wish is quite comparable to children's play, which succeeds their earlier purely sensory technique of satisfaction. If children and primitive men find play and imitative representation enough for them, that is not a sign of their being unassuming in our sense or of their resignedly accepting their actual impotence. It is the easily understandable result of the paramount virtue they ascribe to their wishes, of the will that is associated with those wishes and of the methods by which those wishes operate. (*Totem and Taboo*, 13:84)

Now the artist, too, manages to produce some satisfaction thanks to the play and the illusion of his art. It is true that though the function of the dream is to avoid unpleasure (that is, an increase in tension) by protecting sleep from external excitations, art does not make it possible really to do away with unpleasure or to fight suffering; too much suffering destroys aesthetic enjoyment. But art is a source of "cheap" pleasure which offers some consolation for unpleasure, a consolation that is short-lived for most people, but more lasting for the creator who invests all his affect in the work. "Nevertheless the mild narcosis induced in us by art can do no more than bring about a transient withdrawal from the pressure of vital needs, and it is not strong enough to make us forget real misery" (*Civilization and Its Discontents*, 21:81).[20]

The "magic of art" thus consists in being able to put man to sleep, and in waking life, to restore to him the narcissistic situation of dream; hence the link between narcosis and narcissism. Art aims not so much at pleasure as at nirvana, that is, the zero-degree tension characteristic of primary narcissism. But this effort is hidden, so to speak, by the positive contribution of the real effects of "the magic of art."

> In only a single field of our civilization has the omnipotence of thoughts been retained, and that is in the field of art. Only in art does it still happen that a man who is consumed by desires performs something resembling the accomplishment of those desires and that what he does in play produces emotional effects—thanks to artistic illusion—just as though it were something real. People speak with justice of the "magic of art" and compare artists to magicians. But the comparison is perhaps more significant than it claims to be. There can be no doubt that art did not begin as art for art's sake. It worked originally in the service of impulses which are for the most part extinct today. And among them we may suspect the presence of many magical purposes. (*Totem and Taboo,* 13:90)

Thus, as it produces real effects on all of us by means of a real work which has a definite social status, art, like magic, is intermediary between reality and the imaginary, and differs in this respect from dreams and hallucinatory psychosis. "Art is a conventionally accepted reality in which, thanks to artistic illusion, symbols and substitutes are able to provoke real affects. Thus art constitutes a region half-way between a reality which frustrates wishes and the wish-fulfilling world of the imagination—a region in which, as it were, primitive man's strivings for omnipotence are still in full force" ("The Claims of Psycho-Analysis to Scientific Interest," 13:188). I investigate the question of art's status as intermediary later on, in order to see what that actually means.

We find the counterproof of the magical, and therefore narcissistic, significance of art in the Bible's condemnation of all images and idols, which is not due to any objection to the plastic arts in principle; rather, its aim was to discourage people from practicing magic.[21] The comparison between the Egyptian religion and the Mosaic religion is interesting in this regard, for the latter condemns every kind of magic and sorcery, while in the former they flourish abundantly: "The insatiable appetite of the Egyptians for embodying their gods in clay, stone, and metal (to which our museums owe so much today) is confronted with the harsh prohibition against making an image of any living or imagined creature" (*Moses and Monotheism*, 23:19).

Another important difference between the two religions is that no other people tried as hard as the Egyptians to deny death and ensure their existence in the afterlife, whereas the Jewish religion, on the contrary, had renounced immortality and nowhere alludes to an existence after death.

How can we understand the fact that plastic representation and the search for immortality on the one hand, and the condemnation of images and the renunciation of immortality on the other, go hand in hand? The explanation is that the religion of Moses is monotheism, the religion of the father. With the advent of Moses, therefore, the religious phase that corresponds to the stage at which the libido is directed toward objects is substituted for the first, animistic phase—that of the Egyptians—which corresponds to narcissism. The revolt against "idols" is a way of combatting the belief in the omnipotence of the ideas of the creature who wants to take the place of the creator, and thus is a revolt against the son who wants to take the place of the father. If God is the father (or the father is God) there is no need to fear death, because the father's love clearly ensures immortality. The Egyptians, on the other hand, must provide for their own immortality by projecting themselves into doubles, which is the function they assign to works of art. In "The Uncanny," Freud recalls just this, that originally in Egyptian statuary, the "double" is a means of conquering death.

Moreover, the narcissism of art is not manifested solely in centripetal or centrifugal identifications (as secondary narcissism), or in the belief in the omnipotence of ideas (as primary narcissism). In art as in "primitive" men, primary narcissism is characterized above all by the search for immortality and absolute self-sufficiency, that is, by the aim of being one's own genitor, being the *causa sui*. The artist is a hero, greatly admired by men, because he was capable of "killing" the father; thus the search for immortality and the aim of being the primal cause are correlatives, for the goal of both is to make man a god, which is the same as saying, to replace the father.

The search for immortality is carried out by means of successive identifications with various heroes who have been created or admired, representatives of the ego ideal who serve as substitutes for the image of the father—multiple doubles, constitutive of the identity of the subject who is the same only by virtue of his relation to the Other. Here again the artist proceeds in the same way as the primitive man: "The projected creations of primitive men resemble the personifications constructed by poets; for the latter externalize in the form of separate individuals the opposing instinctual impulses struggling within them" (*Totem and Taboo*, 13:65, n. 2). In "On Transience" Freud denounces artists' desire for immortality as narcissistic, and the theme of "eternal beauty" as ideological. The value of a work of art does not depend on its lasting quality, because its role is to make possible the discharge of certain emotions as a function of the degree of repression proper to a given society.

This search for immortality goes hand in hand with the artist's desire to be the *causa sui*. By identifying with his own characters, whose father he feels he is through identification with his own father, the artist becomes his own father and thus becomes independent of his genitors. It is as though in his transcription of an originary scene, the artist wanted to deny the primal scene: the memory of art aims to erase the real presence of the father; it is originarily deceitful because it covers up a murder. Indeed in the last analysis, isn't wanting to be one's own father tantamount to wanting to give one's mother a child, the work of art? In this sense, the artist could be said to commit incest symbolically. The work of art, in the likeness of its author, appears as a "gift" given to the mother, like the child, of whom the artist would be both the father and the mother. The incestuous attitude toward the mother can go hand in hand with a homosexual attitude (links between homosexuality and narcissism are also found in the paranoid structure).[22] "All his impulses, those of tenderness, gratitude, lustfulness, defiance and independence, find satisfaction in the single wish *to be his own father"* ("A Special Type of Object Choice Made By Men," 11:173).[23]

We would do well here to recall the symbolic and substitutive link between excrement, the penis, the gift, the child, and all forms of production,[24] because to give one's mother a child is also to "save one's mother" phantasmally, just as she saved us from the first danger of birth: the work is a sign of gratitude, a substitutive penis given to the mother.

In a letter of December 15, 1919 to Abraham, Freud says: "Your contribution on the omnipotence of feces was very amusing. After all, they are indeed products like thoughts and desires." This conception of art is party to the theological ideology underlying the notion that the artist is the genitor of his work just as God is of creation. But behind this ideological formulation is the masked, narcissistic desire to be one's own creator, self-sufficient, to be God, one's own procreator.

The case of Leonardo da Vinci is a perfect illustration of the Freudian technique of unmasking.[25] Through identification with his own father, Leonardo said he was "father of his works," and behaved toward them as his father had behaved toward him. He abandoned them in an unfinished state—or at least one he considered unfinished: "There is no doubt that the creative artist feels towards his works like a father. The effect which Leonardo's identification with his father had on his painting was a fateful one. He created them and then cared no more about them, just as his father had not cared about him" (*Leonardo*, 11:121). His inhibited creativity can be explained in the same way, that is, it was parallel to his father's misfortune; out of guilt, Leonardo could not accept being superior to him. His narcissistic object choices, which were homosexual due to his mother's excessive tenderness, repeated his mother's attitude toward him in childhood. It can be said in fact that his works were like substitutes that he offered her in gratitude, and were intended to "save" her from the unhappiness of her existence. The self-sufficient artist, "murderer" of the father, is thus an embodiment of the hero that survives in our culture. The epic poem celebrates him, and tragedy—a substitute for the totemic feast

which is commemorative of the father's death—opens the space of
art as the emblematic staging of its signification. All art, insofar as
it repeats the death of God, is necessarily atheistic.[26] The Oedipus
complex is the originary nucleus of all culture, art, morality, and
religion, which are like so many reaction formations against it.

> In the history of Greek art we come upon a situation which shows
> striking resemblances to the scene of the totem meal as identified
> by Robertson Smith, and not less profound differences from it. I have
> in mind the situation of the most ancient Greek tragedy. A company
> of individuals, named and dressed alike, surrounded a single figure,
> all hanging upon his words and deeds: they were the chorus and the
> impersonator of the hero. He was originally the only actor. Later, a
> second and third actor were added, to play as counterpart to the
> hero and as characters split off from him; but the character of the
> hero himself and his relation to the chorus remained unaltered. The
> hero of tragedy must suffer; to this day that remains the essence of
> a tragedy. He had to bear the burden of what was known as "tragic
> guilt"; the basis of that guilt is not always easy to find, for in the
> light of our everyday life it is often no guilt at all. As a rule it lay in
> rebellion against some divine or human authority; and the chorus
> accompanied the hero with feelings of sympathy, sought to hold him
> back, to warn him and to sober him, and mourned over him when
> he had met with what was felt as the merited punishment for his
> rash undertaking. But why had the hero of tragedy to suffer? and
> what was the meaning of his "tragic guilt"? (*Totem and Taboo*, 13:155–
> 156)

The answer to this question is not the same in *Totem and Taboo* as
in *Moses and Monotheism*, where the analysis is taken up again. In the
first work, the hero represents the primal father, the hero of the real
primal tragedy, which is said to be repeated in tragedy as spectacle,
but in distorted form due to repression. In historical reality, the
members of the chorus were the cause of the hero's suffering,
whereas in tragedy, where the hero causes his own suffering, the
members of the chorus sympathize with him. The crime imputed
to him, namely a revolt against authority, is the product of a projection by the members of the chorus who are the real authors of

the crime; in spite of himself, then, the hero is the redeemer of the chorus.

In *Moses and Monotheism*, Freud seems to have given up the explanation of the crime in terms of displacement and projection. Instead, the hero and the chorus both represent rebellious heroes; both represent the same conspiracy of the brothers against the father (23:87). The suffering is thus interpreted as punishment, but the general meaning still remains the same: Greek tragedy is the different repetition of a murder—the murder of the primal father. The same is true of the representation of Christ's Passion in the Middle Ages and, less clearly, of every work of art insofar as the artist, in creating it, intends to substitute himself for the father. In *Totem and Taboo* Freud writes, "At the conclusion, then, of this exceedingly condensed enquiry, I should like to insist that its outcome shows that the beginning of religion, morals, society and art converge in the Oedipus complex. This is in complete agreement with the psycho-analytic finding that the same complex constitutes the nucleus of all neuroses, so far as our present knowledge goes" (13:156–157).[27]

Thus the key to the theological conception of art is found in the narcissism of the artist and the spectator. Unmasking reveals the regressive and infantile character of artistic activity; as we saw in chapter 3, Freud shows that the artist is not really the "father" of his works, that he is not their master as God is of his creation, that it is instead the works that engender their father and are constitutive of his identity.[28] The structure of the artistic text says more than the artist wants to have it say. He is himself caught in the texture of his own game, surpassed by his "creation" as the father is by his children. If the artist, in relation to his work, is not like God in relation to his creation, it is because the father is not a God, and God is not a father. The demystification of the theological conception of art goes hand in hand with the demystification of a certain finalistic conception of paternity, and with the murder of God: the theological conception of art is the last refuge of theism in a society that considers itself atheistic. In order to be free of this notion one must not kill the father only to set oneself up as his substitute, and thus remain caught in the same closure and the same ideology; rather, one must rethink the concept of paternity and expel what remains of creation from procreation, that is, substitute necessity for finality, and chance and play for seriousness. This is what Freud does, as we shall see in more detail in the last chapter.

The narcissism of art accounts for its fascinating, enigmatic character, and the "uncanny" effect it produces on the spectator; for "we appear to attribute an 'uncanny' quality to impressions that seek to confirm the omnipotence of thoughts and the animistic mode of thinking in general, after we have reached a stage at which, in our *judgment*, we have abandoned such beliefs" (*Totem and Taboo*, 13:86, n. 2).

THE WORK OF THE DEATH IMPULSES

This also means that the work of art is more at the service of the death impulses than of Eros, insofar as its pleasure rests essentially on a saving of expenditure, as "narcosis" and as a product of narcissism. For if narcissism is a search for immortality, the latter can only be achieved by mimicking death in life. Refusal of death is fear of death and thus of life; it is a stockpiling of the self, an economy, a search not so much for a lowering of tensions as for their total dissolution. The nirvana principle is more in command here than the pleasure principle. Narcissism lulls one into sterile self-contemplation or, in the case of collective narcissism, lulls society into contemplation of its own values: art as "reflection" is conservative.

Erected to conquer death, art, as a "double," like any double,[29] itself turns into an image of death. The game of art is a game of death, which always already implies death in life, as a force of saving and inhibition. "The Uncanny" indicates this transformation of the algebraic sign of the double, its link with narcissism and death as the punishment for having sought immortality, for having wanted to "kill" the father. It is perhaps no accident that the model of the "double," erected for the first time by the Egyptians, is found in the figuration of castration in dreams, the doubling of the genital organ. Repetition, like repression, is originary, and serves to fill an originary lack as well as to veil it: the double does not double a presence, but rather supplements it, allowing one to read, as in a mirror, originary "difference," castration, death, and at the same time the necessity of crossing them out.[30]

[The model of castration provided by dreams] led the Ancient Egyptians to develop the art of making images of the dead in lasting materials. Such ideas, however, have sprung from the soil of unbounded self-love, from the primary narcissism which dominates the mind of the child and of primitive man. But when this stage has been surmounted, the algebraic sign of the "double" changes. From having been an assurance of immortality, it becomes the uncanny harbinger of death. . . . When all is said and done, the quality of uncanniness can only come from the fact of the "double" being a creation dating back to a very early mental stage, long since surmounted—a stage, incidentally, at which it wore a more friendly aspect. The "double" has become a thing of terror, just as, after the collapse of their religion, the gods turned into demons (Heine, *The Gods in Exile*). ("The Uncanny," 17:235–236)

Art as a double, an internal division of the self from the self, a repetition (whereas life as pure presence, in accordance with our fantasies, would be pure originality), produces an uncanny effect, as is the case wherever repetition is given when one expects difference. Hence the repetition of the Leonardesque smile in all of his paintings gives Leonardo the idea that there is a terrible fate, something ineluctable that he cannot escape. "Where we would have seen only chance," says Freud, Leonardo finds a destiny, a vocation that uncannily troubles him. The repetition that is linked, in this instance, to the absence to oneself of one's own fantasies (here, the mother's smile)—fantasies stemming from a childhood experience whose meaning is given only in the doubles that infinitely unfold and distort it—this repetition is secondarily, ideologically elaborated and transformed into a theological "finality." "Vocation" is a superstition corresponding to the projection of desire. It is intended to indicate the complete originality of the works, and thus the originality of the author's own person; it is intended to found the necessity of the work, just as the author would like to be founded in existence, elected for himself, by God, wanted by his parents. The idea of "destiny" is intended to bar the absence of difference and the radical originality that he would like to possess— to cross out the possible presence of other beings in the author's place, the presence of new arrivals who might resemble him; in short, it is intended, in its very repetition, to hide the place of chance in life.

The form of the "double" and its secondary elaboration can be related to the compulsion of destiny (see *Beyond the Pleasure Principle*), linked to the repetition compulsion and the death impulse that is its principle of intelligibility.

Finally, the sublimation of the sexual "drive," which is in play in aesthetic pleasure and in "creation," implies an inhibition in the aim of the drive. This inhibition is possible only because the drive is originarily divided from itself, because the death drive effects an originary repression: the possibility of sublimation as a drive deflected from its aim is inscribed in the very being of the drive, insofar as death is always already at work in it. The second inhibition in sublimation, as a "little death," has as its condition of possibility the duality of the drives, and the division of the drive into partial drives. There is no sexual "drive" per se, but only "sexual drives." The transformation of the sexual aim into a cultural aim is mediated by the ego, which transforms object libido into narcissistic libido and imposes on it another aim.[31] Culture is possible, then, only through regression and the liberation of the forces of death.

THE WORK OF EROS

But there could be no culture without Eros, and in art it comes into play at several levels. First, the making of aesthetic pleasure, even when it is masochistic, benefits the pleasure principle; linked to a discharge, it nonetheless produces an increase in excitation. The sexual excitation that accompanies the incentive bonus procures an augmentation of psychic potential.[32] In *Three Essays on the Theory of Sexuality*, pleasure is not conceived of only as a discharge, but as a qualitative variation, the variation of rhythm.

Second, the "double" is not only conceived of as a "reflection," but as an ego ideal. The "double" can also mean "all the unfulfilled but possible futures to which we still like to cling in phantasy, all the strivings of the ego which adverse external circumstances have crushed, and all our suppressed acts of volition which nourish in us the illusion of Free Will" ("The Uncanny," 17:236).

Works of art in their role as "doubles" allow the artist to construct his fantasies, to free himself from them in that very process, and to constitute his identity. Through multiple repetition, the unity of the self is constructed: retrograde movement is linked to a progressive movement of integration, intertwining of the drives, and organization in which the work of Eros can be recognized. Already, at the level of the fantasy—and the work of art, like the fantasy, is a substitute for the meaning of past experience constructed according to the same psychic procedures—the three moments of temporality come into play. In "Creative Writers and Daydreaming," Freud says:

> [A fantasy] hovers, as it were, between three times—the three moments of time which our ideation involves. Mental work is linked to some current impression, some provoking occasion in the present which has been able to arouse one of the subject's major wishes. From there it harks back to a memory of an earlier experience (usually an infantile one) in which this wish was fulfilled; and now it creates a situation relating to the future which represents a fulfilment of the wish. What it thus creates is a day-dream or phantasy, which carries about it traces of its origin from the occasion which provoked it and from the memory. Thus past, present and future are strung together, as it were, on the thread of the wish that runs through them. (9:147–148)

"Creative Writers and Daydreaming" concludes that poetic activity proceeds in the same way as phantasmal activity: "A strong experience in the present awakens in the poet a memory of an earlier experience (usually belonging to his childhood) from which there now proceeds a wish which finds its fulfillment in the poetry. Poetry itself exhibits elements of the recent provoking occasion as well as of the old memory" (p. 151).

Finally, if art, insofar as it is narcissistic, has a conservative function in society, it can also serve to unify the social group, just as it does the individual. The "universal aesthetic feeling" that brings people closer to each other thanks to transnarcissistic identification is in this sense necessary to social life; it fosters the growth of relationships, the formation of groupings larger than the single family unit or the narcissistic closure of the inward-oriented individual. Eros is at work wherever relationships multiply, wherever greater unification occurs. "Beauty," which appears to be the luxury of civilization, can nonetheless serve, however ephemerally, as remedy for its "discontents"—at least, it can do so for those of its participants who are not engaged in exhausting work that makes them incapable of enjoying art.

> As we discovered long since, art offers substitutive satisfactions for the oldest and still most deeply felt cultural renunciations, and for that reason it serves as nothing else does to reconcile a man to the sacrifices he has made on behalf of civilization. On the other hand, the creations of art heighten his feelings of identification, of which every cultural unit stands in so much need, by providing an occasion for sharing highly valued emotional experiences. And when those creations picture the achievements of his particular culture and bring to his mind its ideals in an impressive manner, they also minister to his narcissistic satisfaction. (The Future of an Illusion, 21:13–14)[33]

Thus, in art (and this is true of all cultural and even biological phenomena), both Eros and the death impulses find satisfaction. Nevertheless, it can be said that the death impulses predominate; the key to art is narcissism—a regressive, retrograde activity, a repetition of playful childhood activity, a sublimation.

IMAGINATION, A "NATURAL RESERVE"

But here the death drive is in the service of the struggle against death: the death of the artist who is aiming for immortality; the death of the beloved, since artistic activity fosters the work of mourning by sublimating repressed libido; and the death originarily present in life, since artistic activity is an originary substitutive activity for all of the renunciations imposed by reality and culture. For man cannot really renounce anything—neither the play of his childhood, nor his wishes, even though they have never been fulfilled, except phantasmally; dreams, daydreams, play, and art are originary substitutes, for lack and the absence of meaning are originary. Art seems to be fundamentally a compensation for the harshness of real life and the necessity of death, which are always already there, affecting artist and art lover alike. "In the exercising of an art [psychoanalysis] sees once again an activity intended to allay ungratified wishes—in the first place in the creative artist himself and subsequently in his audience or spectators" ("The Claims of Psycho-Analysis," 13.187).

In the general economy of life and the cultural evolution of man—marked by the passage from the primary to the secondary processes, and instinctual renunciation which is now voluntary rather than automatic, by virtue of submission to the pleasure-unpleasure principle—the function of art is to help us to tolerate the necessity of this passage by repeating the initial state ever-differently. Art, thanks to the phantasmal or imaginative faculty that makes it possible, seems to be an intermediary between the strict pleasure principle, characterized by the struggle against unpleasure, and the reality principle—an intermediary that makes it possible to reconcile them. Here, Freud seems to adopt a perspective which is at once phylogenetic, evolutionist, and finalistic. Judging from his discourse, it would seem that there was an initial state in which the psychic apparatus was governed by the pleasure principle alone—an initial state from the phylogenetic point of view, whose traces remain in each one of us, both in childhood and in the state of sleep. Later on, man gradually came to be governed by the reality principle, at which point life created an intermediary faculty, imagination, to help him to tolerate the harsh submission to the reality principle.

Imagination is part of the "economy" of life. Thanks to imagination, man creates energy *reserves*, and expends less energy struggling against reality in order to change it; thanks to the imaginary realm, wishes are fulfilled by means of hallucinatory gratification.

In "Formulations on the Two Principles of Mental Functioning," a text which is essential for understanding the status of imagination and art as intermediaries, Freud writes:

> A general tendency of our mental apparatus, which can be traced back to the economic principle of saving expenditure [of energy], seems to find expression in the tenacity with which we hold on to the sources of pleasure at our disposal, and in the difficulty with which we renounce them. With the introduction of the reality principle one species of thought-activity was split off; it was kept free from reality-testing and remained subordinated to the pleasure principle alone. This activity is *phantasying*, which begins already in children's play, and later, continued as *day-dreaming*, abandons dependence on real objects. (12:222)

"An Autobiographical Study" emphasizes imagination's economic function as a *reserve*, a reserve acquired at the time of the passage from the pleasure principle to the reality principle: "The realm of imagination was evidently a reserve (*Schonung*) made during the painful transition from the pleasure principle to the reality principle in order to provide a substitute for the gratification of instincts which had to be given up in real life" (20:64).

In the *Introductory Lectures*, Freud compares the "reserve" of imagination to "natural reserves" which perpetuate the "original" state of the earth in places where, regretfully but for reasons of necessity, man has been forced to change it by cultivating it. In these natural reserves everything, even what is harmful, grows freely. Similarly, the reserve of imagination is not subject to any of the laws of reality. Its best-known productions are fantasies, which are the nucleus and the prototype of night dreams; the latter are even less subject to restriction thanks to the liberation of instinctual impulses at night. But these fantasies can be the source of neurotic symptoms, analogous to weeds growing in the natural reserves.

> [Men] have . . . retained a mental activity in which all these abandoned sources of pleasure and methods of achieving pleasure are granted a further existence—a form of existence in which they are left free from the claims of reality and of what we call "reality-testing." Every desire takes before long the form of picturing its own fulfilment; there is no doubt that dwelling upon imaginary wish-fulfilments brings satisfaction with it, although it does not interfere with a knowledge that what is concerned is not real. Thus in the activity of phantasy human beings continue to enjoy the freedom from external compulsion which they have long since renounced in reality. They have contrived to *alternate* between remaining an animal of pleasure and being once more a creature of reason. Indeed, they cannot subsist on the scanty satisfaction which they can extort from reality. . . . The creation of the mental realm of phantasy finds a perfect parallel in the establishment of "reservations" or "nature reserves" in places where the requirements of agriculture, communications and industry threaten to bring about changes in the original face of the earth which will quickly make it unrecognizable. A nature reserve preserves its original state which everywhere else has to our regret been sacrificed to necessity. Everything, including what is useless and even what is noxious, can grow and proliferate there as it pleases. The mental realm of fantasy is just such a reserve withdrawn from the reality principle. (16:374; my emphasis)

It is at the time of this passage from one state to another that a close tie is established between fantasies and the sexual drives. The ego drives are said to adapt more easily to reality than the sexual drives, which have found satisfaction in the body of the child itself. Moreover, during the latency period, the sexual drives are repressed, since the latency period and autoeroticism slow the development of the sexual drives and bring them more surely under the dominance of the pleasure principle. A closer connection is thus made between the ego drives, the activity of consciousness, and the reality principle on the one hand, and the sexual drives, fantasy, and the pleasure principle on the other.[34]

If we were to go only so far as to consider the letter of Freud's discourse, we should have to conclude that on these questions Freud is a prisoner of the traditional conception that separates the imaginary from the real, and makes of imagination a *secondary* substitutive activity which compensates for reality when reality *becomes* unpalatable. The concept of the intermediary would have to be understood in the chronological sense as well as in the sense of mediation between the two principles of psychic functioning which, though separated initially, are secondarily united and reconciled thanks to the imagination. In this, Freud would scarcely be more original than the classical philosophers who always consider imagination a *metaxu*, an intermediary.[35] According to this view, we are *alternately* "animals of pleasure" and "reasonable animals." Freud's comparison of mental life to natural reserves is compatible with this traditional ideology, which presupposes that primal nature—virgin, pure, subject to the pleasure principle alone—is later followed by culture, agriculture, communications, industry, and with them the reign of necessity. Viewed from this angle, Freud's conception is scarcely distinguishable from the fantasies of his own patients who, in accordance with their own desires, always project into the past an idyllic golden age.

But in fact, as we saw in the preceding chapter, Freud's genetic conception is always mythical and its signification, structural. I have already shown that the myth of the primal horde is precisely that—mythical—and that culture is not secondary but always already in place, because "nature" is not a plenitude which accidentally comes to require cultivation. It is originarily conflictual, a difference of itself from itself. The "secondary" processes do not substitute for the "primary" processes, and that is why there could be neither a "passage" from one to the other nor any need for an intermediary to make it tolerable. "Secondary" processes and "primary" processes are both, as such, pure theoretical fictions. The two paradigms Freud gives to indicate the survival of the pleasure principle after the "introduction" of the reality principle—the infant and the state of sleep—amply reveal the mythic nature of the genetic conception.[36]

For if the psychic apparatus of the infant functions through obedience to the pleasure principle alone, it is only thanks to the presence of the mother who satisfies the demand, that is, thanks to an element that takes account of reality. If "the state of sleep is able to re-establish the likeness of mental life as it was before the recognition of reality, because a prerequisite of sleep is a deliberate rejection of reality (the wish to sleep)" ("Formulations," 12:219, n. 3), it is because "reality" is already present; if it were not, there would be no need to reject it. A hallucinatory mode of satisfying desire can be spoken of only in opposition to a real one. And besides, Freud presents both of these models as *fictions*. In *The Interpretation of Dreams*, he says that a psychic apparatus whose functioning is governed by the primary processes alone is a theoretical fiction.

> When I described one of the psychical processes occurring in the mental apparatus as the "primary" one, what I had in mind was not merely considerations of relative importance and efficiency; I intended also to choose a name which would give an indication of its chronological priority. It is true that, so far as we know, no psychical apparatus exists which possesses a primary process only and that such an apparatus is to that extent a theoretical fiction. But this much is a fact. the primary processes are present in the mental apparatus from the first, while it is only during the course of life that the secondary processes unfold, and come to inhibit and overlay the primary ones; it may even be that their complete domination is not attained until the prime of life. (5:603)

Finally, the idea of a "primary" process is contradicted by the idea of an originary repression. The secondary processes thus do not succeed the primary processes, any more than the reality principle succeeds the pleasure principle. Rather, they coexist originarily, because death, deflection, and difference in the Derridian sense are originarily present in life. The coexistence of the two principles overlays that of the death impulses and Eros.

   Freud, who has once again fallen prey to geneticism in his language, is speaking mythically. But originary difference effaces the myth of origin; and yet it is always by means of a myth of origin that Freud tends to help us grasp originary difference. The status of imagination is thus not that of an intermediary. Because "reality" is always already there, because death always originarily inhibits life, because life cannot be totally expended without perishing, because it protects itself by deferring dangerous investment, because it economizes, there is an originary need for a "supplement" to the "pleasure principle": imagination. The substitutive function of imagination is not a compensation that comes second, but an originary supplement. The "reserve" of psychic energy, where desire is expended in hallucination without any constraint and without the economy of death, comes in response to the necessary reserve of life.[37] The fact that reality is always already there institutes an originary repetition in the form of phantasmal activity—it institutes representation as originary. It is in this "economic" sense that we must understand that imagination cannot be creative, but only "reproductive," and not just in the symbolic sense. Symbolic repetition has as its precondition economic repetition; it is because life is reserved that imagination can and must repeat. The process of expenditure of the reserve makes possible the imaginative reserve. Like the "natural reserve" that seems to maintain an original state that never existed as such, imagination stages, mimics the total expenditure that has never taken place. Imagination is a negation of death in life, yet at the same time bears witness to it since it is only phantasmal and implies, insofar as it is an originary repetition, the difference it would like to deny. Imagination, as an originary reserve, opens the door to both pathological repetition and normal repetition in dreams, daydreams, play, and art. Pathological repetition is a negation of originary difference and of reality; it is a desire for full presence, the longing for phantasmal unity, a negation of death. This is the function of the imaginary in the neurotic, and even in the introvert that the artist is: "The artist is once more in rudiments an introvert, not far removed from neurosis" (Introductory Lectures, 16:376).

We will continue to take it that introversion denotes the turning away of the libido from the possibilities of real satisfaction and its displacement onto phantasies which have hitherto been tolerated as innocent. An introvert is not yet a neurotic, but he is in an unstable situation: he is sure to develop symptoms at the next shift of forces, unless he finds some other outlets for his dammed-up libido. The unreal character of neurotic satisfaction and the *effacement of the difference* between phantasy and reality are on the other hand already determined by the fact of lingering at the stage of introversion. (p. 374; my emphasis)

The "freedom" of imagination is not free choice, nor is it free will: this ideological conception goes hand in hand with the famous "license" accorded artists, whose meaning we saw earlier. The freedom of the artist is freedom in regard to the reality that is phantasmally denied.

"The Uncanny" establishes differences between real experience and works of fiction concerning the arousal of the feeling of uncanniness. In fiction, the uncanny is much fuller and richer than in real life; it embraces real life and includes as well things which do not occur under real life conditions. "The realm of imagination depends for its effect on the fact that its content is not submitted to reality-testing" (17:249). The author can multiply the effects imagination can have by creating events which do not occur in reality; the reader goes along with him because "when belief makes him happy, he has to take the acceptance of quite a considerable number of improbable occurrences into the bargain" (*Delusions and Dreams*, 9:18).[38]

The "delusion" of the reader comes in response to the "delusion" of the author, and they have the same basis. The freedom of imagination is the free play of the primary processes, the same freedom that the id enjoys; it must be understood not in a metaphysical sense, but in an economic and topical sense. In terms of categories, the freedom of the primary process is its independence from logical categories, from space and time; from a symbolic standpoint, from the standpoint of representation, this freedom is the play of a combinatory, the play of displacements and condensations;

and from the standpoint of affect, it is the play of transformation of affect—free, unbound energy.

This freedom, therefore, does not rule out constraint and necessity; it is compelled to repeat precisely because of distortion. We have seen how, after painting the *Mona Lisa*, Leonardo was compelled to express himself again, to paint the *St. Anne* in celebration of maternity. Ever-different repetition thus implies both constraint and free play in the variation of forms and the transformation of affect.

The freedom of the primary process in art does not rule out its mastery, either—mastery, that is, by the secondary process of the preconscious system, which is what distinguishes the repetition in art from pathological repetition, and makes art intermediary between imagination, which gives hallucinatory satisfaction to desire, and reality, which frustrates it. In "On Narcissism: An Introduction," Freud writes:

> [The parents] are inclined to suspend in the child's favor the operation of all the cultural acquisitions which their own narcissism had been forced to respect, and to renew on his behalf the claims to privilege which were long ago given up by themselves. . . . Illness, death, renunciation of enjoyment, restrictions on his own will, shall not touch him; the laws of nature and society shall be abrogated in his favor; he shall once more really be the centre and core of creation—"His Majesty the Baby," as we once fancied ourselves. The child shall fulfill those wishful dreams of the parents which they never carried out—the boy shall become a great man and a hero in his father's place, and the girl shall marry a prince as a tardy compensation for her mother. At the most touchy point of the narcissistic system, the immortality of the ego, which is so hard pressed by reality, security is achieved by taking refuge in the child. (14:91)

Thanks to this narcissistic identification, the artist wins love, honor, the wealth he desired, and fame.[39] In "Formulations on the Two Principles of Mental Functioning":

> Art brings about a reconciliation between the two principles in a peculiar way. An artist is originally a man who turns away from reality because he cannot come to terms with the renunciation of instinctual

satisfaction which it at first demands, and who allows his erotic and ambitious wishes full play in the life of phantasy. He finds the way back to reality, however, from this world of phantasy by making use of special gifts to mould his phantasies into truths of a new kind, which are valued by men as precious reflections of reality. Thus in a certain fashion he actually becomes the hero, the king, the creator, or the favourite he desired to be, without following the long round-about path of making real alterations in the external world. But he can only achieve this because other men feel the same dissatisfaction as he does with the renunciation demanded by reality, and because that dissatisfaction, which results from the replacement of the pleasure principle by the reality principle, is itself a part of reality. (12:224)[10]

And in *Introductory Lectures*: "If [the artist] is able to accomplish all this [to fashion a work of art from his fantasies], he makes it possible for other people once more to derive consolation and alleviation from their own sources of pleasure in their unconscious which have become inaccessible to them; he earns their gratitude and admiration and he has thus achieved *through* his phantasy what originally he had achieved only *in* his phantasy—honour, power, and the love of women" (16:376–377).

Thus imagination, an originary reserve, can yield many productions all having the same aim, which is to deny originary difference and death. What essentially distinguishes art from all the others is the contact which, in spite of everything, it maintains with the real, and the collective narcosis it is capable of producing; it is thus distinct from the fundamentally asocial narcissistic satisfactions of dreams or neuroses.

NEUROTIC FORMATIONS AND CULTURAL "CREATIONS"

In every case the starting point is dissatisfaction, and there must be "many favorable circumstances" for the artist—who is moved by extremely strong impulses and dispositions, and has turned away from reality toward imaginary life by virtue of harsh necessity—not to become a neurotic. The favorable circumstances are his great capacity for sublimation and his weakness in effecting repression; and finally his "gift" makes it possible for him to give his fantasies a form such that they lose their personal character entirely and can become a source of enjoyment for others: the sum of pleasure procured thanks to the incentive bonus makes it possible to mask or even, provisionally, to undo repression in others. "The motive forces of artists are the same conflicts which drive other people into neurosis and have encouraged society to construct its institutions" ("The Claims of Psycho-Analysis," 13:187).[41]

Freud compares the great social productions of art, religion, and philosophy to the neuroses. The divergence is essentially that

> the neuroses are asocial structures; they endeavour to achieve by private means what is effected in society by collective effort. If we analyze the instincts at work in the neuroses, we find that the determining influence in them is exercised by instinctual forces of sexual origin; the corresponding cultural formations, on the other hand, are based upon social instincts, originating from the combination of egoistic and erotic elements. Sexual needs are not capable of uniting men in the same ways as are the demands of self-preservation. Sexual satisfaction is essentially the private affair of each individual. The asocial nature of neuroses has its genetic origin in their most fundamental purpose, which is to take flight from an unsatisfying reality into a more pleasurable world of phantasy. (*Totem and Taboo*, 13:73–74)

The different psychic productions—daydreams, dreams, slips of the tongue, bungled actions, art, and other social productions—repeat ever-differently, each in its own completely original way, the same originary conflict, the same lack. Some do this privately, others publicly; but since they all have the same psychic sources, it can be said that there are symbolic relationships between them. Freud goes so far as to establish relations of one-to-one correspondence between the different social productions and the different mental illnesses which echo them. The patients themselves justify the extension of analytic method into regions other than the therapeutic; the totality of productions are but different dialects of a single language: that of the unconscious.

> The different neuroses *echoed* [my emphasis] the most highly admired productions of our culture. Thus hysterics are undoubtedly imaginative artists, even if they express their phantasies mimetically in the main and without considering their intelligibility to other people; the ceremonials and prohibitions of obsessional neurotics drive us to suppose that they have created a private religion of their own; and the delusions of paranoics have an unpalatable external similarity and internal kinship to the systems of our philosophers. It is impossible to escape the conclusion that these patients are, in an asocial fashion, making the very attempts at solving their conflicts and appeasing their pressing needs which, when those attempts are carried out in a fashion that is acceptable to the majority, are known as poetry, religion and philosophy. (Preface to Reik's *Ritual*, 17:261)

But what does "echoed" mean? It means, first, that if the hysteric "mimics" the poet, the obsessional neurotic the religious man, and the paranoiac the philosopher, the reverse is not true. Art, religion, and philosophy are not neuroses; rather, all are social solutions that spare the artist, the religious man, and the philosopher the corresponding neurosis from which he was "not far removed." The echo presupposes an originary sound that it reflects back in distorted form. Cultural productions are not pathological formations, but rather are originary "substitutes" for them. Pathological formations are "caricatures" of cultural productions. But the originary sound was already a repercussion; and the neuroses are echoes of echoes. "The neuroses exhibit on the one hand striking and far-reaching points of agreement with those great social institutions, art, religion and philosophy. But on the other hand they seem like caricatures (*Zerrbild*) of them. It might be maintained that a case of hysteria is a caricature of a work of art, that an obsessional neurosis is a caricature of religion and that a paranoic delusion is a caricature of a philosophical system" (*Totem and Taboo*, 13:73). That is why Freud opposes the assimilation of the artist to the neurotic and the surrealist conception according to which only the primary processes come into play in art. In that case, it would no longer be possible to distinguish one from the other; and that is also why modern art seems dangerous to him.[42]

But in what way is hysteria the neurosis that "echoes" art? The answer is that the process involved in the formation of hysterical fantasies is the same as those at work in artistic production. By means of their symptoms, hysterics establish "events" that unfolded as such only in their imaginations, and that only in the last analysis can be traced back to real events, either as their source, or as materials that aided in their construction. Beginning with Draft N dating from 1897 (1:256), Freud connects the mechanism of poetry with that of hysterical fantasies. Thus he claims that for his *Werther*, Goethe combined one of his experiences (his love for Lotte Kästner) with something he had heard (the fate of young Jerusalem, who committed suicide). As he was toying with the idea of suicide himself, he could identify with Jerusalem, to whom he attributed a motive drawn from his own experience. This was the point of contact which made it possible for him to protect himself, by means of his imagination, from the consequences of his experience. Freud then concludes the draft by saying that Shakespeare was right to juxtapose poetry and madness.

It is thus through their relation to a "memory" that hysteria and works of art correspond. In a letter to Fleiss of April 6, 1897, Freud says that hysterical fantasies refer to things heard by children very early in their lives which are only understood later on.[43] Fantasies are defensive structures, "embellishments" that simultaneously serve as self-justifications. Hysteria, obsessional neurosis, and paranoia all consist in the same elements: fragments of memories, impulses deriving from memories, and protective confabulations. In each case, the compromise formations that constitute the symptoms are different. In hysteria it is the "memories," in obsessional neurosis, the perverse impulses, and in paranoia, the defensive confabulations that creep into ordinary behavior. The fantasies in paranoia differ from the fantasies of hysteria by virtue of their systematic character. The latter are independent of each other and may even be contradictory.[44] But hysteria is only a caricature of a work of art; though they can serve as models for each other, they differ from each other as the pathological does from the normal.

Thus in many respects, works of art are reminiscent of other illnesses, especially paranoia, as I have stressed several times. Moreover, by virtue of their collective character, they are more comparable to other cultural productions than to pathological formations. From this standpoint it is difficult to make a comparison because these productions are not independent of each other, but on the contrary are interwoven like so many collective reaction formations to the Oedipus complex, the common nucleus of neuroses and social life. All are originary substitutes stemming from dissatisfaction and the reign of Ἀνάγκη, necessity. In *Civilization and Its Discontents* Freud speaks of the need for palliative measures. The motivating force of all human activity is utility and a yield of pleasure; all culture is a sublimation of the search for pleasure and has the same instinctual source. The search for happiness directs all man's activities, but since they are all compromises between different demands, no single one of them can procure it. Each individual thus does well to multiply the possible sources of pleasure and to choose the ones that best suit the particular economy of his psyche: "The programme of becoming happy . . . cannot be fulfilled. . . . Happiness, in the reduced sense in which we recognize it as possible, is a problem of the economics of the individual's libido. There is no golden rule which applies to everyone: every man must find out for himself in what particular fashion he can be saved" (21:83).

In the pursuit of happiness and the attempt to avoid suffering, religion is a path open to all. Its technique consists of depreciating the value of life and distorting the image of the real world in a deceitful fashion, by intimidating the intelligence. It is an illusion that presents itself as truth, which makes it dangerous and akin to hallucinatory psychosis. It draws humanity into a mass delusion and keeps it in a state of psychic infantilism, in which the fulfillment of desire, protection, and consolation come from an omnipotent Father. Religion is a fixation of object libido on the parents—a rejection of the death of desire, of the loved one, and of the self. It is death in life out of fear of death. At this price, religion manages to spare people individual neuroses, and this is its sole benefit. But it cannot keep its promise of complete happiness. In the face of suffering, the believer is forced to speak of God's "inscrutable decrees," which is another way of acknowledging the reign of necessity.

Art, too, is an illusion which contrasts with reality, but it presents itself as such and is thus less dangerous. It is less dangerous in this as well, that it affects no one permanently except artists themselves. Though it cannot fight against unpleasure, it nonetheless has a considerable psychic effect because of the importance of imagination in psychic life. But in art the theological illusion is more surreptitiously maintained, and so indirectly, art, though it is always atheistic, supports religion. Atheism—and this is true here for art—can be a disguised form of theism.[45] Ideology considers the artist a hero, a king, a creator, a favorite; like the artist, who considers himself the father of his works and thus father of himself, it helps to sustain the idea of aesthetic "creation," analogous to divine creation. The artist kills God only to put himself in his place. Art is a regression from the stage at which libido is fixated on the parents—the religious stage—to the stage of fixation on the self—the narcissistic stage; or alternatively, it can precede this stage and lead to it. Religion and art are not incompatible; they correspond to the same ideology.

Conversely, in killing the Father as Creator, that is, as God, one must renounce being one's own father as well. True atheism is accompanied by an abandonment of narcissism, which can only be accomplished through the detour of *science*. If he who has art can also have religion, and he who has neither science nor art must have religion, he who has science cannot have religion and cannot help but unmask the ideological conception of art.[46] Of all the cultural disciplines, science is the only lucid one, which is why it is not *echoed* in any neurosis. Whereas religion obeys the pleasure principle alone, and art, in the sense attributed to it above, is an intermediary between the pleasure principle and the reality principle, science essentially obeys the reality principle. It is a powerful detour that makes it possible for man to gain insight into his own misery and accept the reign of necessity, thereby sparing him the detour of religion. Science alone allows one to know illusion to be illusion; it alone contributes to knowledge and can decide on the truth value of discourses other than its own. Still, science is not completely independent of the pleasure principle, and contributes to happiness as well. Insofar as scientific investigation is a sublimation of infantile sexual investigations, it too has its source in the instinctual life of the child, and knowledge is a form of enjoyment. Moreover, the renunciation of wishful illusions is satisfying to the superego: it is only by means of a father substitute in ourselves that we can kill the father and substitute for the theological and narcissistic ideal the scientific ideal that corresponds to the stage of maturity, in which the choice of object is no longer the replica of the parental imago.[47]

One must go by way of illusion in order to denounce it; one must begin by admiring the father—identifying with him, wanting to take his place, then understanding that the father is not a "great man," not really a father—that is, a god—but that he and the child alike are subject to the reign of necessity and chance. Then belief gives way to skepticism, veneration to laughter, and self-love to humor, which procures another saving on expenditure and a yield of pleasure.

Thus in the economy of life, imagination—a "reserve"— is, it could be said with Kant, that "art hidden in the depths of nature," the common source of all human production, pathological and normal, individual or cultural—a "faculty" which is not second and secondary, but fundamental and originary, even as death is, in life.

5

FROM ARTISTIC CREATION TO PROCREATION

The Limits of a Psychoanalysis of Art

But surely infantilism is destined to be surmounted. Men
cannot remain children for ever; they must in the end go out
into "hostile life." We may call this *education to reality.*"
The Future of an Illusion, 21:49.

THE ARTISTIC "GIFT"

In order to destroy the last refuge of the theological illusion and
have done with the corresponding ideology, one must therefore
not only "kill the father," but also renounce being the father of one's
works, renounce being a creator. Yet Freud's texts on the subject
of creation seem, in what they *say*, to fall victim to traditional ideology. If that were the case, my reading would be unfaithful to Freud's
thought.

Now I have indicated that the limits on a psychoanalysis
of art that Freud imposes, in his discourse at least, were precisely

the explanation of the artist's work, on the one hand, and on the other, the explanation of "creation." The latter seems to arise from "genius" and "talent" and to depend upon specific "gifts" that arouse admiration and veneration in the art lover, because thanks to them, the artist can bypass the transformation of reality and procure pleasure. These inexplicable "gifts" are thought to result from the generosity of "kindly nature," a sort of Providence whose beneficence is conferred on a few privileged beings. Numerous writings by Freud affirm that psychoanalysis finds its limits where creation proper begins. *Civilization and its Discontents* affirms that "[the method of satisfying instinctual impulses through art] presupposes the possession of special dispositions and gifts which are far from being common to any practical degree" (21:80).

In Freud's Preface to Marie Bonaparte's *The Life and Works of Edgar Allan Poe*, one finds this statement: "Investigations of this kind are not intended to explain an author's genius" (22:254). In "An Autobiographical Study": "The layman may perhaps expect too much from analysis in this respect, for it must be admitted that it throws no light on the two problems which probably interest him the most. It can do nothing towards elucidating the nature of the artistic gift, nor can it explain the means by which the artist works— artistic technique" (20:65). In "The Claims of Psycho-Analysis to Scientific Interest": "Whence it is that the artist derives his creative capacity is not a question for psychology" (13:187). In *Leonardo da Vinci and a Memory of His Childhood*:

> Leonardo emerges from the obscurity of his boyhood as an artist, a painter and a sculptor, owing to a specific talent which may have been reinforced by the precocious awakening in the first years of childhood of his scopophilic instinct (*Schautrieb*). We should be most glad to give an account of the way in which artistic activity derives from the primal instincts of the mind if it were not just here that our capacities fail us (*versagen*). (11:132)

In "Dostoevsky and Parricide": the "unanalysable artistic gift" (21:179). And in the "Address Delivered in the Goethe House at

Frankfurt," Freud speaks of "the riddle of the miraculous gift that makes an artist" (21:211).

Does Freud accept, then, as the artist and the public do, that there is a paternal relation between the artist and his work? Does he consider the artist a "creator," and renounce the attempt to explain "creation" because it supposedly arises from the miraculous gifts of Providence? Does his conception of art make him the victim of the theological illusion, though he denounces it everywhere else? There appears to be a contradiction of some importance in Freud's thought, which should prompt us to look more closely at the texts cited above.

Their context is always polemical: it is always to defend himself against the accusation that he is doing a reductive psychogenesis, or to fight the resistances aroused by the unmasking of the "idol," that Freud openly declares the limits of the method. In all of these texts, some detail always invites us to reread them otherwise and to do a symptomal reading of them.

Thus in his book on Leonardo, Freud hints at the erotic gain that the use of the method procures for him, and the true "frustration" he would feel if he could not "apply" it to the explanation of the artistic "gift": the term used is *versagen*, which is very strong. In this same text, after having begun by declaring his admiration for the artist and affirming the enigmatic character of his gifts, he says immediately that the pathological and the normal and even the sublime obey precise psychic laws. Whether or not these laws differ from each other, the essential thing is that all psychic phenomena are subject to them. Hence the artist's gift could not escape them and would no longer be miraculous: "[Psychoanalytic research] cannot help finding worthy of understanding everything that can be recognized in those illustrious models, and it believes there is no one so great as to be disgraced by being subject to the laws which govern both normal and pathological activity with equal cogency" (11:63).

Similarly in *Delusions and Dreams in Jensen's 'Gradiva,'* he writes: "There is far less freedom and arbitrariness in psychic life

than we are inclined to assume—there may even be none at all....
What we call arbitrariness in psychic life rests upon laws, which we
are only now beginning dimly to suspect" (9:9).

In all of these texts in which the artist, because of his
"gifts," seems to be a great man in the image of the "father," Freud's
analysis leads to the denunciation of the ideological character of
such a conception and invites us to read his own fascination as
being part of a strategy. This would explain why, after having declared his admiration for Leonardo, he writes: "Indeed, the great
Leonardo remained like a child for the whole of his life in more
than one way; it is said that all great men are bound to retain some
infantile part" (Leonardo, 11:127).

The texts in which Freud attributes the artist's "gifts" to
"kindly Nature" must also be read carefully. Here, Freud borrows
the language of ideology the better to denounce it some pages later
and to show, by juxtaposing ideology with the language of its unmasking, that psychoanalysis has not fallen victim to it. Thus at the
beginning of chapter 14 in his book on Leonardo, he seems to
impute to "kindly Nature" (eine gutige Natur) the artist's "ability to
express his most secret mental impulses ... by means of the works
that he creates" (11:107). But in chapter 5, he denounces the concept
of "kindly Nature" as theological—a concept whose prototype is
the distress of the little child; "kindly Nature" is only an ideological
"repetition" of the kindly and tender mother who had nourished
him in childhood (11:122). Freud recalls a series of dreams of the
ancients which had already established a symbolic relation between
the mother and the earth.[1] When writing about Schreber's fantasies,
he indicates that the sun is the sublimated symbol of the father,
and that the mother is figured by the earth, characterized as a
nurturing mother ("Notes on a Case of Paranoia," 12:54). Moreover,
the animistic concept of nature adhered to by primitives converges
with dream symbolism and delusional fantasies (see Totem and
Taboo). But in the symbolic system of the unconscious, the same
can also signify its opposite and change its algebraic sign, which
is why Mother Earth can also designate Death, insofar as she receives men back into her bosom, she in whom they originated. Thus

Nature, the Earth, is she who bears children, the one who "gives" but also the one who takes away. She is the image of both life and death, identical to the Fates who represent the three images of woman: the childbearer, *die Gebärerin*, the mother, *die Genossin*, the companion, and *die Verderberin*, the destroyer, Death ("The Theme of the Three Caskets," 12:301).[2] Thus "Nature" is only a symbolic mythification of necessity, a distorted projection of human wishes which repress the frustrating character of necessity, that harsh educator. The severity of Nature can thus be seen as merely apparent, since in actuality she is believed to be "kindly," a beneficent Providence.

This conception of nature is correlative to the deification of natural forces, to which primitives attribute the characteristics of the father (or the mother?). In order to struggle against untamed nature, against necessity, which man calls "Fate," and which is deeply humiliating to his narcissism, he humanizes nature; that is, he deifies it by trying to conjure natural forces—appease them, corrupt them, influence them in order to steal part of their power, as a child does with his parents. Thus to believe in "kindly Nature" is to remain a prisoner of the parental imago and to remain at an infantile stage. Freud therefore proposes that we substitute for the terms "Nature," "God," and "Fate," the concepts of Ἀνάγκη, necessity, and λόγος, reason, as the Dutch writer Multatuli had already done.

> The last figure in the series that began with the parents is the dark power of Fate which only the fewest of us are able to look upon as impersonal. There is little to be said against the Dutch writer Multatuli when he replaces the Μοῖρα [fate] of the Greeks by the divine pair Λόγος και Ἀνάγκη; but all who transfer the guidance of the world to Providence, to God, or to God and Nature, arouse a suspicion that they still look upon these ultimate and remotest powers as a parental couple, in a mythological sense, and believe themselves linked to them by libidinal ties ("The Economic Problem of Masochism," 19:168).[3]

It is precisely because Nature is *not* "kindly" that she must not be "charmed" but rather "cultivated"—originarily so. For there are two ways of humanizing nature: one is by means of the lucid knowledge of its laws and laborious transformation, which is an authentic form of "culture"; the other is by means of deification and the adoption of a religious attitude, in which case culture is a mask intended to hide the harshness of necessity.

In *The Future of an Illusion*, Freud denounces the illusion involved in wanting to do away with civilization, and in assuming that this is possible, for the state of nature would mean the reign not of happiness, but of distress. As we saw earlier, the state of nature conceived as a golden age is merely the product of fantasy.

> But how ungrateful, how short-sighted after all, to strive for the abolition of civilization! What would then remain would be a state of nature, and that would be hard to bear. It is true that nature would not demand any restrictions of instinct from us, she would let us do as we liked; but she has her own particularly effective method of restricting us. She destroys us—coldly, cruelly, relentlessly, as it seems to us, and possibly through the very things that occasioned our satisfaction. It was precisely because of these dangers with which nature threatens us that we came together and created civilization, which is also, among other things, intended to make our communal life possible. For the principal task of civilization, its actual *raison d' être*, is to defend us against nature. (21:15)

There follows a description of natural cataclysms, and then this: "With these forces nature rises up against us, majestic, cruel and inexorable; she brings to our mind once more our weakness and helplessness, which we thought to escape through the work of civilization." (p. 16)[4]

Thus when Freud declares that it is "kindly Nature" who bestows genius on the artist, it is now evident that we must understand something else entirely, namely the unmasking of the theological conception of art and of the artist. For if it is not "kindly Nature" who "gives," but rather "necessity," the concept of the "gift" has been totally deconstructed. For there is no gift without a giver, and necessity is not a person; it is part and parcel of the chance element in life. And if there is no such thing as a natural "gift," there is no "genius" either, a term defined in the Littré as "an innate talent, a *natural* inclination toward certain things." To speak of genius is to spare oneself the detour through the work of research, to give a verbal explanation intended to camouflage ignorance and the need for illusion.

In his search for the origin of the monotheism of the Jews, Freud opposes the explanation which relies on the notion of the "religious genius" characteristic of that people: "Genius is well known to be incomprehensible and irresponsible, and we ought therefore not to bring it up as an explanation till every other solution has failed us" (*Moses and Monotheism*, 23:65). In a footnote he adds that this consideration applies to the case of Shakespeare. If there are no special "gifts" accorded the artist which enable him to "create"—gifts which are constitutive of his own distinctive character and which make it possible for him to rise above the common lot—then the work of "genius," "inspired by the author's own inventiveness and sometimes departing from the common rules" (*Littré*) does not exist either. If its status is that of an originary repetition, imagination cannot possibly be "creative" or inventive. The artist does not create, nor does he invent; rather, he recomposes, albeit with the aid of a specific and original form of writing. "The 'creative' imagination, indeed, is quite incapable of inventing anything; it can only combine components that are strange to one another" (*Introductory Lectures*, 15:172).

Thus Freud's declarations regarding the "miraculous" character of the artist's gifts and genius appear to be highly suspect. If they were not, psychoanalysis would scarcely differ from traditional biographies which, when they relate the life of a "great man," "[do] not throw any light on the riddle of the miraculous gift that makes an artist," or "help us to comprehend any better the value and the effect of his works" ("Address Delivered at the Goethe House," 21:211). If they always stumble on these two points, is it not precisely because they consider the artist a great man, a hero, and as such, "untouchable"? Freud, who denounces this conception, ought to be able to explain the "gift," as he manages to "help us to comprehend the value and the effect" of works of art.

And indeed, the text on Goethe affirms that psychoanalysis can do more than ordinary biographies. Even if it cannot explain the "gift," it can at least unravel the threads that link the "gift," "the experiences of the artist," and his works—threads with which the tissue of the artistic text turns out to be woven.

"Psycho-analysis can supply some information which cannot be arrived at by any other means, and can thus demonstrate new connecting threads in the 'weaver's masterpiece' (*Webermeisterstück*) spread between the instinctual endowments, the experiences and the works of an artist" (p. 212). If, in the case of Goethe, Freud admits having failed to help us to understand the work of the "great man," the fault should be imputed not to the method itself but to the lack of information available: "I admit, in the case of Goethe we have not yet succeeded very far. This is because Goethe was not only, as a poet, a great self-revealer, but also, in spite of the abundance of autobiographical records, a careful concealer" (p. 212).

Moreover, psychoanalysis can account for inhibition in an artist's creative activity and show that there is a link between this inhibition and the artist's attitude toward his works or the technique he makes use of. This is what Freud does in his studies of Leonardo da Vinci and Dostoevsky. Leonardo's inhibition is said to be due to his identification with his father, and Dostoevsky's, to a feeling of guilt linked to masturbation in childhood and a vehement unconscious wish for his father's death.

Generally speaking, even if psychoanalysis cannot explain "genius," it can at least show "what motive forces aroused it and what material was offered to [the artist] by destiny. There is a particular fascination in studying the laws of the human mind as exemplified in outstanding individuals" (Preface to Bonaparte's *Poe*, 22:254). It can also say with certainty that an artist's "creation" is simultaneously an outlet for his sexual desire. "We must be content to emphasize the fact—which it is hardly any longer possible to doubt—that what an artist creates provides at the same time an outlet (*Ableitung*) for his sexual desire" (*Leonardo*, 11:132).

Thus Freud himself puts strong restrictions on the limits

he sets for psychoanalysis regarding the explanation of "creation" and the artistic "gift." But to explain "creation"—and to do so only partially at that—does not yet amount to a deconstruction of the concept or a renunciation of theological ideology and the father. It remains to be shown that the artist, who behaves like a father toward his works, is also under an illusion concerning the nature of paternity and the "gifts" he receives from his parents.

It remains to be shown not only that creation is explicable, but that there is no "creation," any more than there is a "gift," either in artistic activity or in procreation.

THE LIMITS OF PSYCHOANALYSIS

Now granted, in his declared intentions, Freud never goes this far. On the contrary, he seems to say that the limits of a psychoanalysis of art stem not only from ignorance but also from the nature of the object under study; the riddle of art could never be completely deciphered since the artistic "gift" and "creation" are, in their very essence, enigmatic. The book on Leonardo da Vinci, especially its first chapter, is of fundamental importance in this regard. Freud says there that he could rightly be accused of having written a "psychoanalytic novel" and that, like many others before him, he has simply fallen under the "spell" of the "great man."

> If in making these statements I have provoked the criticism, even from friends of psycho-analysis and from those who are expert in it, that I have merely written a psycho-analytic novel, I shall reply that I am far from over-estimating the certainty of these results. Like others I have succumbed to the attraction of this great and mysterious man, in whose nature one seems to detect powerful instinctual passions which can nevertheless only express themselves in so remarkably subdued a manner (11:134)

These affirmations are linked to the polemical context in which Freud is defending himself against experts and even against friends of psychoanalysis (what is to be done against the enemies!).

That is why there immediately follows Freud's dutiful acknowledgment of the limits of psychoanalysis: "We must stake out in a quite general way the limits which are set to what psycho-analysis can achieve in the field of biography: otherwise every explanation that is not forthcoming will be held up to us as a failure" (p. 134). The limits are due not to the inadequate methods of psychoanalysis but to the uncertainty and lacunary nature of the material relating to the artist, as was the case with Leonardo and Goethe. The material available to the analyst consists in the data of a person's life history—on the one hand, the chance circumstances of events and background influences, and on the other, the person's reported reactions to them. With his knowledge of psychic mechanisms the psychoanalyst tries, on the basis of the subject's dynamic reactions, to gain deeper understanding of his nature and discover the original motive forces of his mind, as well as their subsequent transformations and development. "If this is successful the behaviour of a personality in the course of his life is explained in terms of the combined operation of constitution and fate, of internal forces and external powers" (p. 135).

But in addition to these chance de facto limits, there are also de jure limits. Even if the analyst had at his disposal all the historical material he wished, and could assess with complete assurance the play of psychic forces in a given person, two important points would still be incomprehensible: first, why a person turned out to be as he was and not otherwise, and second, why his impulses met with one fate rather than another. Now, an artist's gifts and his capacity for artistic activity depend above all of the fate of his drives, his special tendency toward repression, and his remarkable capacity to sublimate. Consequently, "we must admit that the essence of artistic activity is inaccessible to us along psycho-analytic lines" (p. 136). [5]

Thus even if psychoanalysis does not succeed in accounting for the "gift" and the artistic activity that depends on it, at least it unmasks the ideological, theological explanation for it: the gift is not a "gift" from God or from "kindly Nature." It is not innate but is rather the consequence of a double determinism (or double chance): on the one hand, the play of psychic forces, a certain quantity of affects, which is particularly high in artists, and a certain predisposition toward a particular fate of the drives—sublimation; and on the other, the chance experiences that the artist had to live out. What people call "talent," a special inclination, a "gift," is an illusion which can be explained by the fact that a single investment has developed excessive force: any predominant "gift" is merely a dominant drive reinforced by the support of other forces. Hence the problem of the "gift" is first and foremost a quantitative problem, involving the initial quantity of libido, the quantity of repressed libido, and the greater or lesser capacity for sublimation.

SUBLIMATION

In *Civilization and Its Discontents*, Freud writes that the "quantity of instinctual sublimation," which is the capacity of the sexual drive to replace its immediate aim with other aims that can be more highly valued and are not sexual, determines the localization of interests which are narcissistic in nature, and also determines whether a man will become a neurotic or an artist.

However, there is no question of suggesting to a neurotic in analysis that he remedy his ills by sublimating his drives.[6] If he has the capacity to do this, sublimation takes place by itself through the play of psychic forces alone. Analysis can only help to lift inhibitions.

> Not every neurotic has a high talent for sublimation; one can assume of many of them that they would not have fallen ill at all if they had possessed the the art of sublimating their instincts. . . . It must further be borne in mind that many people fall ill precisely from an attempt to sublimate their instincts beyond the degree permitted by their organization and that in those who have a capacity for sublimation the process usually takes place of itself as soon as their inhibitions have been overcome by analysis. ("Recommendations to Physicians Practising Psycho-Analysis," 12:119)

The capacity to sublimate is the measure of each person's capacity to produce cultural works, and it is futile to try to transform man into a purely cultural animal by gradually extending sexual restrictions; though the relation between the quantity of sublimation that is possible and the amount of sexual activity that is necessary varies from one individual to another and from one society to another, total sexual abstinence is harmful to sublimation. In *Five Lectures on Psycho-Analysis*, Freud tells the story of the citizens of Schilda, who had a horse whose consumption of oats, which they deemed excessive, they wanted to reduce gradually. The horse resisted right up to the day he was to have worked without eating— and died (11:53ff).

In the same text Freud compares the work of transforming the drives, by means of sublimation, to the work of transforming heat, by means of machines, into mechanically useful work:

> But just as we do not count on our machines converting more than a certain fraction of the heat consumed into useful mechanical work, we ought not to seek to alienate the whole amount of the energy of the sexual instinct from its proper ends. We cannot succeed in doing so; and if the restriction upon sexuality were to be carried too far it would inevitably bring with it all the evils of soil-exhaustion. (p. 54)

Though it is true that a celibate young *savant* is no rarity, and that he thereby benefits from forces freed for his studies, generally speaking sexual abstinence does not contribute to the training of energetic men of action, original thinkers, and bold reformers. Most of the time, it produces weak men who get lost in the crowd. In any event, "an abstinent artist is hardly conceivable. . . . [He] probably finds his artistic achievements powerfully stimulated by his sexual experience" (" 'Civilized' Sexual Morality and Modern Nervousness," 9:197). Thus, if the capacity for sublimation is given to only a few, it must, in order to remain in the service of Eros, be expended only prudently and parsimoniously. The problem of artistic activity comes down to a problem of libidinal economy. The dynamic conception of the psyche is insufficient: only the economic point of view allows one to understand differences in fate. The conflicts between the drives break out only when certain levels of intensity have been reached; the pathogenic importance of constitutional factors depends upon the quantitative predominance of one partial drive or another, and resistance to neurosis is a quantitative problem.

> I have introduced a fresh factor into the structure of the aetiological chain—namely the quantity, the magnitude, of the energies concerned. We have still to take this factor into account everywhere.... It may even be supposed that the disposition of all human beings is qualitatively alike and that they differ only owing to these quantitative conditions.... It is a matter of *what quota* of unemployed libido a person is able to hold in suspension and of *how large a fraction* of his libido he is able to divert from sexual to sublimated aims. (*Introductory Lectures*, 16:374–375)

Sublimation is thus not merely a word which is meant to baptize the problem of culture; it can be explained if one adopts a metapsychological, or more specifically, an economic point of view. It finds its condition of possibility in the plastic nature of the sexual drive, a plasticity which stems from the death drive inhibiting the aim of the sexual drive and dividing it originally into partial drives. When Freud says that sublimation "derives" from the sexual drive, this term must be understood not in a genetic sense but in the sense of a deviation (*Ablenkung*) and a derivative. Sublimation does not "come from" the sexual drive, but rather is a diversion of sexuality into other paths; the words that signify derivation in German are *Ableitung* and *Ablenkung*. The first of these is also used to indicate a highway detour. The change of aim, which is thus nothing but a change of "road," implies—though all of Freud's texts do not say so explicitly—a change of object. But the "detour" is only possible by means of a transformation of sexual libido into neutral narcissistic libido. The metaphysical metaphor of the "road" here acquires a new, strictly economic meaning: it is intended to signify—and the paradox is that it can do so only with the help of metaphysical language—that sublimation must be understood not as a moral concept but as a metapsychological one, that it is a problem of transforming and redistributing energy. If the sexual drive were a single entity and could be expended without reserve, sublimation would be impossible and would have no raison d'être. But the very incapacity of the sexual drive to obtain complete satisfaction because of the demands of civilization, and especially because of originary repression, establishes culture originarily; "For what motive would men have for putting sexual instinctual forces to other uses if, by any distribution of those forces, they could obtain fully satisfying pleasure? They would never abandon that pleasure and they would never make any further progress" ("On the Universal Tendency to Debasement," 11:190).

It is because the drive cannot achieve its aim, which is always a discharge that gives satisfaction (*Befriedigungsabfuhr*), that investment in an object and a lasting tendency are established, giving the illusion of a special disposition and innate gifts. This is the case with tender feelings that never attain the satisfaction of the sexual drive which is their source. Originary unsatisfaction is what provokes the infinity of desire and the permanence of a substitutive tendency which appears innate, because substitution, derivation, and diversion are originary. Hence the close link between imagination and sublimation in the artist is quite comprehensible: art is one of those diverted paths into which the inhibited sexual drive can be discharged.[7]

The possibility of sublimation and the acquisition of "gifts," "permanent character traits," is thus explained by the capacity of the sexual drive to divide itself up and find paths for discharge other than the sexual path. Plasticity and the change of aim are actually only changes of direction and changes of objects of investment.

Just as sexual disturbances have repercussions for other somatic functions, and any activity exercised with a certain intensity increases sexual excitation, so too—that is, following the same paths—are sexual drives attracted toward nonsexual—that is, sublimated—aims. In the *Three Essays on the Theory of Sexuality*, Freud confesses his ignorance on the subject of these paths, but says that in all probability they must be traversed in both directions (7:206). In order that this diversion into other paths may be possible, it

must also be admitted that the different drives can be substituted
for one another, or shore each other up, reinforce each other: "Instinctual impulses from one source attach themselves to those from
other sources and share their further vicissitudes and . . . in general
one instinctual satisfaction can supplement another" (New Introductory Lectures, 22:96–97).[8]

> Excessively strong excitations arising from particular sources of sex-
> uality . . . find an outlet (Abfluss) and use in other fields, so that a not
> inconsiderable increase in psychical efficiency (Leistungsfähigkeit) re-
> sults from a disposition which in itself is perilous. Here we have one
> of the origins of artistic activity; and, according to the completeness
> or incompleteness of the sublimation, a characterological analysis
> of a highly gifted individual, and in particular of one with an artistic
> disposition, may reveal a mixture, in every proportion, of efficiency,
> perversion and neurosis. A sub-species of sublimation is to be found
> in suppression by reaction-formation, which, as we have seen, begins
> during a child's period of latency and continues in favourable cases
> throughout his whole life. What we describe as a person's "character"
> is built up to a considerable extent from the material of sexual
> excitations and is composed of instincts that have been fixed since
> childhood, of constructions achieved by means of sublimation, and
> of other constructions, employed for effectively holding in check
> perverse impulses which have been recognized as being unutilizable.
> The multifariously perverse sexual disposition of childhood can ac-
> cordingly be regarded as the source of a number of our virtues, in
> so far as through reaction-formation it stimulates their development.
> (Three Essays, 7:238–239)[9]

Most of the time Freud assimilates sexual drives inhibited
in their aim to the sublimated drives. Sometimes, he reserves the
term "sublimated" for inhibited drives which are invested in a cultural object.

Inhibited drives can be mixed in every proportion with
uninhibited ones and can also be changed back into the latter by
following the path of deviation in the opposite direction. The great
advantage the first group has over the second is that, since they
never achieve complete satisfaction, they create lasting ties, "dispositions," "gifts," whereas the uninhibited drives, in being satis-

fied, suffer a loss of energy and must then wait to be restored by an accumulation of sexual libido, during which time they may change the object of investment.[10] Sublimation would not be possible if the sexual drive were a single entity and focused from the beginning on the aim of the function, that is, on the union of two germ cells with a view toward reproduction. The possibility of the sublimation of the drive, as a deviation from its aim, is inherent in the very being of the drive insofar as its aims are multiple from the beginning, and insofar as it is originarily divided into partial drives by the death impulses.

The partial drives arise from various sources, various regions of the body, are fairly independent of each other, and find their satisfaction in organic pleasure; they are originarily perverse and narcissistic. Certain of these drives are later integrated into the organization of the sexual function at the genital stage; others, which are unutilizable, are eliminated by means of repression. Some are sublimated and used to reinforce other tendencies, while still others play secondary roles and serve in the production of fore-pleasure. Most of the forces that can be utilized for cultural activity arise from the repression of perverse elements and their subsequent sublimation. "The constitution of people suffering from inversion— the homosexuals—is, indeed, often distinguished by their sexual instinct's possessing a special aptitude for cultural sublimation" (" 'Civilized' Sexual Morality," 9:190).[11] The sexual drive, which is composite, can be broken down into partial drives which are discharged along paths other than the sexual one and can shore up other tendencies. Thus sublimation arises essentially from a change in the paths of discharge, the substitution of one object of investment for another, the transfer of the libidinal charge of one drive onto another, the shoring up of one drive by another with a view toward working in concert.

Under these conditions the "gift" and artistic activity lose their miraculous character: the "sublime" is merely what is "sublimated," and the riddle changes into an algebra problem to be solved; it is a matter of finding the resultant of a play of multiple forces, endowed with a certain freedom of play.

LEONARDO'S ART AND SCIENCE

This is what Freud tries to do with regard to Leonardo da Vinci. What is referred to as this painter's "special disposition," his "gift," arises from the fact that an investment—that of the thirst for knowledge—has developed in an excessive manner. His drive for knowledge was active from early childhood on and its supremacy was established by impressions from the child's life. The drive for knowledge is not an innate intellectual gift, cannot be counted among the elementary instinctual components, and does not belong exclusively to sexuality. It is linked at once to the sublimation of anal-sadistic drives trying to acquire mastery and to the sublimation of the urge to see (*Schaulust*), with whose energy it works. Its relations to sexual life date from early childhood, for the child's intellectual curiosity is awakened in an interesting way, by the "riddle" of procreation. How is one born from two? Such is the original question (*Three Essays*, 7:194). It is because the drive to know was reinforced, shored up in Leonardo by what were originally sexual drives, that it could subsequently be substituted for a normal sexual life. Indeed wherever a drive has a special intensity, this indicates that it was reinforced by a sexual drive deflected from its aim: "We accept this process as proved whenever the history of a person's childhood—that is, the history of his mental development—shows that in childhood this over-powerful instinct was in the service of sexual interests. We find further confirmation if a striking atrophy occurs in the sexual life of maturity, as though a portion of sexual activity had now been replaced by the activity of the over-powerful instinct" (*Leonardo*, 11:78).

The drive for knowledge in him thus took the place of love, for the deflection of the sexual drive into paths foreign to it is not accomplished without loss. If Leonardo's life was poor in love and artistic activity, it is not because love, art, and science are inherently incompatible, as is proved by the life of Goethe, who knew perfectly well how to reconcile them. Rather, it is because "a conversion of psychical instinctual force into various forms of activity can perhaps no more be achieved without loss than a conversion of physical forces" (p. 75).

While distinguishing between Leonardo's artistic activity and his scientific activity, Freud nonetheless admits of no essential division between the two; though in certain men scientific investigation and artistic activity are found to be separated from one another, it is for reasons linked to the particular economy of their libido, as was the case with Leonardo.

Because of the child's sexual immaturity, the absence of an answer to the question concerning the origin of children results in compensatory phantasmal activity, which is necessarily inadequate. Afterward there ensues a period of sexual repression, with three possible fates awaiting intellectual curiosity: (a) intellectual repression occurs, resulting in neurotic inhibition; (b) intellectual curiosity remains and helps to get around sexual repression through a sexualization of thought (this is the case with Norbert in *Gradiva*, for example); (c) thanks to "special dispositions," the libido evades the fate of repression by being sublimated from the beginning into curiosity and coming to reinforce the drive for research. Research then has a compulsive character; it is a substitute for sexual activity—apparent disinterest in anything sexual being symptomatic of the link of research activity to sexuality. This was the case with Leonardo, who escaped neurosis thanks to certain reinforcements of psychic processes, thanks to his special dispositions for sublimation. Leonardo's disposition toward science is thus not a "gift," but is linked to the history of the libido and to its play. The same can be said of his artistic "gifts."

In order to understand Leonardo's artistic activity it is necessary to complete the picture of the fate of his sexual drive. His libido was not entirely sublimated and did not all go into the reinforcement of the drive for research. A smaller portion continued to have sexual aims, which resulted in an atrophied adult sexual life; "his mother's excessive tenderness was fateful for him; it determined his destiny and the privations that were in store for him" (p. 115). His love for his mother having been repressed, the unsublimated portion of the libido pressed him to adopt a homosexual attitude. The fixation on the mother continued to be preserved in the unconscious, but remained inactive until the encounter with Mona Lisa. Repression, fixation, and sublimation all contributed to the fate of the sexual drive in Leonardo and to his destiny as an artist and a thinker. According to Vasari, his first artistic endeavors were drawings of the heads of laughing women and beautiful boys: he "represented" his repressed sexual objects In his youth, the effect of his identification with his father was that, initially, he had no inhibition. But the excessive repression of his sexual life did not favor the exercise of his sublimated sexual tendencies. All of Leonardo's artistic activity developed in parallel to the regression or development of his sexual life.

In puberty, "the development that turned him into an art ist. . . . was overtaken by the process which led him to be an inves tigator, and which had its determinants in early infancy. The second sublimation of his erotic instinct gave place to the original subli- mation for which the way had been prepared on the occasion of the first repression. He became an investigator, at first still in the service of his art, but later independently of it" (p. 133).

The period of regression linked to the identification with his father influenced his technique and resulted in his tendency not to complete his works. With the loss of his patron, who was a father substitute, regression was only accentuated, and research took the place of artistic production.

But at the age of fifty, when the libido makes a further advance in men, there was a new transformation in the play of affects and the relationship between artistic activity and the activity of research. At this time he encounters Mona Lisa, who awakens his sexuality, lifts the inhibition, and makes possible the return of the repressed in the form of artistic productions celebrating maternity.

> Still deeper layers of the contents of his mind became active once more; but this further regression was to the benefit of his art, which was in the process of becoming stunted. He met the woman who awakened his memory of his mother's happy smile of sensual rapture; and, influenced by this revived memory, he recovered the stimulus

that guided him at the time when he modelled the smiling women.
...With the help of the oldest of all his erotic impulses he enjoyed
the triumph of once more conquering the inhibition in his art. (p.
134)

Thus the life of Leonardo, the relationship between his
love life, art, and science can be explained in terms of the combined
operations of constitution and fate, and the play of internal forces
and external forces. "The accident of his illegitimate birth and the
excessive tenderness of his mother had the most decisive influence
on the formation of his character and on his later fortune, since the
sexual repression which set in after this phase of childhood caused
him to sublimate his libido into the urge to know, and established
his sexual inactivity for the whole of his later life"(p. 135). It seems
that "only a man who had had Leonardo's childhood experiences
could have painted the Mona Lisa and the St. Anne, have secured
so melancholy a fate for his works and have embarked on such an
astonishing career as a natural scientist, as if the key to all his
achievements and misfortunes lay hidden in the childhood phantasy
of the vulture" (p. 136).

What then are the limits of psychoanalytic explanation?
It cannot account for the freedom of play of the drives and their
fate. The repression that followed Leonardo's first erotic satisfactions was not necessary. In someone else it might not have taken
place, or might have taken place in less extensive proportions; "we
must recognize here a degree of freedom which cannot be resolved
any further by psycho-analytic means" (p. 135).

The consequences of this first repression, which were the
sublimation of the libido into the thirst to know, were not necessary
either: in another person repression might have been maintained
and damaged his intellectual activity, or might have procured a
disposition toward obsessional neurosis. The two characteristics of
Leonardo's reactions to the events of his affective life—his tendency
toward instinctual repression and his extraordinary capacity for sublimation—cannot be explained by psychoanalysis. But they are not
"gifts" which are inexplicable in themselves, providential, gratified
by a "kindly Nature": psychoanalytic research only gives place to

biological research: "We are obliged to look for the source of the tendency to repression and the capacity for sublimation in the organic foundations of character on which the mental structure is only afterwards erected" (p. 136).

LIFE AS A GAME

Thus from the Leonardo book onward, Freud indicates that the "wall" which every psychoanalytic explanation comes up against is the rock of the biological. Freud repeats this in one of his last works, "Analysis Terminable and Interminable": "for the psychical field, the biological field does in fact play the part of the underlying bedrock" (23:252).

Now, the tendency for biology is to explain the principal traits of a person's organic constitution as the result of a mixture of male dispositions and female dispositions, a mixture stemming from the chance encounters of a spermatozoon and an ovum.

The problem of artistic "creation" is thus no different from the problem of procreation; the riddle of artistic creation is the riddle of life. The text on Leonardo, as well as "Analysis Terminable and Interminable," ends with this riddle—a riddle because every life, from its inception to its death, is given over to chance, to the play of biological forces, psychical forces, and external forces, and to the play of the encounters of all these forces, so that the fate of the artist is no more specific than any other. A riddle too, because every life, however diverse the expressions of it may be, is a refusal of femininity: "The repudiation of femininity can be nothing else than a biological fact, a part of the great riddle of sex" (p. 252).[12] This refusal of femininity is manifested in the artist by his wish to be a father and to give his mother a penis by weaving a text that masks the holes.

By thus substituting "procreation" for "creation" and "life" for "kindly Nature," does Freud repeat differently the traditional ideology of art, or does he denounce it? To offer an explanation in terms of life and chance is another way of saying, is it not, that "gifts" are inexplicable and that there are privileged beings?

In fact, the difference is considerable, and Freud, by substituting for the problem of creation that of procreation, understood as the "game of life," unmasks a conception of paternity tainted by the theological model which is itself the idealized projection of it. If life is the product of chance, the artist can no more be the father of his works than the father can be a God, or God be a father. For chance is one with necessity (Ἀνάγκη) and stands opposed to finality, choice, the election of one being over another, endowed with exclusive and special gifts. That is why Freud writes, at the end of the study of Leonardo, that the reader will surely be disappointed by an explanation that accords such an important place to chance. Indeed, it eliminates the last bastion where the narcissism of both artist and art lover had taken refuge, and puts an end to the theological conception of art and paternity, whose origin is to be found in infantile wishes. It thus puts an end to the illusion that the parents of each one of us wanted us for ourselves, that we are chosen beings.

If man refuses chance as the explanatory principle of artistic gifts and rejects the psychoanalytic interpretation, it is in order to obliterate the fact that his own life is due to chance, that there is no presence—neither God nor father—that chose him. At the origin of life there is not a full unity, but rather a multiplicity of seeds which fertilize haphazardly, and the entire process of embryonic development proceeds by means of successive divisions: development is ongoing differentiation and implies an originary difference. In the life of each individual, life is having a "go," one of the many it has in its game; the subject is "played" by the combinatory of parental signifiers, and plays them as well. But the artist who recognizes that his genius is due to chance loses the assurance of his identity. It is no longer possible for him to want to take the place of the father in order to be his own founder, if the father himself cannot serve as a foundation, since he himself has no foundation. The entire traditional ideology of art was intended to repress the absence of foundation of all life. If there is no longer a God who is the *causa sui*, it is no longer possible to want to take his place. To renounce one's illusions and accept necessity is the only lot that remains. Such is the lesson to be drawn from the end of the Leonardo study.

> Everything to do with life is chance, from our origin out of the meeting of spermatozoon and ovum onwards — chance which nevertheless has a share in the law and necessity of nature, and which merely lacks any connection with our wishes and illusions. The apportioning of the determining factors of our life between the "necessities" of our constitution and the "chances" of our childhood may still be uncertain in detail; but in general it is no longer possible to doubt the importance precisely of the first years of our childhood. We all still show too little respect for Nature which (in the obscure words of Leonardo which recall Hamlet's lines) "is full of countless causes that never enter experience." [A footnote supplies the Italian, from M. Herzfeld's *Leonardo da Vinci* (1906), p. 11: "La natura é piena d'infinite ragioni che non furono mai in isperienza."] Everyone of us human beings corresponds to one of the countless experiments in which these "ragioni" of nature force their way into experience. (11:137)[13]

It is thus life itself which is the "artist," and Freud proposes that we substitute for the idolatry of the artist as a great man, correlative to the idolatry of the Father (=God), the respect for nature. The riddle of art is the riddle of life as an artist: the "kindness" of nature is not the kindness of a divine Providence, but rather comes down to the varied richness of its game. To respect nature is not to replace one idol with another; instead, it is to recognize necessity and submit to its laws, to accept reality, death, and "originary difference," as well as femininity, insofar as it is the symbol of these things.

What men find charming in art is the illusion it gives them of being masters of creation and, by that very means, of procreation, the illusion of being able to dominate death and to be the *causa sui*.

When, at the end of the Leonardo study, Freud openly

declares the limits of psychoanalysis in its "application" to art, it is not because he is still dependent upon theological ideology. The reference to biology is the sign neither of an abdication nor of blind confidence in the sciences of nature: the latter are no better at explaining life, even though they pretend to be. Rather, Freud is indicating that there is no point in giving a "reasoned" account of life. To give a reason would be to find a "foundation," and to continue to believe in "reasons." The only "reasons" are those of life, whose time is not linear but circular. Life in its eternal return repeats differently the same eternal game.

Thus, Freud's interpretation of art takes us from a theological conception of the world to a scientific conception—one that is nonetheless different from the traditional ideology of the sciences which, by virtue of their wish for a total explanation, also remain prisoners of theology. It takes us from the conception of a divine and finalized world to a world of chance and necessity, from childhood which takes games seriously, to the game of seriousness, that is, to the innocence of life; it takes us from tragedy to comedy and humor.[14] Comedy, because the Freudian method of demystifying is a method of unmasking, and when the masks fall, there is nothing left to do but laugh. In studying the comic in *Jokes and Their Relation to the Unconscious*, Freud defines unmasking as a set of procedures which degrade a man's dignity by showing the weaknesses he shares with all humanity, and especially by revealing that his psychic activity is dominated by bodily needs (8:202–203). Unmasking comes down to saying: "such and such a person, who is admired as a demigod, is after all only human like you and me." And indeed, this is what the Freudian interpretation does in inviting us to abandon our veneration for this hero, this king, this favorite that the artist is, and to substitute for it the "respect for Nature."

Though the comic procedure is not said to be an *Aufdeckung* but rather an *Entlarvtung*, it seems to me all the more admissible to consider the two together, since Freud gives as a prime example of unmasking "the efforts at laying bare the monotonous psychical automatism that lies behind the wealth and apparent freedom of psychical functions," and since he himself assimilates the *Entlarvtung* to the *Aufdeckung*, for instance in the Schreber case.

Now, behind the unmasking of the artist, we must read the unmasking of the father, and here one cannot help thinking of Freud's father, the "great man" stooping to pick up his hat at a Christian's command[15]—a scene about which one can either cry or laugh, but which brings disappointment that can only lead to the end of admiration for the father and with it, the death of the sacred. However, instinctual renunciation is possible only thanks to the superego and its satisfaction: it is still through the father that one overcomes the father. Yet the greatest proof of one's faithfulness to him is to "kill" him, not in order to put oneself in his place, but to construct a new concept of paternity stripped of sanctification. The yield of pleasure obtained by the superego in renouncing its infantile illusions is humorous pleasure. "Humor seems to say· Look! there is the world that seems so dangerous! A mere child's game! The best thing to do is joke about it! . . . When the superego tries, by means of humor, to console the ego and protect it from suffering, this in no way contradicts its origin in the parental agency" ("Humor," 21:166).

Thus through his interpretation, Freud denounces the theological illusion down to its last stronghold, and uncovers narcissism as the foundation of artistic activity. It is therefore impossible to renounce ideology without weaning oneself psychically, for this alone enables one to adopt a "scientific" attitude which must not rest until it has unmasked, in all human activity, the presence of illusions stemming from the survival of infantile wishes which man cannot renounce: "It is simply a fact that the truth cannot be tolerant, that it admits of no compromises or limitations, that research regards every sphere of human activity as belonging to it and that it must be relentlessly critical if any other power tries to take over any part of it" (*New Introductory Lectures*, 22:160).

In concluding, I would like to emphasize how much this "scientific" attitude of Freud's is comparable in every point with the viril skepticism of Nietzsche. As is the case for Nietzsche, it goes hand in hand with the abandonment of heaven and the love of the earth: "We leave Heaven to the angels and the sparrows," says Freud in *the Future of an Illusion*, quoting Heine, one of his "fellow unbelievers" (21:50). For Nietzsche as for Freud, the world is only an innocent "child's game" guided by chance, and the true art is the art of life which, in its eternal return, repeats differently sorrows and joys, "creations" and "decreations."

APPENDIX

DELUSION AND FICTION

Concerning Freud's *Delusions and Dreams in Jensen's 'Gradiva'*

A STRANGE FASCINATION

The study of Jensen's *Gradiva* (1906) does not, strictly speaking, inaugurate the "application" of the analytic method to a field other than that of pathology. *Jokes*, which precedes it by one year, already provides a good example of the "application," and in numerous letters (in particular Letters 71, 91, 92, and 100 to Fliess dating from 1897–1898, and those to his wife dated August 26, 1882, January 26, 1883, and October 5, 1883),[1] one finds that Freud has already broached an interpretation of Conrad Meyer's *Die Richterin* [The Woman Judge] and outlined analyses of Sophocles' *Oedipus Rex* and Shakepeare's *Hamlet*, which are taken up again and further elab-

The first version of this essay appeared in *Europe* (March 1974), no. 539, pp. 165–184. It is excerpted from a larger study on *Gradiva*, a part of which has already been published as "Résumer, interpréter" in *Critique* (October 1972), no. 305, pp. 892–916; reprinted in *Quatre romans analytiques* (Paris: Galilée, 1974).

orated in 1900 in *The Interpretation of Dreams* and subsequently in other works as well. Very early on, one finds in Freud's works scattered literary or artistic references which denote his status as a highly cultivated man, and which also function as signs of the very special interest psychoanalysis has in art: though Freud is interested in the "masterpieces" of world literature, he also turns his attention to works that are deemed to be of secondary importance or are completely neglected by specialists, professional aestheticians, such as *Gradiva* by Jensen (1837–1911), a novelist and short story writer from Northern Germany.

Freud says of *Gradiva* that it "has no particular merit in itself" ("An Autobiographical Study," 20:65). But the free-floating attention of the psychoanalyst is open to what is usually neglected, catching details which escape the professionals. This apparently inexplicable attraction to Jensen's novella is analogous to that of the hero of the story, Norbert, who is also captivated, fascinated by a statuette which has nothing remarkable about it from an archeological standpoint. How strange this fascination is, which constitutes the riddle of the story and prompts the story, a narrative that begins and ends with the solution to the riddle. It is this riddle that the psychoanalyst proposes to solve and that he considers to be the fundamental issue in the text.

> The interest taken by the hero of the story in this relief is the basic psychological fact in the narrative. It was not immediately explicable. "Dr. Norbert Hanold, Lecturer in Archaeology, did not in fact find in the relief anything calling for special notice from the point of view of his branch of science." "He could not explain to himself what there was in it that had provoked his attention. He only knew that he had been attracted by something and that the effect had continued unchanged ever since." (*Delusion and Dreams*, 9:11)

If Freud's interest in the narrative and the pleasure he takes in reading it recall and are of the same nature as the interest and pleasure experienced by Norbert, an understanding of the affect felt by the psychoanalyst should make the hero's emotions comprehensible as well.

Freud learns that Jung was the first to have become interested in the novella.[2]

> It happened that in the group of men among whom the notion |of conducting this type of research| first arose there was one who recalled that in the work of fiction that had last caught his fancy there were several dreams whose features had seemed somewhat familiar and invited him to attempt to apply to them the method of *The Interpretation of Dreams*. He confessed that the subject-matter of the little work and the scene in which it was laid may no doubt have played the chief part in creating his enjoyment.... During the treatment of this genuinely poetic material the reader had been stirred by all kinds of thoughts akin to it and in harmony with it. (pp. 9–10)

Jung's pleasure and Freud's, the hero's pleasure, and Jensen's possible pleasure—all these pleasures echo one another.[3] In each of these figures, the pleasure felt is mixed, impure, composed of fore-pleasure, an incentive bonus given by the beauty of the work (the poetic narration, the beauty of the statue), to which is added a deeper pleasure made possible by the diversion of the charmed ego's attention, a pleasure arising from the discharge of repressed impulses. The discharge takes place on the condition that something in the work can touch the reader or the spectator, something that is recognized as familiar yet whose origin is not recognized. The effect produced by the work is always that of the uncanny (*unheimlich*). The Gradiva statuette arouses in Norbert this strange impression whose meaning he will understand only once his delusion comes to an end. In turn, Jensen's narrative produces the same effect on Jung and Freud, an effect which is doubled for them since the text stages a world that is familiar to the analyst (the world of dreams and delusions). What is strange about this is that such a world is so perfectly described not by a psychiatrist or a psychoanalyst but by a fiction writer who entitles his work a "fantasy." How can the novelist possess this knowledge, having spared himself the trouble of following analytic procedures? This is the second instance of uncanniness, another riddle for the psychoanalyst.

THE RIDDLE

The *Gradiva* essay is the narrative account of a riddle which figures in miniature the riddle constituted by the work of art as such. Whereas Freud modestly declares that he simply wants to interpret the few dreams scattered throughout the novella and thus "gain some small insight into the nature of poetic production" (p. 9), in what he actually *does* he has already taken the step that leads from the analysis of fictional characters, considered to be real persons, to an inquiry into the nature of poetic production. The hero Norbert is like Jensen's "double": Norbert's "delusion" is a "double" of the work, while Zoe, by contrast (or so it seems), plays the role of therapist and is the locus of truth within the riddle of the delusion; she is the double of the psychoanalyst who possesses the truth of both the delusion and the work. At least, that is what Freud means to suggest by establishing a parallel between dreams and delusions on the one hand, and poetic production on the other. The same terms, the same metaphors, describe delusional or dream production and fictional production. The riddle they constitute is a text to be deciphered, a tissue which conceals a truth and must be unraveled thread by thread. The continuous character of the text, the coherence of the web, functions as a lure: it hides the holes in the text, the missing links, just as the web of delusion is a veil that hides and serves as protection against the return of the repressed. Behind the riddle there is not another text which is taken to be the truth, the latent content of the riddle. There is is but a single text which speaks and cloaks the real: only from certain traces within the manifest content which open a space of legibility within the text (traces which prove that the production of illusion has failed to some extent, as has the tissue in its function as lure, in its continuity) can the riddle be deciphered, the holes, discontinuities, and lacunae reappear, and the riddle appear as such. The dream, the delusion, and the work are texts whose structure is such that it authorizes a double reading. Freud terms such texts riddles: "A group of men who regarded it as a settled fact that the essential riddles of dreaming have been solved by the efforts of the author of the present work . . . "(p. 7).

"To what impression of the previous day are we to relate the 'lady colleague' who in the dream replaces the famous zoologist Eimer?" Freud asks (p. 74). (Here there is a riddle because there are missing links between the dream images and the daytime events: these links are what the dream's work of transformation causes to disappear by producing other links and constituting another text. Consider in this connection the "strangely absurd" dream in which "all the impressions of the day were afterwards woven together"(p. 72), which is, as it were, the very paradigm of the dream; that is, of its enigmatic character and its function as an illusion.) Freud says of his patients that "once they have understood, they themselves bring forward the solutions of the final and most important riddles of their strange condition" (p. 38). "Zoe has solved the riddle of the delusion and provides the key to her ambiguous words" (p. 85; see also pp. 77–78 and 66). "The author presents us with a further riddle by making the dream, the discovery of the supposed Gradiva in the street, and the decision to undertake the journey as a result of the singing canary succeed one another as a series of chance events. . . . This obscure region of the story is made intelligible to us by some explanations which we derive from the later remarks of Zoe Bertgang" (p. 66).

The metaphor of the tissue is applied to the *dream*: "the weaving of the dream" (p. 67 in Jensen's text) and to the *delusion*: "Evidently he was completely cured of his delusion and had risen above it; and he proved this by himself tearing the last threads of the cobweb of his delusion" (p. 37). "Mental patients go to the most extreme lengths to weave together plausible absurdities and lend them a thread of coherence" (p. 72). "The young man who just spoke is spinning a strange web in his mind; it seems to me he imagines that a fly is buzzing in his head. But then doesn't everyone have a spider on his ceiling?" (p. 152 in Jensen).

This metaphor is not directly applied to the work itself; but in what he *does*, Freud tears the threads of the text by breaking the narrative up into discontinuous fragments. Indeed, to the metaphor of the web is added a series of architectural metaphors: because the tissue protects and defends, the delusion is also described as an edifice which must be torn down and broken to pieces, in order to reconstruct a new edifice afterward. At the same time that Freud speaks of a "crumbling of the delusion," he refers, at the beginning of part 2 of his study, to the dismantling of the work that he has just carried out, thus once again assimilating to one another delusional and fictional production. " 'Gradiva' herself had demonstrated the incorrectness of the hypotheses [Norbert] had assembled and had given him the most natural explanations of all the things he had seen as riddles" (p. 87), Freud observes; he refers to "a curious new piece of delusion" (p. 78), and a need "to understand the origin of this addition to the delusion and to look for the fresh piece of unconscious discovery which was replaced by the fresh piece of delusion" (p. 78).

THE SYMBOLICS OF POMPEII

The architectural metaphor finds its very model in the main activity of the hero, who is an archeologist with a fondness for the remains of the classical past, for its fragments. The Gradiva statuette too, as the "Postscript to the Second Edition" tells us, is just a fragment of a larger relief. The whole, which depicted three figures, could be reconstituted by bringing together fragments which had been scattered in different museums. Freud uses this metaphor to describe the activity of psychoanalysis.[4] Thus by making the delusion crumble and breaking up Jensen's text, he establishes a link between the delusional construction and Norbert's past, and suggests a possible link between the work and the author's past.

Norbert, like Oedipus, is able to decipher all the external riddles—the ones inscribed on the walls of Pompeii. He has the knowledge, but he fails to recognize the Pompeii inside himself. His science is no longer of any help to him and will leave him stranded at the most critical moments of his adventure. In *Gradiva*, Jensen remarks upon this discrepancy in Norbert between knowledge and truth: "In N.H.'s eyes, the word *caupa* seemed to stand out from the scribbling, but perhaps it was an illusion, for he could not have said so for certain. He was very adept at deciphering these graffiti which were so hard to make out, and he had had successes in this area which had won glorious recognition" (p. 49). And yet he needs Zoe in order to emerge from his burial, to decipher his own riddles. Thus Freud says that he is played with by the symbolics of Pompeii, that he makes use of it in his delusion as a disguise for his repressed memory, but that he is unaware of the symbolics of repression as such.[5] He has only an endopsychic perception of it, whereas Zoe, like the psychoanalyst, is said to play with these symbolics deliberately. Freud writes: "There is, in fact, no better analogy for repression, by which something in the mind is at once made inaccessible and preserved, than burial of the sort to which Pompeii fell a victim and from which it could emerge once more through the work of spades.[6] Thus it was that the young archaeologist was obliged in his phantasy to transport to Pompeii the original of the relief which reminded him of the object of his youthful love" (p. 40).

Jensen, who puts the same symbolics into Zoe's mouth, shows the function of the symbol which to those who can understand it simultaneously conceals and reveals through the very force that masks and disguises, just as the return of the repressed arises from the very force that represses. Jensen thus seems to be perfectly familiar with repression and with the laws governing the return of the repressed. Nevertheless, he has no concept of repression, but only stages it in the symbolics of Pompeii. The author no longer seems to share at all his hero's delusions, but instead places himself on the side of Zoe and the psychoanalyst. Yet though Jensen's invention of this symbolics shows that he has written a novel that is psychologically true, he is unaware that he has this perception, and that in writing a fiction he in turn is played with by symbolics. He is unaware of everything in his past that is buried in his work, unaware that the symbolics of Pompeii played out by his hero is also played out by him; he merely has an endopsychic perception of the symbolics which is precisely what makes it possible for him to describe it, without knowing it, perfectly truthfully. Like the hero, he possesses knowledge but not truth (as Lacan defines these terms). Only the Freudian reading interprets the symbolics of Pompeii at work in the text as being the symbolics of repression. Indeed, many meanings can be read in this symbolics, and many interpretations can be given: the symbolic text is polysemous and admits of a plural truth. The city of Pompeii as such signals this pluralism of meaning. It is ambiguous by nature, and Jensen, by setting most of the narrative in this city, places the novella under the sign of duplicity. Pompeii is the epitome of undecidability, hesitation, and oscillation, the city of delusion and crisis in which all certainty is shaken. In *Gradiva* Pompeii is above all Vesuvius, and the Vesuvio that takes people out of their usual state:

> It seemed to him that, on the ground, the black silhouettes of the treetops and the buildings were not standing perfectly straight. But it is true that this phenomenon was in no way frightening in a land which has been constantly shaken from time immemorial. For the underground play which everywhere impatiently awaits eruption finds an outlet by going up into the vines and the grapes of which Vesuvio is made, the Vesuvio which was not N.H.'s usual drink every evening. (p. 66)

Pompeii is at once a new and ancient city (p. 42), burned by light and sun but also cloaked in grey smoke and submerged in ashes and lava—a dead city but also the city of initiation into the mysteries of life and love, as the surviving frescoes attest (pp. 92, 151, 152); a city of two languages, that of the living who speak German, and that of the dead who speak Latin and Greek or maintain an empty silence (pp. 41, 48, 51). This duplicity makes of Pompeii the epitome of the city of dreams, a city in which the hero is between consciousness and unconsciousness and, having fled the return of his erotic desires, encounters love, which is one with life. It is a treacherous city which functions like a *pharmacon* (in the Derridian sense), for those who sojourn there seem to be strange and enigmatic in nature, whether dead or alive, woman or man, ghost or spirit; it is a neutral city in which it is possible to go from death to life, from the cold and darkness of the wintry north to the spring-time warmth of Italy, from science to imagination and delusion, from unconsciousness to consciousness. These are traditional rhetorical antitheses that make of Jensen's narrative a lovely symbolic tale which can be interpreted, like the tale of Sleeping Beauty, as a myth of initiation into love and life.[7] In Freud's view, every other interpretation refers to the analytic interpretation as its truth Thus Freud shatters the different symbolic layers of the text and retains only a single one which determines the text's meaning, dispelling the ambiguity of the city and delivering the hero from crisis. The symbols are treated as symptoms and have, in Freud's view, the same function as compromise and lure.

Once again, the text is treated as a delusional production.

THE MURDER OF THE AUTHOR

Freud's text itself demands a double reading: it openly acknowledges that its primary aim is to show that the normal or pathological behavior of fictional characters obeys the same laws as the behavior of real people. It is mainly in this respect that Jensen's text interests him.

Gradiva offers confirmation of psychoanalytic discoveries and support against traditional psychology. The novelist, who is closer to popular superstition and the beliefs of antiquity than to science and modern psychiatry, has written not a work of "fantasy," but a perfectly correct psychiatric study. In conformity with psychoanalytic precepts, he has shown that dreams do not consist in a mere play of somatic excitations, but are rather psychic formations capable of transforming waking psychic life, dictating, for example, the hero's departure for Italy, and favoring the formation of his delusion.[8] He has been able to describe perfectly the genesis and cure of a delusion, and to show that an apparently arbitrary and fanciful product obeys psychic laws, holds the sick person's past in confinement in distorted and transposed form, and thus has in it what Freud calls historical, if not material, truth.[9] Just as the words in a dream are replicas of words heard the previous day, albeit perhaps in altered form (pp. 73–74), so the hero's delusional formations are replicas of his childhood memories.

But at another level of reading, Freud wants to show that the work of fiction in turn, though it is taken to be arbitrary and fanciful and presents itself as such, also obeys laws, and that nothing, however delusional it may seem to be, is left to chance. In this sense the author is completely comparable to his character. He presents the truth as illusion and does so under an illusion. He too is deluded without knowing it, and Freud wants to suggest that his work too is a distorted echo of his childhood. At the same time that Freud dismantles Jensen's text in order to interpret Norbert's dreams, he commits the murder of the author as the father of the work. There are parallels between the metaphors that describe the products of dreams and delusions and those that describe the products of fictions, and also parallels implied by the repetition of the same terms applied sometimes to delusion, sometimes to the work. Both are initially said to be "arbitrary products" (according to the traditional conception). Thus regarding the hero's invention of the name "Gradiva," Freud says, "These products of his phantasy seem arbitrary enough" (p. 50). And later, "Such products of the imagination would seem to us astonishing and inexplicable if we met them in someone in real life. Since our hero, Norbert Hanold, is a fictitious person, we may perhaps put a timid question to his author, and ask whether his imagination was determined by forces other than its own arbitrary choice" (p. 14).

The production of delusion is described as the production of a work of fiction. Norbert, in his fascination with the statuette, gives her a name, makes up a story of her origins, and assigns her a specific place which is apparently contingent: "He convinced himself ... that she must be transported to Pompeii" (p. 11). Norbert's turn of mind predisposes him toward delusion as much as toward becoming a writer.

> This division between imagination and intellect destined him to become an artist or a neurotic; he was one of those whose kingdom is not of this world. Thus it was that it could come about that his interest was attached to a relief representing a girl stepping along

in a peculiar fashion, that he wove his phantasies around her, imagined a name and an origin for her, placed the figure he had created
in the setting of the Pompeii that was buried more than eighteen
hundred years before... (p. 14).

Through this description of delusional "creation" Freud likens the
mechanism of hysteria to that of poetic production, just as he had
done before in 1897 in Draft N concerning Goethe's *Werther*, where
he had quoted Shakespeare's assimilation of poetry to madness.
Later on, *Totem and Taboo* defines hysteria as a caricature of poetry,
a distorted echo of it.

   These different comparisons do not constitute an attempt
to reduce a work of literature or culture to a psychotic or neurotic
illness, since the latter is but a caricature of the former; instead,
they try to show that both are originary and original substitutes for
a past whose meaning has never been perceived as such. Fantasies
and works of art are original memories of some kind, substitutes
for a memory that is always already absent. They are protective
fabulations, embellishments which serve as counter investments to
memory that is always already repressed. Since both replicate the
past in some sense, neither could be an arbitrary "creation." Given
the fact that literature, as Freud emphasizes in "The Uncanny," is
not subject to the test of reality, and that the writer has a certain
poetic license, this license is merely the other side of an instinctual
necessity that it camouflages. Thus in *Gradiva*, Jensen seems to use
poetic license to authorize the introduction of improbable elements
into his tale despite the psychological truth of his descriptions, and
to give his tale a happy ending which conforms to the psychology
of the reader rather than to reality. One of these improbable elements is the "inexplicable" resemblance between an ancient Greek
statuette and a young German woman of our time; the other is to
have Norbert and Zoe meet by chance in Pompeii.

   But here the author intervenes helpfully, and smoothes things out
   by making Gradiva appear at this juncture and undertake the cure
   of the delusion. By the power he possesses of guiding the people of
   his creation towards a happy destiny, in spite of all the laws of
   necessity which he makes them obey, he arranges that the girl, to
   avoid whom Hanold had fled to Pompeii, shall be transported to that

very place. In this way he corrects the folly to which the young man was led by his delusion—the folly of exchanging the home of the living girl whom he loved for the burial-place of her imaginary substitute.... [This set of circumstances] certainly seems to justify the author's description of his story as a "Pompeian phantasy," but it seems also to exclude any possibility of measuring it by the standards of clinical reality. (pp. 69–70)

These improbable developments are readily accepted by the reader, who in connivance with the author, with whom he has so to speak signed an implicit contract, believes for the duration of the reading in spirits and ghosts, in exchange for the benefit of the pleasure offered him by the incentive bonus. This belief in the extraordinary is of course also found in ordinary life when we are disoriented, and this faith brings us happiness (see p. 71).

Freud shows, however, that these improbable developments themselves answer to definite psychic laws. The appeal to chance is not simply a *deus ex machina*: "This second provision of the author's, however, involves no violent departure from actual possibility; it merely makes use of chance, which unquestionably plays a part in many human histories; and furthermore he uses it to good purpose, for this chance reflects the fatal truth that has laid it down that flight is precisely an instrument that delivers one over to what one is fleeing from" (p. 42). The first improbability seems more difficult to dispel. Yet the fact that the author gives no explanation for the resemblance between Zoe and Gradiva is perhaps a way of indicating that this resemblance must be accounted for on the basis of the delusion.

Nevertheless, on closer consideration this delusion of Hanold's seems to me to lose the greater part of its improbability. The author, indeed, has made himself responsible for one part of it by basing his story on the premiss that Zoe was in every detail a duplicate of the relief. We must therefore avoid shifting the improbability of this premiss on to its consequence—that Hanold took the girl for Gradiva come to life. Greater value is given to the delusional explanation by the fact that the author has put no rational one at our disposal. (p. 70)

What is more, if we questioned the author, says Freud, we would be in a good position to show "once again how what was ostensibly an arbitrary decision rested in fact upon law" (p. 43). The arbitrariness would disappear if we had knowledge of the novelist's psychic sources. But since we do not have access to the sources of the author's psychic life, we will grant him the right to construct a realistic development upon an improbable premise as Shakespeare had done, for example, in *King Lear*.[10]

THE DOUBLE

Thus to speak of arbitrariness is to confer a baptismal name upon ignorance. The advancement of the notion of "poetic license" obscures the relation of replication between the work and the life of the author, just as the delusional aspect of the delusion hides its historical foundation and truth. Replication does not mean the projection of preexisting fantasies or the translation or expression of a previous text, even though Freud sometimes uses terms which could lead one to believe that he remains a prisoner of the traditional logic of the sign. The only existing text is the text of the work, which is one with the text of life: it is through the text of the work that life is structured as a text, and that fantasies can be structured; that is, organized in such a way that they can be read as such and such a fantasy. The work is not a double of the author understood as the reflection of a being or of a preexisting life; it is an originary double, a replica which is necessary precisely because the text of life is lacunary, and because the ego does not exist prior to what it produces, as a presence full of meaning whose products would be merely second and secondary representations. The work is a "supplement," an originary substitute; it is not added like a surplus to a text full of meaning—what life is taken to be—but rather is added as a complement which makes it possible for life to be constituted as a text. Based on the parallel established between it and delusional production, it can be said that the text of the work and the text of the life relate to each other as echoes or replicas.

Now granted, these two metaphors might precisely lead

one to believe that there exists an originary text which precedes its representation: the echo seems to presuppose a originary sound of which it is thought to be the distorted repercussion, the replica of an original model. In what he *says*, Freud seems to establish a relation of derivation and translation between two texts, and seems dependent on the traditional conception of art as mimesis. For example, concerning the invention of the name and origin of the statuette presented initially as arbitrary and contingent, Freud writes: "We had already guessed that the Greek origin of the imaginary Gradiva was an obscure result of the Greek name 'Zoe'; but we had not ventured to approach the name 'Gradiva' itself, and had let it pass as the untrammelled creation of Norbert Hanold's imagination. But, lo and behold! that very name now turns out to have been a derivative—indeed a translation—of the repressed surname of the girl he had loved in the childhood which he was supposed to have forgotten. . . . He felt free, for his delusion had now been replaced by the thing of which it could only have been a distorted and inadequate replica" (p. 38). "These [fantasies], as we learned later, were echoes of his memories of his youthful love, derivatives of those memories, transformations and distortions of them, after they had failed to make their way into his consciousness in an unmodified form" (p. 50). Hanold's decision to leave for Italy is "an echo of the dream" (p. 13), just as the slap he gives Zoe on the hand repeats the blows the two had exchanged as children. The term "echo" is always used to cancel out arbitrariness and the radical inventiveness of behavior or production. "Creation" is only repetition; there is never any creation *ex nihilo*:

> And now the discovery dawns upon us that the young archaeologist's phantasies about his Gradiva may have been an echo of his forgotten childhood memories. If so, they were not capricious products of his imagination, but determined, without his knowing it, by the store of childhood impressions which he had forgotten, but which were still at work in him. It should be possible for us to show the origin of the phantasies in detail, even though we can only guess at them. (p. 31)

And yet, it is because these childhood impressions have never been lived in the full possession of their significance that there is repetition. It is because the originary text is absent that there is the echo, the second text, which is thus originary in its secondness. "As we learn later in the story, Hanold was not different from other children. . . . It is in attachments such as this, in combinations like this of affection and aggressiveness, that the immature erotism of childhood finds its expression; its consequences only emerge later, but then they are irresistible, and during childhood itself it is as a rule recognized as erotism only by doctors and novelists" (p. 46).

Thus the metaphor of the echo indeed introduces the idea of a repetition, but of an originary and original repetition. By looking beyond what Freud *says* to what the hero *does* in his delusional production, it can be seen that the echo retains only certain traces of the original sound, certain elements from which a new play of sound is constituted. For example, Norbert imagines that Gradiva is of Greek origin on the basis of the girl's Greek given name, "Zoe," a repressed, forgotten name. Such a displacement is possible only because the delusion plays on the double meaning of the word "origin" by condensing, as in a play on words, the etymology of a term and the genealogy of a person. The play on words does not appear, since the signifier "Zoe" is barred. In order for this displacement to occur, the signifier "Zoe" must be disconnected from its particular referent, Zoe, a girl who is German and not Greek, a childhood friend of the deluded man. These disconnections between signifier and signified which make possible the delusional construction are the expression, at the level of language, of the negative hallucination from which Norbert is suffering. The hallucination makes him deaf and blind to everyday reality, to the point that his investment in it is completely withdrawn in favor of a neo-reality created by his fantasies. The Greek origin which is said to be an echo of the Greek word *Zoe* therefore is not the translation of a prior language into another one. Instead, it is a complete remodeling of reality, the invention of another story and of a poetic language, precisely because everyday language is reduced to a play of signifiers cut off from any referent. Norbert's language itself is now merely a trace of language, reduced to a play of traces, to its strict literalness, to the elements of the language on the basis of which it is possible to play, to construct a new reality. There is thus connivance between poetic language and delusional language by virtue of this same divestment of the real.

The deluded person, however, rather than playing in this way with the traces of his past, is played with by his past without knowing it. For Zoe, who has knowledge of Norbert's past, the present delusion "echoes" the past. Zoe plays the role of an ideal psychoanalyst, one who can only exist in a work of fiction—a psychoanalyst who, far from being limited to making guesses about the genesis of the fantasies (p. 31), could both be familiar with her patients' past and respond to their transference. In real treatment, the psychoanalyst can only generate delusions along with his patient (see "Constructions in Analysis," 23:257–269) or else build the novel of his childhood; in any case he never holds the key to his patient's delusion.

This same metaphor of the echo makes it possible to understand the relation between pathological productions and cultural "creations." Thus hysteria and creative fiction echo one another.

> The forms assumed by the different neuroses echoed the most highly admired productions of our culture. Thus hysterics are undoubtedly poets, even if they express their phantasies *mimetically* in the main and without considering their intelligibility to other people; the ceremonials and prohibitions of obsessional neurotics drive us to suppose that they have created a private religion of their own; and the delusions of paranoiacs have an unpalatable external similarity and internal kinship to the systems of our philosophers. It is impossible to escape the conclusion that these patients are, in an *asocial* fashion, making the very attempts at solving their conflicts and appeasing their pressing needs which, when those attempts are carried out in a fashion that is acceptable to the majority, are known as poetry, religion, and philosophy. ("Preface to Reik's *Ritual*," 17:261)

Hysteria and poetry each play out the past in their own way and are played out by the past. The "creator" is in no way superior to his "creatures," any more than the normal person is to the sick person; nor should fictional characters be treated differently from real people. When Freud pretends to distinguish between them, for example at the end of his study—"But we must stop here, or we may really forget that Hanold and Gradiva are only creatures of their author's mind" (*Delusions and Dreams*, 9:93)—he does so only the better to emphasize ordinary illusion, since his entire study has as its necessary consequence the cancellation of the oppositions inherited from an entire metaphysical tradition.

   Thus Jensen's knowledge is merely a pseudo knowledge that the novelist possesses without knowing it and that is played out by him, an endopsychic perception common to artists, people who are superstitious or animistic in their beliefs, and certain deluded people, a shadowy perception in which the repressed relations of the unconscious are projected outward into a work of art, a myth, or a delusion. Thus, after having repeatedly declared for strategic reasons that the writer's knowledge is superior to that of science and is its precursor (see especially pp. 8, 45–49, and 52–55), Freud shows surprise at this and casts suspicion on it.

> When, from the year 1893 onwards, I plunged into investigations such as these of the origin of mental disturbances, it would certainly never have occurred to me to look for a confirmation of my findings in the works of novelists and poets. I was thus more than a little surprised to find that the author of *Gradiva*, which was published in 1903, had taken as the basis of its creation the very thing that I believed myself to have freshly discovered from the sources of my medical experience. How was it that the author arrived at the same knowledge as the doctor—or at least behaved as though he possessed the same knowledge? (p. 54)

   Though the psychoanalyst and the novelist arrive at the same results, they proceed differently. The poet can do without the analytic method because he is tuned into his unconscious; the repressed is projected outward into the work. The novelist is under an illusion without knowing it; he calls his work a fantasy and is irritated by the analytic interpretation of it. This play of knowledge, says Freud, is characteristic of artistic creation. Concerning Stefan Zweig's "Four-and -Twenty Hours in a Woman's Life," he later writes in "Dostoevsky and Parricide" that "it is characteristic of the nature of artistic creation that the author, who is a personal friend of mine, was able to assure me, when I asked him, that the interpretation which I put to him had been completely strange to his knowledge and intention, although some of the details woven into the narrative seemed expressly designed to give a clue to the hidden trace of it" (21:192). To someone who knows how to read it then, the text tells much more that the author tells us about it; his declared intentions serve as a facade and conceal an unconscious meaning. Like a symptom, the work is a compromise in which either a literal meaning or an unconscious meaning may be read, depending whether or not it is subjected to the analytic method.

THE WORK, A SYMPTOM TO DECIPHER

Thus in relation to his other writings on art, Freud's study of *Gradiva* can be considered a pivotal work. Before the *Gradiva* essay, Freud's relation to art is one of fascination, corresponding to the child's admiration of the great man, the father. At this point, works of art serve as testimony to and confirmation of psychoanalysis, providing it with paradigms for both normal and pathological psychic processes. This first attitude is present in the study of *Gradiva*. Corresponding to it are Norbert's fascination with the statuette and the reader's willingness to go along with Jensen's narrative, since he is taken with the work's charm. Reading it as a fantastic work, he has faith in the hero's fantasies, identifies with him completely, and shares his delusions. This is a naive reading which allows the reader to play with his fantasies without feeling guilty, a reading in which the author pays the reader for empathizing with his character. No reading pays unless there is affective contact between the reader and the characters. Freud comments, "The author wishes to bring the hero closer to us so as to make 'empathy' easier; the diagnosis of *dégénéré*, whether it is right or wrong at once puts the young archaeologist at a distance from us, for we readers are the normal people and the standard of humanity" (p. 45). And later, "[The hero] still appears to us as incomprehensible and foolish; we have no idea how his peculiar folly will be linked to human feeling and so arouse our sympathy. It is an author's privilege to be allowed to leave us in such uncertainty. The charm of his language and the ingenuity of his ideas offer us a provisional reward for the reliance we place in him and for the still unearned sympathy which we are ready to feel for his hero" (p. 14).

This first stage is followed by a second, also present in the study of *Gradiva*, which marks a turning point in Freud's interest in art. The work can offer support to psychoanalysis on the condition that it already be read analytically: this is the insurmountable circle of hermeneutics. Though Freud declares that Jensen's text provided both text and commentary, there is nonetheless a discrepancy marked by the subtitle, "fantasy"; though the commentary is made on the basis of the text, the text is no longer considered in its literalness alone. The analytic reading introduces a double reading into every text. From now on the work of art is no longer a model for science but an object of investigation, a text to be deciphered. The task is to find the laws that govern poetic production, even though in the *Gradiva* essay Freud only announces this project very cautiously and with false modesty.

> But even this sobering thought does not damp our interest in the fashion in which writers make use of dreams. Even if this enquiry should teach us nothing new about the nature of dreams, it may perhaps enable us from this angle to gain some small insight into the nature of poetic production. Real dreams were already regarded as unrestrained and unregulated structures—and now we are confronted by unfettered imitations of these dreams! There is far less freedom and arbitrariness in mental life, however, than we are inclined to assume—there may even be none at all. What we call chance in the world outside, can, as is well known, be resolved into laws. So, too, what we call arbitrariness in the mind rests upon laws, which we are only now beginning dimly to suspect. Let us, then, see what we find! (p. 9)

This second stage is marked by the murder of the text and of the author as father of his work. It puts an end to fascination. It involves a change in the reader as well, for he is now distanced from the hero and, after passing through a phase of disappointment, comes to feel superior to him. The reader's disappointment arises from the fact that the hero with whom he had identified up to that point is now seen as deluded. It is at this point that the hero is murdered. The reader has the feeling that the author has played him for a fool by promising him something marvelous and fantastic and then coming up with nothing but a scientific riddle to solve. He is obliged to renounce playing with his fantasies and to come back to reality; his ego must no longer let itself be charmed by the beauty of the writing but must try instead to understand it. Learning that the hero is deluded puts an end to the reader's delusion.

> What a humiliation for us readers! So the author has been making fun of us, and, with the help, as it were, of a reflection of the Pompeian sunshine, has inveigled *us* into a delusion on a small scale, so that we may be forced to pass a milder judgment on the poor wretch on whom the mid-day sun was really shining. Now, however, that we have been cured of our brief confusion, we know that Gradiva was a German girl of flesh and blood—a solution which we were inclined to reject as the most improbable one. And now, with a quiet sense of superiority, we may wait to learn what the relation was between the girl and her marble image, and how our young archaeologist arrived at the phantasies which pointed towards her real personality. (p. 18)

THE READER'S DELUSION

What difference is there between the reader and the hero? What makes it possible for the reader to emerge from the delusion that characterized his naive reading? What prevents the hero from emerging from his delusion as quickly as the reader? One answer would be as follows: at the same time that the author moves his narrative toward the solution of the riddle and the resolution of the delusion, he also tends to delay the answer and the cure, since both necessarily bring the story to an end. It could thus be said that the very structure of the narrative produces the divergence between the reader and the hero.[11] But in this case the tension in the reader might just as well have lasted right up to the last moment. Nothing in the structure of an enigmatic narrative justifies having the reader stop identifying with the hero at a certain point. The reason for the divergence must then be sought in the psychology of the reader. The reader represents normality. Yet to a certain extent this normal person is deluded whenever he remains at the first level of reading. This is what Freud wants to show: there is no reason to oppose the normal to the pathological, and every day each one of us crosses the fictional and conventional boundary separating the two. "But the frontier between states of mind described as normal and pathological is in part a conventional one and in part so fluctuating that each of us probably crosses it many times in the course of a day" (p. 44).

Thus in the novella, Norbert's amorous fascination with a stone statuette, the image of a woman from another century, differs only in degree from so-called normal passion, and pathology is what makes it possible to understand "normal" behavior. A person who is in love is possessed, captivated by the object of his passion. What is more, Norbert's fascination can be considered as the larger-than-life model of all love which, like Norbert, is in search of a lost object that was loved in childhood, the father and/or the mother. "We may suspect, of course, that...our case of pathology might end up as a 'commonplace' love-story. But...was not our hero's possession by his Gradiva sculpture a complete instance of being in love, though of being in love with something past and lifeless?" (p.22).[12]

If the difference between the normal and the pathological must be read under erasure, it remains to be explained how it is possible for the reader to emerge from his delusion more quickly than the hero. Since the reader started reading he has been in a difficult position and has been subject to great tension by virtue of being unable to say to what literary genre the novella belongs. This position becomes more and more untenable as his hesitation and disorientation increase. The reader can only come out of his crisis by opting for one of three hypotheses concerning the nature of the apparition in Pompeii: "Is she a hallucination of our hero, led astray by his delusions? Is she a 'real' ghost? or a living person?" (p. 17). The reader's disorientation comes in response to the hero's loss of balance; both—and this is diagnosed by Freud as the very trademark of delusion—radically separate the real from the imaginary, delusion from truth, and ghosts from real people. Because the problem has been posed incorrectly, the most improbable hypothesis will turn out to be the truest. The real person is also a spirit and a hallucination, because the hallucination has its source in reality, and the spirit and midday ghost are merely the mythic projection of repressed psychic relations.[13]

The reader and the hero are ignorant of these links, and this ignorance is the cause of their uneasiness: they want to clear up the matter once and for all. The reader is able to do this faster than Norbert because the reader puts his reading of events to the test of reality, something which he should not be able to do, strictly speaking, since he does not know what kind of literary work he is dealing with. But he is forced to make a decision precisely because of the tension in which he is being held. The hero, on the other hand, remains untouched by the test of reality; he always finds a new elaboration that enables him to deny reality in order to accommodate it to his delusion, rather than the other way around. The reason for this is that the delusion has its psychic roots in the hero's psyche and not in the reader's; the hero can emerge from his delusion only by means of an energetic treatment.

> Not that we need believe in ghosts to draw up this list of hypotheses. The author, who has called his story a "phantasy," has found no occasion so far for informing us whether he intends to leave us in our world, decried for being prosaic and governed by the laws of science, or whether he wishes to transport us into another and imaginary world, in which spirits and ghosts are given reality. As we know from the examples of Hamlet and Macbeth, we are prepared to follow him there without hesitation. If so, the imaginative archaeologist's delusion would have to be measured by another standard. Indeed, when we consider how improbable it must be that a real person could exist who bore an exact resemblance to the antique sculpture, our list of hypotheses shrinks to two: a hallucination or a

mid-day ghost. A small detail in the account soon cancels the first possibility. A large lizard was lying motionless, stretched out in the sunshine, but fled at the approach of Gradiva's foot and darted away across the lava paving-stones. So it was no hallucination, but something outside our dreamer's mind. But could the reality of a *rediviva* startle a lizard? (p. 17)

Because, to a certain extent, the particular madness of the hero is distinct from ours, we cannot identify with him all the way through,[14] and we move to a second level of reading now guided not by the search for enchantment but by the pleasure of deciphering a riddle. This pleasure is still closely tied to the earlier one; it is not disinterested since the desire to know also has libidinal roots. The pleasure of solving the riddle is given as a substitute for the pleasure brought by the supernatural; thus the reader is disappointed again when he learns that the heroine is just Norbert's neighbor. The riddle is too simple. So the novelist consoles the reader for his double disappointment by giving him a happy ending as part of the fiction. Indeed, the supernatural had been reestablished by grasping, detail by detail, the links between delusional creation and everyday reality. Which is to say that if psychoanalysis deconstructs one incarnation of the fantastic, it gives us another one in its place by showing, as Plato had already done in *Phaedrus*, that the supernatural is inside us. The pleasure of knowing—a substitute for the pleasure of seeing—is nonetheless a pleasure.

A second stage is thus marked by the murder of the text, of the father, and of the hero, and by the end of naive reading.

FREUD AND METAPHYSICS

In his treatment of the work, Freud at once opposes an entire metaphysical tradition and remains dependent upon it. He is dependent upon Plato, who considers that the poet does not know what he is saying: he is inspired. For this theological term Freud substitutes the term "endopsychic perception." Inspiration is the fact of being subject to the play of the primary processes. Moreover, for

Plato as for Freud, art is the power of illusion that, by means of disguises and embellishments, aims above all at charming and bringing pleasure.[15] But Freud moves away from Plato and joins Aristotle in maintaining that illusion is distinct from falsehood. By means of illusion, the artist—himself under an illusion—nonetheless tells the truth. He presents a psychic truth, stages it without knowing it. All that is needed to possess the truth is to convert poetic language, the language of disguise, into a metapsychological language,[16] just as for Aristotle one must go from metaphoric language, which potentially possesses truth, to the conceptual language of reason, in order actually to have truth. Myth is the childhood of philosophy for Aristotle, just as for Freud, art is the childhood of psychoanalysis. Art occupies an intermediate position between the pleasure principle and the reality principle and reconciles them to one another.[17]

The study of *Gradiva* thus marks a turning point in Freud's attitude toward art. It is a pivotal text, as Freud emphasizes repeatedly in his recapitulative works.[18] In the "Postscript to the Second Edition" of the *Gradiva* study, written five years later, it is said that

> in the five years that have passed since this study was completed, psycho-analytic research has summoned up the courage to approach literary production with yet another purpose in view. It no longer merely seeks in them for confirmations of the findings it has made from unpoetic, neurotic human beings; it also demands to know the material of impressions and memories from which the author has built the work, and the methods and processes by which he has converted this material into a work of art. It has turned out that these questions can be most easily answered in the case of writers who (like our Wilhelm Jensen, who died in 1911) were in the habit of giving themselves over to their imagination with a spontaneous joy in creating. Soon after the publication of my analytic examination of *Gradiva* I attempted to interest the elderly author in these new tasks of psycho-analytic research. But he refused his co-operation. (p. 94)

In this postscript Freud tries to establish the link between the work and Jensen's past not by using a genetic method, but by means of a method which can very tentatively be termed structural. He compares Jensen's different texts, pointing out that many motifs return again and again, and that the central situation in *Gradiva* and the same setting are reproduced: the apparition, in the heat of a summer day, of a girl who is dead or believed to be dead. These repetitions are such that the different works echo one another, and because of this continual return we may suppose that the works are replicas of the author's past.

NOTES

1. THE DOUBLE READING

1. See "The Claims of Psycho-Analysis to Scientific Interest," in *The Standard Edition of the Complete Psychological Works of Sigmund Freud*, James Strachey, ed. and tr., 24 vols. (London: Hogarth Press and The Institute of Psycho-Analysis, 1953), 13:165–190, esp. section F, "The Interest of Psycho-Analysis from the Point of View of the Science of Aesthetics," pp. 187–188. [Volume and page numbers following quotations from and references to the works of Freud refer to this edition. Where necessary, I have modified the translation.——Trans.]

2. See "On the History of the Psycho-Analytic Movement," 14:3–66, and "Resistances to Psycho-Analysis," 19:213–222, esp. p. 218.

3. Though I am not unacquainted with the copious literature on the subject I am attempting to treat in this book, I have decided, barring exceptions, to use only Freud's texts with the intention of making them known to the French public, which, because translations are lacking or inadequate, is unacquainted with most of Freud's works.

4. Here Freud refers to Otto Rank and his work (*The Incest Motif in Poetry and Legend*).

5. See the beginning of the text "The Moses of Michelangelo," 13:211 ff.

6. We know from Freud's correspondence that he preferred literature to the other arts and particularly appreciated it. From a letter to Fliess on August 18, 1897, we know that it was on the latter's suggestion that he went to Florence, where he took pleasure in visiting the museums, but found religious art dull, especially Christian art. In Milan, he liked only Leonardo da Vinci's *Last Supper*. From a letter of October 5, 1883, we can measure the extent of Freud's literary and philosophical knowledge. The two works that made the greatest impression on him at this time were *Don Quixote* and *The Temptation of Saint Anthony*. [The Fliess letter appears in *The*

Origins of Psycho-Analysis, Marie Bonaparte, Anna Freud, and Ernst Kris, eds. (New York: Basic Books, 1977), pp. 214–215. Passages of Freud's October 5 and July 26, 1883 correspondence with his wife concerning Dickens, *Don Quixote*, and *The Temptation of St. Anthony* are quoted by Ernest Jones in *The Life and Works of Sigmund Freud*, 3 vols. (New York: Basic Books, 1981), 1:174–175.— TRANS.] But Freud's literary tastes and knowledge are especially evident in the examples taken from the field of literature which adorn the entire body of his work. The authors that appear most often are Shakespeare, Goethe, Sophocles, Heine, Ibsen, Flaubert, Rabelais, Zola, Diderot, Boccaccio, Oscar Wilde, George Bernard Shaw, Dostoevsky, Molière, Swift, Homer, Horace, Tasso, Hoffmann, Schiller, Mark Twain, Aristophanes, Thomas Mann, Stefan Zweig, Hebbel, Galsworthy, Cervantes, Hesiod, Macaulay, and many others of lesser reknown. His knowledge of tales, legends, and folklore is equally remarkable. In order to become acquainted with Freud's tastes and the various criteria he uses to assess literary works, it is interesting to refer to his "Contribution to a Questionnaire on Reading" (9:245–247), where he distinguishes between the most *magnificent* books (those of Homer and Sophocles, Goethe's *Faust*, Shakespeare's *Hamlet* and *Macbeth*), the most *significant* books (those of Copernicus, Johann Weier, and Darwin), and his *favorite* books (Milton's *Paradise Lost* and Heine's *Lazarus*).

Among the *good* books he cites:

—Multatuli (who replaced the Μοῖρα, fate, of the Greeks with Λόγος, reason, and ἀνάγλη, necessity, as does Freud himself), *Letters and Works*
—Kipling, *The Jungle Book*
—Anatole France, *Sur la pierre blanche*
—Zola, *Fécondité*
—Merezhkovsky, *Leonardo da Vinci*
—Keller, *Leute von Seldwyls*
—C. F. Meyer, *Huttens letzte Tage*
—Macaulay, *Essays*
—Gomperz, *Griechische Denker*
—Mark Twain, *Sketches*

He ends this questionnaire by saying that he wishes above all to be able to throw light on the relation between the author and his work.

7. See the last chapter of *Leonardo da Vinci and a Memory of His Childhood*, 11:59–137; "Dostoevsky and Parricide," 21:175–194; and "Address Delivered in the Goethe House at Frankfurt," 21:208–212.

8. See *Totem and Taboo*: "Anyone approaching the problem of taboo from the angle of psycho-analysis, that is to say, of the investigation of the unconscious portion of the individual mind, will recognize, after a moment's reflection, that these phenomena are far from unfamiliar to him" (13:26).

9. See also "On Psycho-Analysis," 12:207–211, esp. p. 210: "The psycho-analytic method of investigation can accordingly be applied equally to the explanation of normal psychical phenomena, and has made it possible to discover the close relationship between pathological psychical products and normal structures such as dreams, the small blunders of everyday life, and such valuable phenomena as jokes, myths and imaginative works." See also "Two Encyclopaedia Articles" ("Psycho-Analysis" and "The Libido Theory"), 18:235–259, where Freud also indicates

the link between the history of religions, culture, mythology, literature, and psycho-analysis, expressing surprise, since originally psychoanalysis had the sole aim of understanding neurotic symptoms. The bridge linking these phenomena to one another is dream analysis; it shows that the mechanisms which produce pathological symptoms are also at work in the normal man: "Thus psycho-analysis became a *depth-psychology* and capable as such of being applied to the mental sciences, and it was able to answer a good number of questions with which the academic psychology of consciousness was helpless to deal. . . . The significance of the Oedipus complex began to grow to gigantic proportions and it looked as though social order, morals, justice and religion had arisen together in the primaeval ages of mankind as reaction-formations against the Oedipus complex" (p. 253).

10. Note added in the third edition; I have since analyzed this text in "Le double e(s)t le diable" in *Quatre romans analytiques* (Paris: Galilée, 1974).

11. See "On Psycho-Analysis," 12:207–211.

12. This does not mean that psychoanalysis is an art rather than a science, as it has been reproached for being.

13. [Here Kofman is using the term "writing" (*écriture*) in the strong sense it has acquired in recent critical theory, especially in France. As Leon S. Roudiez says in his introduction to Julia Kristeva's *Desire in Language* (New York: Columbia University Press, 1980), "*Ecriture* is what produces 'poetic language' or 'text' (in the strong sense of *that* word . . .)" (p. 19). Roudiez defines "text" as "a body of words in a state of ferment and *working*, like 'beer when the barm is put in' (Bacon, as quoted in *Webster* 2)" (p. 12).——TRANS.]

14. It is interesting to note the religious vocabulary here, which is symptomatic of art's sacrosanct status.

15. Freud makes this distinction, for example, in "Moses, His People, and Monotheistic Religion" in *Moses and Monotheism: Three Essays*, 23:129.

16. See "Dostoevsky and Parricide," 21:175–194. Freud distinguishes three aspects of Dostoevsky's personality: the neurotic, the moralist, and the creative artist. Just as he is beginning to address the last and speak of the success of Dostoevsky's works, Freud abruptly drops the subject and moves on to the study of a work by Stefan Zweig, "Four-and-Twenty Hours in a Woman's Life." Although, as I shall show, this shift can be justified on methodological grounds, one cannot help but see in it the mark of Freud's ambivalent feelings toward Dostoevsky.

Regarding Freud's ambivalence toward Dostoevsky, see also M. Th. Neyraut-Sutterman, "Parricide et épilepsie," *Revue française de psychanalyse*, July 1970.

17. See "On the History of the Psycho-Analytic Movement": "These problems . . . are among the most fascinating in the whole application of psychoanalysis" (14:37).

18. See "Repression": "Repressions that have failed will of course have more claim on our interest than any that may have been successful; for the latter will for the most part escape our examination" (14:153).

19. I am transposing onto the realm of art what Freud says about religion.

20. In a letter of September 25, 1913, he tells his wife that he goes to see the *Moses* every day. [In fact the date of the letter is September 25, 1912; see Jones, *The Life and Work of Sigmund Freud*, 2:365.—— TRANS.

21. Letter to Weiss, April 12, 1933, in *Letters of Sigmund Freud*, Ernst L. Freud,

ed., and Tania Stern and James Stern, trs. (New York: Basic Books, 1960), p. 416. [The editor notes that Freud has actually mistaken the date, which was 1912.—— TRANS.]

22. Freud himself explains this anonymity in a reply of April 6, 1914 to a letter from Abraham, who thought that readers would nonetheless surely recognize Freud's stamp: The 'Moses' piece is anonymous on the one hand for fun, and on the other, because I am ashamed of its obviously dilettantish character which, at all events, is difficult to avoid in works for Imago, and finally because, even more than usual, I have doubts about the results and published it only because the editors pressed me to do so." [My translation of Kofman; in The Life and Work of Sigmund Freud, 2:366, Jones excerpts and paraphrases similar remarks of Freud's to Abraham, but gives January 6, 1914 as the date of the letter.——TRANS.] Here again we cannot stop at Freud's declarations. The reasons he gives seem weak to me—all the more so since he himself showed the importance of the name for the unconscious, and specifically the proper name. The counterproof is the taboo on proper names so common in primitive societies. For the unconscious the name represents the person. Certain names must not be uttered, for to do so is to come into contact with the person himself, to risk committing a murder or incest, or run the risk of death oneself. To bring words into relation with each other is, for the unconscious, a union analogous to the one between the sexes. It is for this reason that Jewish ritual forbade the utterance of the name of the divinity. Instead of "Jehovah" one was supposed to say "Adonai." Even theophoric proper names retained a taboo quality.

Cf. "The Significance of Vowel Sequences," 12:341; "Group Psychology and the Analysis of the Ego," 18:69–143; and especially Totem and Taboo: "Even a civilized adult may be able to infer from certain peculiarities in his own behaviour that he is not so far removed as he may have thought from attributing importance to proper names, and that his own name has become to a very remarkable extent bound up with his personality" (13:56).

Note added in the third edition: See also the "Dream of the Three Fates" in The Interpretation of Dreams, 4:207, where Freud reports that the slightest play on his name was intolerable to him. See as well Jokes and Their Relation to the Unconscious (vol. 8), and the way aggressive Witz exploits proper names.

23. Note added in the third edition: Anne Berman's French translation deletes "least of all by someone who is himself one of them." I am lifting this remarkable instance of censorship which dates—and this is no accident— from the 1940s.

24. See Totem and Taboo, 13:90.

25. See "Group Psychology and the Analysis of the Ego": "It was then, perhaps, that some individual, in the exigency of his longing, may have been moved to free himself from the group and take over the father's part. He who did this was the first epic poet; and the advance was achieved in his imagination. This poet disguised the truth with lies in accordance with his longing. He invented the heroic myth. The hero was a man who by himself had slain the father—the father who still appeared in the myth as a totemic monster. Just as the father had been the boy's first ideal, so in the hero who aspires to the father's place the poet now created the first ego ideal.... The myth, then, is the step by which the individual emerges from group psychology.... The poet who had taken this step and had in this way set himself free from the group in his imagination, is neverless able (as Rank has further

observed) to find his way back to it in reality. For he goes and relates to the group his hero's deeds which he has invented. At bottom this hero is no one but himself. Thus he lowers himself to the level of reality, and raises his hearers to the level of imagination. But his hearers understand the poet, and, in virtue of their having the same relation of longing towards the primal father, they can identify themselves with the hero" (18:136–137).

26. In *Totem and Taboo* Freud shows that all touching is taboo and dangerous, except voluntary touching. So it is that kings, who are also substitutes for the paternal imago, cured scrofula by mere contact. As we shall see, the artist, too, has a kind of magic power.

27. Freud also vacillates on the status of the hero in tragedy.

28. See *Totem and Taboo*, 13–90. It would be interesting to compare what Freud says here with Auguste Comte's "law of the three states."

29. See "Group Psychology and the Analysis of the Ego": "But it is precisely the *sight* of the chieftain that is dangerous and unbearable for primitive people, just as later that of the Godhead is for mortals. Even Moses had to act as an intermediary between his people and Jehovah, since the people could not support the sight of God; and when he returned from the presence of God his face shone—some of the *mana* had been transferred on to him, just as happens with the intermediary among primitive people" (18:125).

30. The other two wounds were inflicted by Copernicus and Darwin. See "A Difficulty in the Path of Psycho-Analysis," 17:139ff.

31. See Derrida's distinction between concept and discourse. [For example, in "Differance," in *Speech and Phenomena*, David B. Allison, tr. (Evanston, Ill.: North western University Press, 1973), pp. 129–160.——TRANS].

32. [One translator of Freud, Katherine Jones, makes this remark in *Moses and Monotheism* (New York: Vintage Books, 1967) about the phrase "instinctual renunciation," which appears in the *Standard Edition* as well: "I use this phrase (*Triebversicht*) as an abbreviation for 'renouncing the satisfaction of an urge derived from an instinct' " (p. 144).——TRANS.]

33. At the end of this chapter I can protest against all the hasty criticisms leveled against Freud's conception of art, which is deemed to be a prisoner of bourgeois ideology. I am thinking for example of a note in Philippe Sollers' article on Lautréamont, "La Science de Lautréamont," in *Logiques* (Paris: Editions du Seuil, 1968). Here I am quoting this text and note 1 which accompanies it:

> "Freudian theory's inability to approach 'literature' arises precisely from this limited orality (the metaphysical space of speech).
> "For Freud, the 'creative writer' is an 'exceptional personality' who stirs others without knowing why himself, but with the aim of obtaining 'honor, money, and women.' He is like 'the child at play,' play being defined as the opposite of reality; the 'poet' creates for himself 'an imaginary, unreal world' and thus discloses—but with an 'incentive bonus'—the mechanism of fantasy, fantasy which is present in everyone and is revealed by the neurotic. It is true that Freud intends to treat only 'the less pretentious writers of romances, novels, and stories who are read all the same by the widest circles of men and women' ("Creative Writers and Daydreaming," 9:143–153). It is hardly necessary to stress the astounding naiveté of such a conception. Yet most

analytical researches on the so-called literary text are still oriented toward
the signified alone. On this problem, cf. Derrida's 'Freud et la scène de l'é-
criture.' [Translated as "Freud and the Scene of Writing" in Writing and Difference,
Alan Bass, tr. (Chicago: University of Chicago Press, 1978), pp. 196–231.——
TRANS.] Not a single one of Freud's individualist and petit bourgeois prejudices
has been dislodged." (p. 254)

In his text "Freud et la création littéraire," Jean-Louis Baudry makes ap-
proximately the same criticisms:

"Freud's conception or, one might say, his 'representation' of 'literary creation'
(which is hinted at in his use of the words 'creation,' 'creator,' 'work,' etc.)
thus seems to be dominated and guided by the idea, the ideologeme of
representation. This ideologeme, marking Freud's tie to his time and a class,
at once impregnates the bourgeoisie's conception of 'art' and is diffracted in
the texts themselves in such a way that their very textuality is hidden by it.
In Freud's wake—but departing from the paths that he had broken elsewhere—the psychoanalytic movement and the thought inspired by it have
displayed the same incomprehension, a remarkable impotence with regard
to the written word, undoubtedly because of its representatives' attachment
to a metaphysics, an ideology, and the interests of a class to which they
belong in spite of everything." (Tel quel [Winter 1968], 32:83)

The accusation of naive reading could be turned back against Philippe
Sollers. It is regrettable to see pejorative epithets or ready-made categories such as
"petit bourgeois" and "individualist" substituted for arguments. Baudry's text appears to be better argued, but does not take account of the totality of the Freudian
corpus, nor of the distinction I have introduced between what Freud says and what
he does. The reference our two critics make to Derrida therefore requires considerable
qualification.

2. FASCINATION BY ART

1. See especially Letters 71, 91, 92, and 100 dating from the years 1897–
1898, in The Origins of Psycho-Analysis, Marie Bonaparte, Anna Freud, and Ernst Kris,
eds. (New York: Basic Books, 1977), pp. 221–225, 255–259, and 270.
2. Freud makes use of the myth of Empedocles in the third doctrine on
the drives, as counterproof and as paradigmatic model. See my article "Freud et
Empédocle" in Critique (June 1969), 265:525–550; rpt. in Quatre romans analytiques (Paris:
Galilée, 1974).
3. See Jean Starobinski, "Hamlet et Freud," Les Temps modernes (June 1967),
253:2113–2135.
4. The example of Oedipus Rex appears in most of Freud's works, sometimes
as a counterproof of the Oedipus complex, sometimes to be itself subjected to an
interpretive analysis. The most important texts on this subject are his letter to Fliess
of October 15, 1897 (Letter 71 in The Origins of Psycho-Analysis); The Interpretation of

Dreams, 1900; *Introductory Lectures on Psycho-Analysis,* 1916; "Dostoevsky and Parricide," 1927; and "A Short Account of Psycho-Analysis," 1938.

5. See also *The Psychopathology of Everyday Life,* where Freud speaks of "the universal human application of the Oedipus myth as correlated with the Fate which is revealed in the oracles" (6:178), and of "the 'Oedipus dream,' as I am in the habit of calling it, because it contains the key to the understanding of the legend of King Oedipus. In the text of Sophocles a reference to such a dream is put into Jocasta's mouth" (p. 178, n. 2).

6. See also the comparison of Hamlet and Oedipus in "An Autobiographical Study," 22:64.

7. See also *The Interpretation of Dreams,* where Freud expresses his agreement with James Sully's essay "The Dream as Revelation." Sully writes: "Like some letter in a cypher, the dream-inscription when scrutinized closely loses its first look of balderdash and takes on the aspect of a serious, intelligible message. Or, to vary the figure slightly, we may say that, like some palimpsest, the dream discloses beneath its worthless surface-character traces of an old and precious communication" (4:135, n. 2).

See also *Introductory Lectures,* 15:229 ff., where for essentially polemical reasons, Freud compares dreams to nonlinear pictographic and ideogrammatic forms of writing. They were once thought to be indecipherable and meaningless, but the opposite has been proved. The indeterminate nature of their characters (each syllable has an average of ten meanings in the Chinese language) does not necessarily result in equivocal or polysemous meanings. The linguist Abel shows that contrary meanings assigned to root words did not result in ambiguous communications. Tone and gesture indicated the meaning in the spoken language. As for the written language, the meaning is designated by a pictorial sign which is not intended to be pronounced. The same indeterminacies are to be found in the Hebrew and Egyptian languages. Indeterminacy in the latter is exacerbated by the arbitrariness of the writer, who can arrange the images from right to left or from left to right. He could also arrange the signs vertically "and in making inscriptions on comparatively small objects he allowed considerations of decorativeness and space to influence him in altering the sequence of the signs in yet other ways. The most disturbing thing about hieroglyphic script is, no doubt, that it makes no separation between words" (p. 230).

These features can be applied analogically to the writing of dreams. The most important aspect of the comparison is that the Chinese language, for example, has so to speak no grammar and is composed almost exclusively of raw materials, "just as our thought-language is resolved by the dream-work into its raw material, and any expression of relation is omitted" (p. 231).

8. See Jacques Derrida, "Freud and the Scene of Writing" in *Writing and Difference,* Alan Bass, tr. (Chicago: University of Chicago Press, 1978). Derrida discloses the specificity, even the singularity, of the writing of dreams, which cannot be deciphered by any code and has its own grammar. Hence the limits encountered by the deciphering method and the impossibility of using a fixed key to dreams. In psychic writing the difference between signified and signifier is not fundamental.

Hence also the limits of any possible translation of the specific writing into the language of consciousness. "Translation is possible only if a permanent code allows a substitution or transformation of signifiers while retaining the same signified, always present, despite the absence of any specific signifier. This fundamental possibility of substitution would thus be implied by the coupled concepts signified/signifier = sign" (p. 210). [I have slightly modified Bass' translation.—TRANS.]

9. Artaud proposes to institute a form of staging based on equilibrium between the forces of expenditure and the forces of reserve, the yin and the yang of the Chinese, masculine and feminine forces comparable to Eros and the death drives respectively. This new mise en scène will be something other than a mere appendage of the text. Speech will no longer play a privileged role, but rather will have the same status as in dreams. It will be used "in a concrete and spatial sense, and in combination with everything in the theater that is spatial and of significance in the concrete realm" ("Oriental Theater and Western Theater," in Antonin Artaud: Selected Writings, Susan Sontag, ed., and Helen Weaver, tr. [New York: Farrar, Straus & Giroux, 1976], p. 270).

This mise en scène will make use of new signs—veritable moving hieroglyphs displaying their meaning through the violence of the effect they have, rendering useless "any translation into a logical and discursive language." The stage is a sort of "speech anterior to words" (see "On the Balinese Theater," Antonin Artaud, p. 220), whose grammar is yet to be found. Artaud's conception of the mise en scène is thus very close to that of the dream, as Freud speaks of it. It is therefore not surprising to see Artaud take painting as an exemplary model of what this mise en scène at the theater is or should be. In his "Quatrième lettre sur le langage" of May 28, 1933 he writes, "Any silent staging should, through its movement, its numerous characters, its lighting, its settings, rival what is most profound in paintings such as van den Leyden's Daughters of Lot, certain Sabbaths by Goya, certain Resurrections and Transfigurations by El Greco, the Temptation of Saint Anthony by Bosch and the disquieting and mysterious Dulle Griet by Breugel the Elder.... It is a silent theater, but which speaks much more than if it had received a language in which to express itself. All these paintings have a double meaning and, apart from their purely pictorial dimension, they contain a lesson and reveal mysterious or terrible aspects of nature and the mind." [Unless Antonin Artaud cited as source, translations of Artaud are mine.——TRANS.] See also "Mise en Scène and Metaphysics," in Antonin Artaud, pp. 227–239.

10. [Regarding Kofman's term "signifiance," I shall refer once again to Roudiez's "Notes on the Translation and on Terminology" in Kristeva's Desire in Language (New York: Columbia University Press, 1980): " 'Signifiance' ... refers to operations that are both fluid and archaic—with the latter word restricted to its Freudian sense (See Introductory Lectures on Psychoanalysis, Lecture 13). It refers to the work performed in language ... that enables a text to signify what representative and communicative speech does not say" (p. 18).——TRANS.]

11. ["Combinatory," which exists in English as an adjective but is not normally used as a noun, is modeled on the French term combinatoire. It is borrowed from linguistics and defined as "the set of linguistic constraints which determine the combinations of elements that make up an utterance" (Grand Larousse Dictionary). Kofman's term "symbolic combinatory" bears testimony to the fact that, particularly in France, Saussurian linguistics informs readings of Freud and the phenomena he studied. Her use of the term in connection with the analysis of dreams, works of art, and other psychic and cultural productions is in keeping with her view of these phenomena as texts to be deciphered according to the rules that govern their production and functioning.——TRANS.]

12. |I have replaced the term "representability," which appears in the *Standard Edition*, with "figurability," in accordance with Kofman's challenge to earlier readings of Freud.——TRANS.|

13. See also *New Introductory Lectures* (Lecture 29): "We had learnt to make use for our interpretations even of the purely formal features of the manifest dream—that is, to transform them into material coming from the latent dream-thoughts" (22:26).

14. Text cited in Michel Deguy's article "La Folle de Saussure," *Critique*, (January 1969), 260:21.

15 See *New Introductory Lectures*, 22:26.

16 |Schiller's letter is in fact addressed to Korner.——TRANS.|

17. Letter of December 1, 1788, cited by Freud in *The Interpretation of Dreams*, 4:103.

18. In "The Claims of Psycho-Analysis to Scientific Interest," Freud remarks, "The unconscious speaks more than one dialect."

19. See "The Unconscious," 14:161–204.

20. Concerning this paragraph, cf. Derrida, "Freud and the Scene of Writing."

21. See *The Interpretation of Dreams*, 4:278.

22. See *Delusions and Dreams in Jensen's 'Gradiva,'* 9:10.

23. See for example *Civilization and Its Discontents*, 21:68–69, and "Constructions in Analysis," 23:259–260, in which the analytic method is compared to and differentiated from the archeological method. See also "Notes Upon a Case of Obsessional Neurosis": "Every effort was made to preserve Pompeii, whereas people were anxious to be rid of tormenting ideas" (10:176–177).

24. There are numerous other texts in which Freud declares his admiration for the knowledge of poets and artists in general. Let me cite, for example, *The Psychopathology of Everyday Life* (1905): "In view of the interest that is lent to our theory of slips of the tongue by support of this nature from great writers, I feel justified in citing a third such instance which has been reported by Ernest Jones," (6:98), and he cites Shakespeare in *Richard II* and *The Merchant of Venice*. Later, concerning a Galsworthy novel: "A very instructive and transparent example of the sureness with which imaginative writers know how to employ the mechanism of parapraxes and symptomatic acts in the psychoanalytic sense is contained in [this] novel" (pp. 132 - 133). And later: "I have already been able again and again to produce evidence that creative writers think of parapraxes as having a meaning and a motive, just as I am arguing here. We shall not be surprised, therefore, to see from a fresh example how a writer [Theodor Fontane] invests a clumsy movement with significance, too, and makes it foreshadow later events" (p. 176).

With regard to symptomatic acts concerning rings: "The theme of the ring leaves one once again with the impression of how hard it is for a psycho-analyst to discover anything new that has not been known before by some poet" (p. 205).

In *The Interpretation of Dreams*: "The importance of day-dreams has not escaped the unerring vision of imaginative writers" (5:491). In this work, numerous literary works illustrate his analyses.

In "Notes Upon a Case of Obsessional Neurosis" ("The Rat Man"; 1909): "Poets tell us that in the more tempestuous stages of love the two opposed feelings may subsist side by side for a while as though in rivalry with each other" (10:239).

In "The Claims of Psycho-Analysis to Scientific Interest": "Psycho-analysis has done justice to the sexual function of man by making a detailed examination of its importance in mental and practical life—an importance which has been emphasized by many creative writers and by some philosophers, but which has never been recognized by science" (13:180).

In the later texts, there are fewer references to poetry. We may however still cite the Introductory Lectures, 16:260, and Moses and Monotheism, 23:89, where Freud says that, strangely enough, Goethe had already accepted without any evidence the idea that Moses had been murdered; and in the New Introductory Lectures, Lecture 23, "Femininity," ends—not without irony perhaps—with this sentence: "If you want to know more about femininity, enquire from your own experiences of life, or turn to the poets, or wait until science can give you deeper and more coherent information" (22:135).

The examples of knowledge gained through painters are more sparse. Let me cite, in the Introductory Lectures (15:135), the analysis of The Prisoner's Dream, a painting by Schwind in the Schack Gallery in Munich, which shows how accurately the artist has grasped that the dream arises from the dominant situation.

25. See also Letter 78 to Fliess, December 12, 1897, in The Origins of Psycho-Analysis, p. 237.

26. See The Interpretation of Dreams, 4:97, n. 1, added in 1909.

27. Note added in the third edition: On Gradiva, see the appendix of this volume, "Delusion and Fiction," and my "Résumer, interpréter" in Quatre romans analytiques; see also Mary Jacobus' fine article "Is There a Woman in this Text?" in New Literary History (Autumn 1982), 14 (1):117–141; and Jean Bellemin-Noël, Gradiva au pied de la lettre (Paris: Presses Universitaires de France, 1983).

3. FREUD'S METHOD OF READING

1. See The Interpretation of Dreams, 4:29–30.

2. This term is generally used by Freud to describe his method as one of solving riddles. It is sometimes replaced by entlarvten, which is the same as the term used to designate the comic process of unmasking. For instance he writes, concerning one of President Schreber's delusions, of "the 'miracled' birds which [after we have unmasked them (entlarvten)] have been shown to be girls" ("Notes on a Case of Paronoia," 12:53).

3. See "From the History of an Infantile Neurosis," 17:43, n. 1 and what I have said above in this regard.

4. On the problematic of the mask that reveals even as it hides, cf. Nietzsche, for example in Beyond Good and Evil, section 5, where the philosophical text, Spinoza's Ethics, is presented as a mask which hides and reveals the sickly nature of the philosopher and which he uses like a shield to defend himself. The text is also a tissue that protects against transgression of the prohibition and possible punishment for it.

5. Nietzsche also attributes this enigmatic quality to woman and says that her primary virtue is modesty. It would be dangerous to unveil her, for then one could see that behind her veils woman is hiding nothing. See the Preface to Beyond

Good and Evil, The Gay Science, sections 64–68; and Thus Spoke Zarathustra, "On Little Old and Young Women." For example, in the Preface to Beyond Good and Evil [in fact, it is in the Preface to The Gay Science——TRANS.]: "One should have more respect for the bashfulness with which nature has hidden behind riddles and iridescent uncertainties. Perhaps truth is a woman who has reasons for not letting us see her reasons? Perhaps her name is—to speak Greek— Baubo?" (Walter Kaufmann, tr. [New York: Vintage Books, 1974], p. 38) Note added in the third edition: In L'Enigme de la femme: La Femme dans les textes de Freud (Paris: Galilée, 1980), I show the difference between Freud's and Nietzsche's conceptions of the enigma and also their similarities, based on their treatment of woman's narcissistic self-sufficiency. [Translated as The Enigma of Woman: Woman in Freud's Writings, Catherine Porter, tr. (Ithaca, N.Y.: Cornell University Press, 1985).——TRANS.]

    6. Cf. "Analysis Terminable and Interminable," 23:250–253.

    7. Freud's last doctrine on the drives would then be close to the Chinese conception of yin and yang.

    8. See Totem and Taboo. I shall come back to this comparison.

    9. My emphasis. See also Introductory Lectures, 16:367–370. The fairy tale can also function as a screen memory; see 12:281 ff.

    10. See also "The Wolf Man," 17:50 ff, esp. p. 55: "A child, like an adult, can produce phantasies only from material which has been acquired from some source or other."

    11. See "The Wolf Man," 17:45, n. 1 and "The Rat Man," 10:206–207, n. 1. Cf. André Green, "La Diachronie dans le freudisme," Critique (March 1967), 238:359–385.

    12. See "The Rat Man," 10:206–207, n. 1; Leonardo, 11:83 ff.; Moses and Monotheism, 23:66–67; and The Psychopathology of Everyday Life, 6:43 ff.

    13. Regarding this entire analysis, see esp. Moses and Monotheism, 23:66 ff.

    14. See "Remembering, Repeating, and Working Through," 12:148.

    15. See Totem and Taboo, 13:151 and Moses and Monotheism, 23:70.

    16. See Totem and Taboo, 13:14.

    17. Jacques Derrida, "Freud and the Scene of Writing," in Writing and Difference, Alan Bass, tr. (Chicago: University of Chicago Press, 1974), p. 214.

    18. See "Note Upon the 'Mystic Writing Pad'," 19:227–232.

    19. This problematic of the trace can already be found in Plato, especially in the myth presented in the Gorgias. The shift from Kronos' reign to that of Zeus brings about a change in the manner of judging souls. In Kronos' time, that is, before the institution of a true cosmic order—a time that corresponds to judgment by tribunals as practiced in the real city—the living judged the living fully dressed, that is, arrayed in fair bodies, rank, and wealth, and accompanied by numerous witnesses. These raiments are masks that hide the true nature of the soul. Similarly, the judges have before their souls a screen made of their own bodies. The sensible world prevents the soul from presenting itself to itself directly. Zeus' reign, on the other hand, institutes a cosmic order, the symbol of an ideal order in the city and in the soul, that is, the subordination of ἐπιθυμία, desire, and θῡμός, soul, to νοῦς, mind, or reason. Zeus orders that souls be judged naked, stripped of all things sensible that mask and deceive. To be judged naked is to be judged dead, in the realm of Hades, the god of the invisible; that is, in the simple presence of the self to the self. But still, the soul cannot save itself; it can only be judged through the inter-

mediary of others, symbolized in the myth by one of the judges of the underworld: Minos, Rhadamanthus, or Aeacus. Moreover, since even the naked soul, separated from the body, retains the traces of the way it has lived, the judgment is made from these traces. Presence is given therefore only in its traces, in a kind of writing, since it is no longer a question here of distorting traces stemming from the sensible world. For instance, the soul is said to be striped with the blows of the whip, covered with scars left by perjury and iniquity, "marks imprinted on the soul of this man by each of his actions." There are thus raiments that hide and traces that reveal.

20. It is for these two reasons that in his article "Nietzsche, Freud, Marx," in *Nietzsche* (Paris: Cahiers de Royaumont, 1967), Michel Foucault is able to oppose hermeneutics to semiotics, which believes in the absolute existence of signs and "institutes the reign of terror of the index."

21. "Constructions in Analysis," 23:257. Note added in the third edition: For a detailed reading of this text, see my *Un Métier impossible* (Paris: Galilée, 1983).

22. |Bracketed interpolations are Kofman's.——TRANS.|

23. On the comparison of psychoanalysis to archeology, see the references already given above and esp. *Civilization and Its Discontents*, 22:68–69, where Freud emphasizes that the continuation of all the stages of development previously passed through into the final stage is possible only in the psychic sphere. In this book Freud also refers to the paradigm of evolution in animals, in which primitive elements are preserved alongside newer ones, but he rejects it as insufficient.

24. |The German title of the essay, "Der Dichter und das Phantasieren," in fact contains no possessive adjective.——TRANS.|

25. See "On the Sexual Theories of Children": "A knowledge of infantile sexual theories in the shapes they assume in the thoughts of children can be of interest in various ways—even, surprisingly enough, for the elucidation of myths and fairy tales" (9:211).

26. See *Introductory Lectures*: "|Day-dreams| are the raw material of poetic production, for the creative writer uses his day-dreams, with certain remodellings, disguises, and omissions, to construct the situations which he introduces into his short stories, his novels, or his plays. The hero of the day-dreams is always the subject himself, either directly or by an obvious identification with someone else" (15:99).

27. The importance of staging in the game with the wooden reel was suggested to me by Dr. Green during a seminar at the Institut de Psychanalyse. My work owes much to this seminar, which I attended for two years. Cf. André Green, "Répétition, différence, réplication," *Revue française de psychanalyse*, May 1970.

28. Note added in the third edition: See also Jean-Claude Bonne, "Le Travail d'un fantasme,"*Critique* (August/September 1973), 315/316:725–753.

29. See also "The Wolf Man": "Of the wishes concerned in the formation of the dream the most powerful must have been the wish for the sexual satisfaction which he was at that time longing to obtain from his father. The strength of this wish made it possible to revive a long-forgotten trace in his memory of a scene which was able to show him what sexual satisfaction from his father was like" (17:35–36).

30. The division of an image into two figures following upon an unconscious identification could be likened to the division characteristic of paranoid psychoses. Whereas hysteria condenses, the latter divide, or rather, "paranoia resolves once

more into their elements the products of the condensations and identifications which are effected in the unconscious.... |Schreber's| decomposition of the persecutor |the father| into Flechsig and God |is| a paranoid reaction to a previously established identification of the two figures or their belonging to the same class" ("Notes on a Case of Paranoia," 12:49–50).

This division can also be compared to the one found in myths and in the child's family romance. According to the psychoanalytic interpretation, the two families are one except that they are separated in time. In both cases (and this justifies the date Freud assigns Leonardo's cartoon), identification comes first and division, second.

Doesn't Freud's interpretation go against what Leonardo himself says about the role of sketches as a means of varying forms and playing with them freely?

"Painter of narrative compositions, do not paint the elements of your painting with sharp outlines, for the same will happen to you as to many painters of all kinds who want the least little stroke of charcoal to be definite; and these may very well acquire riches but not fame for their art, since the creature represented often does not have movements appropriate to the intention, but when the artist has finished a beautiful and agreeable arrangement of elements, it seems damaging to him to move them either higher or lower, or more to the back or to the front. These masters do not deserve any praise for their art.

"Have you never seen poets compose their verses? They do not become tired of writing beautiful letters and do not object to crossing out certain verses in order to write them again better. Therefore, painter, compose the limbs of your figures in general terms, and first see to it that the movements are appropriate to the state of mind of the beings who occupy your composition, and only then think of the beauty and the quality of the details.

"For you must understand that if this unfinished sketch does happen to agree with your idea, it will be all the better when it is enhanced by the perfection of all its parts. I have seen clouds and stains on walls which have stimulated me to make beautiful inventions on different subjects; and these stains, although in themselves devoid of any perfection in any part, did not lack perfection in the movements and other effects. (The Genius of Leonardo da Vinci, André Chastel ed., and Ellen Callmann, tr. |New York: Orion Press, 1961|, p. 205)

In fact, Freud's interpretation does not rule out Leonardo's. Instead, it allows us to understand why, in this play of forms, one ends up being adopted rather than another, or after another.

31. Note added in 1919, p. 115. |In fact, Freud is talking about Mary's drapery in this passage.—— TRANS.|

32. In Pfister's letter to Freud of April 3, 1922, he refers to Rorschach's method as "truly remarkable." In his reply of April 6, 1922, Freud says that Pfister is overestimating Rorschach as an analyst.

33. It would be interesting to compare Freud's conception of the relationship between the work of art and the past with the Proustian conception. Proust is clearly aware of this relationship, as he proposes the "remembrance of things past" as the aim of his work. Remembrance is supposed to yield the very essence of things,

a spiritual equivalent of eternity. But the work of art seems to him to be the transcription of a book which has already been written within, of which the writer is merely the translator. Hence the sense of constraint at the time of creation.

To translate is to make an individual experience communicable. Art has the privilege of enabling individual consciousnesses to break out of their solitude, "as if our finest ideas were like tunes which, as it were, come back to us although we have never heard them before and which we have to make an effort to hear and to transcribe" (*Remembrance of Things Past*, C. K. Scott Moncrieff and Terence Kilmartin, trs., with Andreas Mayor [London: Chatto and Windus, 1982], p. 912).

"Whether I considered reminiscences of the kind evoked by the noise of the spoon or the taste of the madeleine, or those truths written with the aid of shapes for whose meaning I searched in my brain, where—church steeples or wild grass growing in a wall—they composed a magic scrawl, complex and elaborate, their essential character was that I was not free to choose them, that such as they were they were given to me. And I realised that this must be the mark of their authenticity.... As for the inner book of unknown symbols (symbols carved in relief they might have been, which my attention, as it explored my consciousness, groped for and stumbled against and followed the contours of, like a diver exploring the ocean-bed), if I tried to read them no one could help me with any rules, for to read them was an act of creation in which no one can do our work for us or even collaborate with us....

"This book, more laborious to decipher than any other, is also the only one which has been dictated to us by reality, the only one of which the 'impression' has been printed in us by reality itself.... The book whose hieroglyphs are patterns not traced by us is the only book that really belongs to us.... Only the impression, however trivial its material may seem to be, however faint its traces, is a criterion of truth and desires for that reason to be apprehended by the mind, for the mind, if it succeeds in extracting this truth, can by the impression and by nothing else be brought to a state of greater perfection and given a pure joy. The impression is for the writer what experiment is for the scientist, with the difference that in the scientist the work of the intelligence precedes the experiment and in the writer it comes after the impression....

"I had then arrived at the conclusion that in fashioning a work of art we are by no means free, that we do not choose how we shall make it but that it pre-exists us and therefore we are obliged, since it is both necessary and hidden, to do what we should have to do if it were a law of nature, that is to say to discover it." (pp. 913–915)

"So that the essential, the only true book, though in the ordinary sense of the word it does not have to be 'invented' by a great writer—for it exists in each one of us—has to be translated by him. The function and task of a writer are those of a translator." (p. 926)

"Through art alone we are able to emerge from ourselves, to know what another person sees of a universe which is not the same as our own." (p. 932)

"And I understood that all these materials for a work of literature were simply my past life; I understood that they had come to me, in frivolous

NOTES: FREUD'S METHOD OF READING   215

pleasures, in indolence, in tenderness, in unhappiness, and that I had stored
them up without divining the purpose for which they were destined." (p. 935)
    "There is a feeling for generality which, in the future writer, itself
picks out what is general and can for that reason one day enter into a work
of art." (p. 937)

    Proust, even more than Freud, seems to be dependent upon the traditional
logic of the sign. Moreover, a voluntary transcription of the past no longer "puts it
into play." The unconscious primary processes should no longer intervene. In this
case, can we still be talking about a work of art?
    34. See *The Interpretation of Dreams*, 4:333–334 and *New Introductory Lectures*,
22:26
    35. Freud addresses this same problem in a letter to Fliess of January 9,
1892. On the overdetermination of the meaning of works of art, see also the different
interpretations of the tale of the three wishes in *The Interpretation of Dreams*, 5:557 and
581, n. 1.
    36. Letter 100, December 5, 1898, in *The Origins of Psycho-Analysis*, Marie
Bonaparte, Anna Freud, and Ernst Kris, eds. (New York: Basic Books, 1977), p. 270.
    37. Letter of July 26, 1883 to his wife, quoted in Ernest Jones, *The Life and
Work of Sigmund Freud*, 3 vols. (New York: Basic Books, 1981), 1:175.
    38. See "Notes on a Case of Paranoia,'" where Freud writes concerning
Byron's *Manfred*: "It is plausible, by the way, to connect the plot of *Manfred* with the
incestuous relations which have repeatedly been asserted to exist between the poet
and his half-sister. And it is not a little striking that the action of Byron's other play,
Cain, should be laid in the primal family, where no objections could exist to incest
between brother and sister" (12:44–45, n. 2).
    39. Note added in the third edition: Cf. "Judith" in my *Quatre romans ana-
lytiques* (Paris: Galilée, 1974), and Mary Jacobus, "Judith, Holophernes, and the Phallic
Woman" in *Reading Woman* (New York: Columbia University Press, 1985).
    40. Cf. Artaud, "Oriental Theater and Western Theater," in *Antonin Artaud:
Selected Writings*, Susan Sontag, ed., and Helen Weaver, tr. (New York: Farrar, Straus
& Giroux, 1976): "True expression hides what it manifests.... Every powerful emotion
awakens in us the idea of emptiness. And the clear language which prevents this
sense of emptiness also prevents poetry from appearing in the mind. That is why
an image, an allegory, a figure of speech which disguises what it wants to reveal
has more meaning for the mind than the clarity provided by the analytical properties
of speech" (pp. 269–270).
    41. I demonstrated the circular character of the method in chapter 2. Works
of art served as models for understanding the dream processes, and dream symbolism and its processes served, in turn, to interpret works of art. What Freud did
with regard to art he later generalized to include all productions of culture.
    In the *Introductory Lectures*, Freud writes: "We may enquire how we in fact
come to know the meaning of these dream-symbols, upon which the dreamer himself
gives us insufficient information or none at all. My reply is that we learn it from very
different sources—from fairy tales and myths, from buffoonery and jokes, from folklore (that is, from knowledge about popular manners and customs, sayings and
songs) and from poetic and colloquial linguistic usage. In all these directions we
come upon the same symbolism, and in some of it we can understand it without

further instruction. If we go into these sources in detail, we shall find so many parallels to dream-symbolism that we cannot fail to be convinced of our interpretations" (15:158–159; see also p. 166).

In "Revision of the Theory of Dreams," Freud gives examples of this parallel:

"An instance of this sort is the symbol of an overcoat or cloak (*Mantel*). We have said that in a woman's dreams this stands for a man. I hope it will impress you when you hear that Theodor Reik (1920) gives us this information: 'During the extremely ancient bridal ceremonial of Bedouins, the bridegroom covers the bride with a special cloak known as "Aba " and speaks the following ritual words: "Henceforth none save I shall cover thee!' " (Quoted from Robert Eisler, 1910.) We have also found several fresh symbols, at least two of which I will tell you of. According to Abraham (1922) a spider in dreams is a symbol of the mother, but of the phallic mother, of whom we are afraid; so that the fear of spiders expresses dread of mother-incest and horror of the female genitals. You know, perhaps, that the mythological creation, Medusa's head, can be traced back to the same *motif* of fright at castration." (22:24–25)

The American art critic Meyer Shapiro seems to have relied on this essay in his interpretation of *La Nativité du Maître Flemalle*, which forms part of the triptych of the Mérode altar.

And finally, Freud writes in "The Wolf Man": "If in my patient's case the wolf was merely a first father-surrogate, the question arises whether the hidden content in the fairy tales of the wolf that ate up the little goats and of 'Little Red Riding Hood' may not simply be infantile fear of the father" (17:32).

42. Is it a demand of consciousness to admit that everything is meaningful? In the polemical essay "The Unconscious" (14:161–204), where Freud wants above all to denounce the internal contradictions in philosophies of consciousness, the hypothesis of the unconscious, which eliminates incoherence and incomprehension, seems to be the necessary and legitimate consequence of a philosophy of consciousness. But from a metapsychological point of view it can be said that it is a demand of Eros. It is only in dementia, where the death drive seems definitively to have won out and the symbolic is submerged by the economic, that this demand for meaning cannot find satisfaction.

43. See Freud's letter to his wife of October 5, 1883; quoted by Jones in *The Life and Work of Sigmund Freud*, 1:174.

44. See also "An Autobiographical Study," 20:64, and *Totem and Taboo*, 13:17. On the relation between the Oedipus complex and tragedy, cf. André Green's *Un Oeil en trop: Le Complexe d'Oedipe dans la tragédie* (Paris: Editions de Minuit, 1969), esp. p. 18.

45. In *Delusions and Dreams in Jensen's 'Gradiva,'* the same concern with what is eternally human is evident. Freud writes of Norbert: "We have not yet grasped by what route his particular form of madness could enter into relation with humanity as a whole in order to command our interest."

46. See esp. *Totem and Taboo* and *Moses and Monotheism.*

47. André Green, "Répétition, différence, réplication," p. 282.

48. See "Analysis Terminable and Interminable," 23:236ff.

49. Letter of July 20, 1938, in *Letters of Sigmund Freud*, Ernest L. Freud, ed., and Tania Stern and James Stern, trs. (New York: Basic Books, 1960), pp. 448–449.

50. See "Dostoevsky and Parricide," 21:193–194.

51. At the end of this chapter I should like to cite the introduction to the second part of *Moses and Monotheism*, which seems to me to be a good paradigm of artistic creation as Freud conceives it. He presents the second part as a different repetition of the first. But the first part was itself already a *répétition*, or rehearsal, in the theatrical sense of the term. Repetition is second and originary—the text of art repeats the text of life which is itself repetition. "The part of this study which follows . . . is nothing other than a faithful (and often word-for-word) repetition of the first part, abbreviated in some of its critical enquiries and augmented by additions relating to the problem of how the special character of the Jewish people arose. I am aware that a method of exposition such as this is no less inexpedient than it is inartistic. I myself deplore it unreservedly." The last sentence is obviously ironic, as it serves to denounce the misrecognized repetition that is proper to art and to oppose it to Freud's voluntary repetition. What follows clearly shows that this text is a paradigm.

"Why have I not avoided it? The answer to that is not hard for me to find, but it is not easy to confess. I found myself unable to wipe out the traces of the history of the work's origin, which was in any case unusual. Actually it has been written twice: for the first time years ago in Vienna, where I did not think it would be possible to publish it. [This corresponds to excessive psychic censorship blocking the return of the repressed.] I determined to give it up; but it tormented me like an unlaid ghost [the repressed tries to reappear in spite of censorship, pushes toward expression, but can return only in the form of a compromise], and I found a way out by making two pieces of it independent and publishing them in our periodical *Imago*: the psycho-analytic starting point of the whole thing 'Moses an Egyptian,' and the historical construction erected on this 'If Moses was an Egyptian . . .' [the first part leaves aside what would arouse too much resistance and would thus be subject to the blows of censorship]. The remainder, which included what was really open to objection and dangerous . . . I held back, as I thought, forever."

Freud leaves for England where censorship is less harsh—a change in conditions which makes possible the return of the repressed.

"I had scarcely arrived in England before I found the temptation irresistible to make the knowledge I had held back accessible to the world, and I began to revise the third part of my study to fit it on to the two parts that had already been published. This naturally involved a partial rearrangement of the material [a new combinatory in the return]. I did not succeed, however, in including the whole of this material in my second version; on the other hand I could not make up my mind to give up the earlier versions entirely [if all of the repressed is not expressed in one work, there have to be several of them, for man is unable to renounce *anything*]. And so it has come about that I have adopted the expedient of attaching a whole piece of the first presentation to the second unchanged—which has brought with it the disadvantage of involving extensive repetition. . . . There are things which should be repeated and which cannot be said often enough. But the reader must decide of his own free will whether to linger over the subject or to come back to it. He must not be surreptitiously led into having the same thing put before him twice in one book. It is a piece of clumsiness for which the author must take the blame. Unluckily an author's creative power does not always obey his will: the work proceeds as it can, and often presents itself to the author as something independent or even alien." (23:103–104)

The text closes with the point about the constraint placed on creation, and the independence of the work in relation to its author; the author as father is dead.

4. ART IN THE ECONOMY OF LIFE

1. See also his letter of January 26, 1883 to his wife on the effect the reading of The Temptation of St. Anthony had on him. [See Ernest Jones, The Life and Work of Sigmund Freud, 3 vols. (New York: Basic Books, 1981), 1:175, for an excerpt from Freud to his wife on St. Anthony; Jones gives July 26, 1883, however, as the date of the letter.——TRANS.]

2. Note added in the third edition: I elaborate this point of view in a forthcoming essay.

3. Note added in the third edition: The commentary by Phillippe Lacoue-Labarthe that accompanied his translation of this essay has been reprinted as "La Scène est primitive," in Le Sujet de la philosophie (Paris: Aubier-Flammarion, 1979).

4. The importance of aesthetic emotion, especially at the theater, was already noticed by Plato in Book 10 of The Republic, and by Aristotle in his famous conception of catharsis. After Freud, it is Artaud who comes closest to this conception, for he wants to establish a theater that produces the same magical effect that acupuncture has on the organism: a balance between feminine and masculine, the forces of reserve and of expenditure, and of Eros and death. See Artaud's "An Emotional Athleticism" and "The Theater of the Seraphim" in Antonin Artaud: Selected Writings, Susan Sontag, ed., and Helen Weaver, tr. (New York: Farrar, Straus & Giroux, 1976), pp. 259–267 and 271–276; and his letter to Orane Demazis of December 30, 1933, in Oeuvres Complètes (Paris: Gallimard, 1956), in which he writes: "For this action I am talking about is organic, it is as sure as the vibrations of a music capable of charming snakes. It directly affects the organs of nervous sensitivity, just as the sensitizing points in Chinese medicine affect the organs of sensation and the command functions of the human body. All of this to say, coming back to the idea of the theater, that it acts, and one only has to know how to manipulate it" (5:224).

Unlike the use contemporary theater has made of it, Artaud's theater is not a theater of pure spontaneity, but of spontaneity governed by almost mathematical laws, analogous to those of the Kabbala to control breathing, and the laws of Chinese medicine. Forces are never expressed except through the forms that hide them. The theater of cruelty precedes the separation of force and meaning. In "Le Théâtre et la culture," Artaud writes, "The intensity of forms exists only to charm and capture a force which, in music, awakens a rending keyboard" (Oeuvres Complètes, 4:15). And in "The Theater of the Seraphim," "And yet, and this is the secret, just as IN THE THEATER, the force will not come out. The active masculine will be repressed. And it will retain the energetic will of the breath. It will retain it for the whole body, and on the outside there will be a scene of the *disappearance* of force at which the SENSES WILL BELIEVE THEY ARE PRESENT" (*Antonin Artaud*, p. 273)

5. See *Beyond the Pleasure Principle*, 18:17.

6. For a critique of the disinterested character of aesthetic feeling, cf. Nietzche, *Beyond Good and Evil*, section 33, and *Twilight of the Idols*.

7. Since the sexual roots of aesthetic feeling are repressed, it is not surprising that the latter can serve as a counterinvestment to repressed sexual feelings. This is what happens with President Schreber, in whom aesthetic feeling serves as a cover for sexual feeling. Thus "the idea . . . occurred to him while he was half asleep, to the effect that that it must be nice to be a woman submitting to the act of copulation" ("Notes on a Case of Paranoia," 12:20). But the repressed is revealed by the fact that he has only to draw female buttocks on his body, or simply to imagine doing so, in order to acquire a feeling of sensual well-being which gives him a foretaste of the sexual enjoyment of the woman during copulation. Generally speaking there is in Schreber an an aestheticization of the sexual and an eroticization of beatitude, symptomatic of the repressed link between the sexual and the beautiful. For him, defecation is accompanied by an intense voluptuousness of the soul, just as religious beatitude is described as a state of constant sexual enjoyment. Voluptuousness is a bit of beatitude given to men in advance, so to speak. Thanks to a whole system of rationalizations, he can thus manage to reconcile the belief in God and a feminine type of sexual enjoyment: for him, the cultivation of voluptuousness is a duty. It is interesting to consider the Priscillian episode in Buñuel's film *The Milky Way* from this perspective.

8. See the essay "Repression," 14:143ff.

9. Note added in the third edition: But not without modifying it somewhat.

10. Freud is citing Fechner's *Vorschule der Äesthetik* (Leipzig, 1897), vol. 1, chap. 5, p. 51.

11. In order to understand this last point, it is important to know that according to Freud, psychic effort must be made in the production of representations; every representation is accompanied by slight movements that mimic it. These movements require a greater or lesser expenditure of energy, depending on whether the content of the representation connotes an idea of greater or lesser value, or something of greater or lesser size or importance. The difference between two efforts is always marked by a discharge of energy, that is, pleasure, unless it is reutilized elsewhere.

12. Ernst Gombrich, "L'Esthétique de Freud," *Preuves*, April 1969.

13. See for example Paul Klee, *On Modern Art*, Paul Findlay, tr. (London: Faber & Faber, 1969): "From this point given mastery of the medium, the structure can be assured foundations of such strength, that it is able to reach out into dimensions far removed from conscious endeavor" (p. 29).

14. On the same theme, cf. "An Autobiographical Study," 20:63, and *Introductory Lectures*, 16:331.

15. Cf. also Jacques Lacan, "Le Stade du Miroir" in *Ecrits* (Paris: Editions du Seuil, 1966); in English, "The Mirror Stage" in *Ecrits: A Selection*, Alan Sheridan, tr. (New York: Norton, 1977).

16. Letter of August 26, 1882, quoted in Jones, *The Life and Work of Sigmund Freud*, 1:175.

17. It first appears in a note in the second edition of the *Three Essays on the Theory of Sexuality*, in 1910.

18. See also *New Introductory Lectures*, Lecture 32: "When later on we began to study the ego itself more closely and arrived at the conception of narcissism, this distinction [between the ego instincts and the sexual instincts] itself lost its foundation. In rare cases one can observe that the ego has taken itself as an object and is behaving as though it were in love with itself. Hence the term 'narcissism,' borrowed from the Greek myth" (22:102). See also "A Difficulty in the Path of Psycho-Analysis," 17:139.

Leonardo himself would not have rejected this interpretation, which emphasizes narcissism both in his life and in his work, for it was he who wrote:

> "The painter who has misshapen hands will give similar ones to his figures, and he will do the same for all the other members unless long study has prevented it.... For, if you are brutish, your figures will be the same and without grace; and in the same manner, everything that you, painter, have within you, whether it leans more toward good or toward evil, will be revealed in your figures in some way.... Look at the good parts of a great number of beautiful faces, whose beauty is confirmed by public opinion rather than by your own judgment, for you might make the mistake of selecting faces similar to your own. If fact, it does happen that we love that which resembles us.... It is the greatest defect in painters to repeat the same movements and the same faces and draperies in a composition and to make most of the faces resemble their author.... And thus, every characteristic of the painting corresponds to a characteristic of the painter himself. Having repeatedly thought about the cause of this defect, it seems to me one must believe that the soul, which rules and governs the body, also forms our judgment, even before we have formed it ourselves; thus it is the soul that has shaped the whole figure of the man as it judges best, with the nose long, or short, or flat, and in the same way determined the height and general appearance; and this judgment is so powerful it moves the arm of the painter and makes him copy himself, because it seems to the soul that this is the true way to paint a man, and that whoever does not do as it does, is mistaken. And when it finds someone who resembles the body it has composed, it likes him and often falls in love with him; and that is why many men fall in love with and marry women who resemble them and often the children born to them resemble their parents." (*The Genius of Leonardo da Vinci*, André Chastel, ed., and Ellen Callmann, tr. [New York: Orion Press, 1961], pp. 193–195)

19. Cf. *Totem and Taboo*, 13:90.

20. Religion is also characterized by Freud as a "narcotic": "The authorities were weaned from the narcotic of religion." See also *Moses and Monotheism*.

21. See *Totem and Taboo*, 13:80, n. 1.

22. See for example "The Wolf Man," where Freud shows how the child's incestuous desire for his mother is to a certain extent a desire to return to the womb, thus to receive the father's seed, and consequently, to have a passive, homosexual attitude toward him.

23. On the relation between the creator and his desire to be the *causa sui*,

see de M'Uzan, "Aperçus sur le processus de la création littéraire," *Revue française de psychanalyse* (1965), no. 1.

24. See "The Wolf Man" and *Leonardo da Vinci and a Memory of His Childhood,* 11:121.

25. There is also the case of Artaud. See especially "Here Lies," in *Antonin Artaud,* pp. 540–551, where Artaud claims to be both his genitors at once: "I am my father, my mother, my son, and me."

26. Here one could compare Freud's conception to Malraux's.

27. On the meaning of tragedy, see also "Psychopathic Characters on the Stage," 7:305–310.

28. Cf. Lautréamont who, as Marcelin Pleynet shows in *Lautréamont* (Paris: Editions du Seuil, 1976), signs his works "Isidore Ducasse" only after writing *Les Chants de Maldoror;* the text created its author.

29. See J.-P. Vernant, "La Catégorie psychologique du double" in *Mythe et pensée chez les Grecs* (Paris: Petite Collection Maspero, 1965): "The double is a reality that is external to the subject, but which in its appearance stands in opposition to everyday objects and the ordinary setting of life by virtue of its unusual character. It functions on two contrasting planes at once: at the moment it shows its presence, it reveals that it is not of this world, that it belongs to an inaccessible other realm" (p. 70). "The Colossos, as double, always creates a link between the living and the infernal world" (p. 73).

30. Note added in the third edition: This pharmaceutic function of the double should be compared to that of the Apollinian in Nietzsche's *The Birth of Tragedy.* See my *Nietzsche et la scène philosophique* (Paris: U.G.E. 10/18, 1979).

31. See "The Ego and the Id," 19:30.

32. See "Psychopathic Characters on the Stage," 7:305–310.

33. On collective identification through art, cf. Nietzsche, *The Birth of Tragedy:* "The gulfs between man and man give way to an overwhelming feeling of unity |identification| leading back to the very heart of nature" (Walter Kaufmann, tr. |New York: Vintage Books, 1967|, p. 59).

34. On this development, see "Formulations on the Two Principles of Mental Functioning."

35. For example, for Descartes, to imagine "is to apply the soul to the body." The imagination serves to demonstrate the possibility of the union of soul and body in the "Sixth Meditation": it is intermediary between the soul and the body.

For Spinoza, to imagine is to think according to the order of the affections of the human body. The imagination is intermediary between the understanding and the emotions.

For Kant, the transcendental imagination is intermediary between the categories of understanding and the intuitions of the senses. The transcendental scheme plays the role of mediator. But Kant sees in the transcendental imagination an "art hidden in the depths of nature" that is perhaps a common foundation of the categories and the intuitions. In order to unify the two the intermediary must be the common foundation; in this respect Kant is close to Freud.

36. See "Formulations on the Two Principles of Mental Functioning," 12:215–226.

37. This conception of the stored quantity that the psychic apparatus maintains to preserve its functioning is already laid out in the 1871 Draft.

38. [Freud is quoting Jensen.——TRANS.] It can be said that Norbert's belief in his delusion figures in miniature the reader's belief in the author's fiction.

39. See *Introductory Lectures*, 16:376–377.

40. See also "An Autobiographical Study," 20:64.

41. Artaud, too, perceived the fundamental unity of artistic formations and other psychic productions. In "Oriental Theater and Western Theater" he writes of Flemish painting: "The nightmares of Flemish painting... have their source in those dreamlike states which give rise to abortive gestures and absurd slips of the tongue" (in *Antonin Artaud*, p. 270). [I have modified the translation.——TRANS.]

42. In a letter to Abraham of December 26, 1922, Freud writes: "I have received the drawing which is supposed to represent your head. It is horrible. I know what [an] excellent person you are, and I am all the more shocked that such a trifling flaw in your character as your tolerance or sympathy for modern 'art' has to be so cruelly punished. I learn from Lampl that the artist declares that this is how he sees you! People like him should be the last to have access to analytical circles, for they are the all-too-undesirable illustration of Adler's theory that it is just the people with serious congenital defects of vision who become painters and draughtsmen"; in *Letters of Sigmund Freud*, Ernest L. Freud, ed., and Tania Stern and James Stern, trs. (New York: Basic Books, 1960), p. 340.

43. Letter 59 in *The Origins of Psycho-Analysis*, Marie Bonaparte, Anna Freud, and Ernst Kris, eds. (New York: Basic Books, 1977), p. 193.

44. See 1:244 and 247 (Letter 61), and 1:253 (Draft M).

45. It would be interesting to consider this in relation to the texts in which Nietzsche shows that there are many ways of killing God, and that some of them merely repeat the theistic attitude. See for example *Beyond Good and Evil*, section 53: "Why atheism today?—'The father' in God has been thoroughly refuted; ditto, 'the judge,' 'the rewarder.' Also his 'free will': he does not hear—and if he heard he still would not know how to help. Worst of all: he seems incapable of clear communication: is he unclear? This is what I found to be causes for the decline of European theism, on the basis of a great many conversations, asking and listening. It seems to me that the religious instinct is indeed in the process of growing powerfully— but the theistic satisfaction it refuses with deep suspicion" (Walter Kaufmann, tr. [New York: Vintage Books, 1966], p. 66).

46. [Kofman is alluding here to *Civilization and Its Discontents* (21:74), where Freud quotes Goethe's *Zahme Xenien* IX: "Wer Wissenschaft und Kunst besitzt, hat auch Religion;/Wer jene beide nicht besitzt, der habe Religion!"——TRANS.]

47. Here again, see Nietzsche: it is only by means of morality that morality can be overcome. (See *Beyond Good and Evil*, section 32).

5. FROM ARTISTIC CREATION TO PROCREATION

1. It is interesting to note that for the most part the footnotes added to the book date from 1911; that is, one year after the publication of *Leonardo*. See *The Interpretation of Dreams*, 5:398, n. 1.

2. On the earth as the place of origin of *homo sapiens*, see "Preface to Bourke's *Scatological Rites of All Nations*," 22:336.

3. Freud addresses this same theme in *Civilization and Its Discontents*, 21:126–127, and in a letter to Pfister of April 6, 1922. Note added in the third edition: This demystification of nature does not keep Freud from resorting to it as an explanation and appealing to its finality in order to conceal very different ends. On this problem, see my *L'Enigme de la femme: La Femme dans les textes de Freud* (Paris: Galilée, 1980) [*The Enigma of Woman: Woman in Freud's Writings*, Catherine Porter, tr. (Ithaca, N.Y.: Cornell University Press, 1985)], and "Ça cloche," in my *Lectures de Derrida* (Paris: Galilée, 1984).

4. On necessity as a harsh educator, see also *Introductory Lectures*, 16:355 and 430. (Note added in the third edition: See also "The Dream of the Three Fates," 4:204–208 and 233.) Freud's αυάγκη, necessity, should be considered in relation to what Artaud calls "cruelty." See "An End to Masterpieces," in *Antonin Artaud: Selected Writings*, Susan Sontag, ed., and Helen Weaver, tr. (New York: Farrar, Straus & Giroux, 1976), pp. 252–259.

5. [This passage summarizes Freud's argument using Freud's words (rendered into French): in translating it into English, I have relied on the *Standard Edition*, 11:134–136 ——TRANS.]

6. In this regard, Freud opposes Pastor O. Pfister's conception of the issue, among others.

7. See *New Introductory Lectures*, 22:96ff.

8. On the plasticity of the sexual tendency and the ease with which it changes its aim, substituting one satisfaction for another and playing for time, see especially 22:97.

9. See also "Character and Anal Erotism," 9:175.

10. See *Group Psychology*, 18:137 ff.

11. See also *New Introductory Lectures*, 22:181, and "Two Encyclopaedia Articles," 18:256.

12. Note added in the third edition: On this problem, see my *L'Enigme de la femme* [*The Enigma of Woman*].

13. In *The Psychopathology of Everyday Life*, Freud contrasts his belief in external "chance" with the belief of superstitious people. The superstitious believe in "internal chance," whereas for Freud, all psychic production obeys definite laws. Conversely, the superstitious, who project psychic motivations into the external world, see in every event the coming of a destiny guided by an intention, a transcendent finality.

"I do not believe that an event in whose occurrence my mental life plays no part can teach me any hidden thing about the future shape of reality; but I believe that an unintentional manifestation of my own mental activity does on the other hand disclose something hidden, though again it is something that belongs only to my mental life. I believe in external (real) chance (*Zufall*), it is true, but not in internal (psychical) accidental events (*Zufälligkeit*). With the superstitious person it is the other way round. He knows nothing of the motivation of his chance actions and parapraxes, and believes in psychical accidental events; and, on the other hand, he has a tendency to ascribe to external chance happenings a meaning which will become manifest in real events, and to regard such chance happenings as a means of expressing something that is hidden from him in the external world. The differences between myself and the superstitious person are two: first, he projects outwards a motivation which I look for within; secondly, he interprets chance as due to an event, while I trace it back to a thought. But what is hidden from him corresponds to what is unconscious for me, and the compulsion not to let chance count as chance but to interpret it is common to both of us. . . . *Because* the superstitious person knows nothing of the motivation of his own chance actions, and *because* the fact of this motivation presses for a place in his field of recognition, he is forced to allocate it, by displacement, to the external world." (6:257–258)

14. The humorous attitude toward life, the passage from tragedy to comedy, should be considered in relation to Nietzsche's *The Gay Science* and his laughter. See for example section 1 of *The Gay Science*:

"To laugh at oneself as one would have to laugh in order to laugh *out of the whole truth*—to do that even the best so far lacked sufficient sense for the truth, and the most gifted had too little genius for that. Even laughter may yet have a future. I mean, when the proposition 'the species is everything, *one* is always none' has become part of humanity, and this ultimate liberation and irresponsibility has become accessible to all at all times. Perhaps laughter will then have formed an alliance with wisdom, perhaps only 'gay science' will then be left. For the present, things are still quite different. For the present, the comedy of existence has not yet 'become conscious' of itself. For the present, we still live in the age of tragedy, the age of moralities and religions." (Walter Kauffman, tr., [New York: Vintage Books, 1974], p. 74)

15. Note added in the third edition: It is interesting to recall that for Freud the hat is a symbol of the genital organ and that its meaning derives from that of the head "in so far as a hat can be regarded as a prolonged, detachable head." Taking off one's hat "has the meaning of an abasement before the person saluted" ("A Connection Between a Symbol and a Symptom," 14: 339–340). On the relationship between the head, the hat, and castration anxiety, see Neil Hertz's fine article "Medusa's Head: Male Hysteria Under Political Pressure," *Representations* (Fall 1983), 4:27–54.

APPENDIX: DELUSION AND FICTION

1. [The numbering of the Fliess letters refers to their appearance in *The Origins of Psycho-Analysis*, Marie Bonaparte, Anna Freud, and Ernst Kris, eds. (New York: Basic Books, 1977), pp. 221–225, 255–259, and 270. For discussion and excerpts from Freud's 1882 and 1883 letters to his wife concerning his reading, see Ernest Jones, *The Life and Work of Sigmund Freud*, 3 vols. (New York: Basic Books, 1981), 1:174–175.——TRANS.]
2. It is Ernest Jones who informs us of this.
3. See *Leonardo da Vinci and a Memory of His Childhood*: "Kindly Nature has given the artist the ability to express his most secret mental impulses, which are

hidden even from himself, by means of the works that he creates; and these works have a powerful effect on others who are strangers to the artist, and who are themselves unaware of the source of their emotion" (11:107).

4. See especially "Constructions in Analysis," 23:257–269, and *Civilization and Its Discontents*. Cf. the foregoing analyses in the present work and my *Un Métier impossible* (Paris: Galilée, 1983).

5. Pompeii is given as a metaphor for repression in "The Rat Man": "I made some short observations upon the psychological differences between the conscious and the unconscious." Then Freud remarks upon the inalterable character of psychic productions in the unconscious: "The destruction of Pompeii was only beginning now that it had been dug up" (10:176)

6. The spade here recalls the two-pronged pitchfork, a metaphor for both repression and the law of the return of the repressed, in the line from Horace quoted by Freud: "Naturam furca expellas semper redibit." ["You may drive out Nature with a pitchfork, but she will always return." The *Standard Edition* points out that Freud actually misquoted a line from Horace's *Epistles*, 1, 10, 24, which reads "Naturam expelles furce, tamen usque recurret."——TRANS.]

7. Cf. also Balzac's *Sarrasine* and Roland Barthes' *S/Z* (Richard Miller, tr. [New York: Hill and Wang, 1974]), and my "Résumer, interpréter," *Critique* (October 1972), 539:165–184, rpt. in *Quatre romans analytiques* (Paris: Galilée, 1974), in which I develop all of this.

8. Between dream and delusion there is but a difference in the degree of conviction. Dream is the nocturnal delusion of each one of us. Delusion is "characterized by the fact that in it 'phantasies' have gained the upper hand that is, have obtained belief and have acquired an influence on action" (*Delusions and Dreams*, p. 45).

9. See for example *Moses and Monotheism*.

10. It is no matter of indifference that Freud has chosen the example of *King Lear* here. As I have shown elsewhere, all of *Gradiva* can be read as a variant of *King Lear*. (See my "Resumer, interpréter.")

11. This is one of the codes of reading advanced by Roland Barthes in *S/Z* concerning Balzac's *Sarrasine*.

12. In the same way, it is said that the conviction that accompanies delusion is not exceptional; it has the same psychic foundations as "normal" conviction (p. 80).

13. See "The Uncanny," 17:219–252.

14. See "Psychopathic Characters on the Stage," 7:305–310, in which it is shown that only a neurotic spectator can identify with a neurotic hero, and Freud advises the dramatist to place characters on the stage in whom the spectator can both recognize and fail to recognize himself.

15. See *Contributions to the Psychology of Love*, 11:165 ff.

16. "We must render the author's accurate representation in the technical terms of psychoanalysis" (p. 47).

17. The Hegelian character of such an approach could be demonstrated as well, since Hegel is very close to Aristotle. This text of Freud's is therefore not "simple"; like all texts, it is heterogeneous.

18. See especially "An Autobiographical Study," 20:65, and "On the History of the Psychoanalytic Movement," 14:36.

WORKS OF FREUD CITED

The following list refers to volumes of *The Standard Edition of the Complete Psychological Works of Sigmund Freud*, James Strachey, ed. and tr., 24 vols. (London: Hogarth Press and The Institute of Psycho-Analysis, 1953). Dates in parentheses indicate the date of publication; letters which follow differentiate essays published in the same year, as cited in the *Standard Edition* bibliography (vol. 24); dates in brackets indicate the date of composition.

Vol. 1   Draft M (May 25, 1897), pp. 250–253.
           Draft N (May 31, 1897), pp. 254–257.
Vol. 2   "Studies on Hysteria" (1895d).
Vol. 3   "The Aetiology of Hysteria" (1896c), pp. 191–221.
           "Screen Memories" (1899a), pp. 303–322.
Vol. 4   *The Interpretation of Dreams* (1900a).
Vol. 5   *The Interpretation of Dreams*, pp. 339–632.
Vol. 6   *The Psychopathology of Everyday Life* (1901b).
Vol. 7   *Three Essays on the Theory of Sexuality* (1905d), pp. 125–243.
           "On Psychotherapy" (1905a [1904]), pp. 257–268.
           "Psychopathic Characters on the Stage" (1942a [1905 or 1906]), pp. 305–310.
Vol. 8   *Jokes and Their Relation to the Unconscious* (1905c).
Vol. 9   *Delusions and Dreams in Jensen's 'Gradiva'* (1907a [1906]), pp. 3–93.
           "Creative Writers and Daydreaming" (1908e), pp. 143–153.
           "Character and Anal Eroticism" (1908b), pp. 169–175.

" 'Civilized' Sexual Morality and Modern Nervousness" (1908d), pp. 179–204.

"On the Sexual Theories of Children" (1908c), pp. 209–226.

"Contributions to a Questionnaire on Reading" (1906f), pp. 245–247.

Vol. 10   "Notes Upon a Case of Obsessional Neurosis" ("The Rat Man") (1909d), pp. 155–249.

Vol. 11   Five Lectures on Psycho-Analysis (1910a [1909]), pp. 7–55.

Leonardo da Vinci and a Memory of His Childhood (1910c), pp. 63–137.

"A Special Type of Object Choice Made by Men" (1910h), pp. 165–175.

"On the Universal Tendency to Debasement in the Sphere of Love" (1912d), pp. 179–190.

"The Taboo of Virginity" (1918a [1917]), pp. 193–208.

Vol. 12   "Notes on a Case of Paranoia" (1911c [1910]), pp. 9–82.

"Recommendations to Physicians Practising Psycho-Analysis" (1912e), pp. 111–120.

"Remembering, Repeating, and Working Through" (1914g), pp. 147–156.

"On Psycho-Analysis" (1913m [1911]), pp. 207–211.

"Formulations on the Two Principles of Mental Functioning" (1911b), pp. 215–226.

"The Theme of the Three Caskets" (1913f), pp. 291–301.

"Preface to Bourke's Scatalogic Rites of All Nations" (1913k), pp. 335–337.

"The Significance of Vowel Sequences" (1911d), p. 341.

Vol. 13   Totem and Taboo (1912–1913), pp. 1–161.

"The Claims of Psycho-Analysis to Scientific Interest" (1913j), pp. 165–190.

"The Moses of Michelangelo" (1914b), pp. 211–238.

Vol. 14   "On the History of the Psycho-Analytic Movement" (1914d), pp. 3–66.

"On Narcissism: An Introduction" (1914c), pp. 69–102.

"Repression" (1915d), pp. 143–158.

"The Unconscious" (1915e), pp. 161–204.

"A Metapsychological Supplement to the Theory of Dreams" (1917d [1915]), pp. 222–235.

"Thoughts for the Times on War and Death" (1915b), pp. 275–300.

"A Connection Between a Symbol and a Symptom" (1916c), pp. 339–340.
Vol. 15 *Introductory Lectures on Psycho-Analysis*, Parts I and II (1915–1916).
Vol. 16 *Introductory Lectures on Psycho-Analysis*, Part III (1916–1917).
Vol. 17 "From the History of an Infantile Neurosis" ("The Wolf Man") (1918b [1914]), pp. 3–122.
"A Difficulty in the Path of Psycho-Analysis" (1917a), pp. 137–144.
"On the Teaching of Psycho-Analysis in Universities" (1919j [1918]), pp. 171–173.
"The Uncanny" (1919h), pp. 219–252.
"Preface to Theodor Reik's *Ritual: Psycho-Analytic Studies*" (1919g), pp. 259–263.
Vol. 18 *Beyond the Pleasure Principle* (1920g), pp. 7–64.
"Group Psychology and the Analysis of the Ego" (1921c), pp. 69–143.
"Two Encyclopaedia Articles" ("Psycho-Analysis" and "The Libido Theory") (1923a [1922]), pp. 235–259.
Vol. 19 "Remarks Upon the Theory and Practice of Dream-Interpretation" (1923c [1922]), pp. 109–121.
"The Economic Problem of Masochism" (1924c), pp. 159–170.
"A Short Account of Psycho-Analysis" (1924f [1923]), pp. 191–209.
"Resistances to Psycho-Analysis" (1925e [1924]), pp. 213–222.
"Note Upon the 'Mystic Writing Pad'" (1925a [1924]), pp. 227–232.
Vol. 20 "An Autobiographical Study" (1925d [1924], pp. 7–74.
Vol. 21 *The Future of an Illusion* (1927c), pp. 3–56.
Civilization and Its Discontents (1930a [1929]), pp. 59–145.
"Humor" (1927d), pp. 161–166.
"Dostoevsky and Parricide" (1928b [1927]), pp. 175–194.
"Address Delivered in the Goethe House at Frankfurt" (1930e), pp. 208–212.
Vol. 22 *New Introductory Lectures on Psycho-Analysis* (1933a), pp. 3–182.
"Preface to Marie Bonaparte's *The Life and Works of Edgar Allen Poe*" (1933d), p. 254.
Vol. 23 *Moses and Monotheism: Three Essays* (1939a [1934–1938]), pp. 3–137.
"Analysis Terminable and Interminable" (1937c), pp. 211–253.
"Constructions in Analysis" (1937d), pp. 257–269.

INDEX

"Address Delivered in the Goethe House at Frankfurt," Freud, 19, 151, 155–56

Adulthood, 20

Aesthetic pleasure, 105–12, 121, 130–32, conditions for, 114; in Jensen's *Gradiva*, 177

Aesthetics, 11–12; economic view, 107–12, 113; psychoanalysis and, 6–13

"The Aetiology of Hysteria," Freud, 72

Affect: and representation, 13; transformation of, 34, 106–8, 112, 140

Affective discharge of art work, 77

Amusing effect of jokes, 106–7

Analysis, termination of, 72

"Analysis Terminable and Interminable," Freud, 169

Analytic cures, 13

Analytic method, 65, 73–74, 84–85

Andersen, Hans Christian, "The Emperor's New Clothes," 25–26, 57

Animism, primitive, and narcissism, 121

Animistic phase, 18, 20, 46

Anonymity of Freud, 16, 204n22

Arbitrariness in psychic life, 151–52, 187

Archeological construction, 68–70

Aristotle, 198

Art, 133; and death drive, 128–32; dream as paradigm, 53–54; and dream interpretation, 24–51; and fantasy, 75–85; Freud's views, 8–13, 192–93, 198, 201–2n6, 209–10n24; magic of, 121–22; and neuroses, 143–47; and Oedipus complex, 21, 126–27; and play, 112–14; psychoanalysis of, 1–5, 11, 15–17, 20, 21; and science, 13; social function, 105–6, 132; theological conception, 10, 49, 125, 127, 154, 157, 170

Artist, 10, 112–14, 123–24; cult of, 18; Freud's views, 13–18, 23, 49; "gift" of, 150–59, 164, 169–74; identification with father, 125–28; imagination of, 138–39, 140–41; and neurosis, 141–42; psychic knowledge of, 40–44; sublimation capacity, 109; symbolic murder, 15–17, 20

Artistic activity of Leonardo, 166–67

Artistic creation, 5, 156–57, 149–51, 217–18n51

Artistic license, 95, 187

Artistic phase, 18

Art works, 31; interpretation of, 64–75
Association, principles of, 56
Atheism, 126, 146, 222n45
Attention, diversion of in drama, 116
Author: fantasies of, 87; murder by
    analysis, 184–86; see also Artist
"An Autobiographical Study," Freud,
    50, 99, 134, 150

Bacchus, Leonardo, 84
Beauty, 109–10; analysis of, 11–12; and
    knowledge, 43; social function, 132
Beyond the Pleasure Principle, Freud, 76–
    77, 107
Bible, 122; repression in, 94–95
Biography, 19–20; psychoanalysis of,
    158–59
Biological limits, psychoanalysis and,
    169–74
Bisexuality, 57
Bonaparte, Marie, The Life and Works of
    Edgar Allan Poe, Freud's Preface to,
    150, 156
Brandes, Georg, 87
The Brothers Karamazov, Dostoevsky, 91–
    92

Castration, 7–8; dream model, 129; fear
    of, 57; universal fantasy, 97–98
Cathartic function of art, 111, 117
Censorship, 32, 56, 102; of dreams, 33–
    34
Chance, 128, 170–71, 223n13; in Jen-
    sen's Gradiva, 186
Character, 163
Child, relationship to parents, 18–20
"Childhood Memories and Screen
    Memories," Freud, 58–59
Childhood memory, 59–60, 75, 188–89;
    and daydreams, 33; and fantasy, 60–
    61; and poetry, 76
Childhood play, 112, 121
Chorus, Greek drama, 126–27
Circular method of analysis, 26, 28–29,
    41, 50, 97–98
Civilization, and nature, 154

Civilization and Its Discontents, Freud, 12,
    96, 109, 121, 145, 150, 159
" 'Civilized' Sexual Morality and Mod-
    ern Nervousness," Freud, 160, 164
"The Claims of Psycho-Analysis to Sci-
    entific Interest," Freud, 2, 30, 122,
    133, 142, 150
Comedy, 112, 172–73, 224n14; in child-
    hood, 113
Comparative structural analysis, 41–42
Composite images, formation of, 35
Concealed subject matter of dreams,
    36
Condensation process, 34–35
Conflict: father-son, 27; in tragedy, 115
Construction, 64–75
"Constructions in Analysis," Freud, 68,
    71
Contact, psychic, 56
Content of art, 12–13
Continuity, association by, 56
Counterproofs, 50
Creation, 188; artistic, 5, 10, 149–51,
    156–57, 205–6n33
Creative imagination, 78, 155
Creative works: and neuroses, 190–91;
    structural analysis, 87–88
"Creative Writers and Daydreaming,"
    Freud, 46, 76, 114–15, 131
Cultural evolution, 133
Cultural productions, and neuroses,
    142–47
Culture, 136, 145; and death drive, 130;
    and Eros, 130; and sublimation, 162

Dali, Salvador, Freud's views, 102–3
David Copperfield, Dickens, 98
Daydreams, 133, 134, 212n26; and
    childhood memory, 33
Death: denial of, 123–24; refusal of,
    128
Death drive, 128–32; in art, 55–56, 58,
    132, 133
Death of family members, dreams of,
    27
Decoding of dreams, 67–68
Deification: of hero, 18; of nature, 154

Delusion, 187, 225n8; inspiration as, 49; in Jensen's *Gradiva,* 179–80, 183–85, 186, 189–90; psychotic, 15; of reader, 194–97
Delusions and Dreams in Jensen's 'Gradiva,' Freud, 23, 24, 40–51, 139, 151–52, 175–99
Derrida, Jacques, 30, 66
Destiny, 130
Details, 39; of text, 9; of dreams, 67–68
Determinants of pleasure, convergence of, 110
Determinism, and artistic gifts, 158–59
Dickens, Charles, 98
Discharge of affect, in art work, 77
Displacement, childhood memory, 59
Distortion: in art, 39; from censorship, 33–34; in childhood memory, 59; in dreams, 25, 39, of text, 55; and truth, 100, 101
Diversion of attention, in drama, 116
Don Quixote, Cervantes, 119
Dostoevsky, Feodor Mikhailovich, 156; *The Brothers Karamazov,* 91–92; Freud's views, 14, 87, 88, 90, 203n16
"Dostoevsky and Parricide," Freud, 48, 85, 150, 191–92
Doubles, 118, 128–30, 131, 221n29; heroes as, 88; in Jensen's *Gradiva,* 178, 187–92; and search for immortality, 123–24
Drama: incest theme, 99; narcissism of, 125 26; pleasure sources, 115–19
Dreams, 120, 133, 207n7; and art, 24–51, 53–54; and delusion, 225n; and imagination, 135; interpretation of, 58, 67–68, 203n9; in Jensen's *Gradiva,* 183–84; and jokes, 24; and memory, 71; of single night, 85–86; symbolism of, 7–8, 97, 215–16n41

Echo metaphor, 189, 190
"The Economic Problem of Masochism," Freud, 153
Economic theory of art, 107–12, 134; and play, 113; and sublimation, 160–62

Education in psychoanalysis, 7
Ego, 3, 5; and identification in drama, 116; and reality, 135–36; and sexual aim, 130
Egypt, ancient, religion of, 122–23
Elaboration, artistic, 76
Ellis, Havelock, 61
"The Emperor's New Clothes," Andersen, 25–26, 57
Endopsychic perception, 44, 45–46, 191, 197; in Jensen's *Gradiva,* 181–82
Enigma, and art, 39–40, 54–58, 81
Enjoyment of art, 12
Enstellung, 67
Epic poetry, 18, 62–64, 125, 204–5n25
Eros, 130–32, in art work, 55–56, 58
Excrement, symbolism of, 125
Exhibitionism, and dreams, 26–27
Expressiveness: of art, 12–13, 31–32; of dreams, 31–32, 36
Expressive procedures, 39
Extraordinary, belief in, 186
Eye: pleasure from, 111; symbolism of, 7–8, 97

Family romance of child, 18
Fantastic creations, 35
Fantasy, 131, 134–35; of artist, 90; and art work, 75–85, 87; of author, 96; literary, 185; and memory, 58–64; and neurosis, 144; universal, and dreams, 24–26
Fate, 153
Father: artist as, 170; deification of, 18; hero identified with, 20; Leonardo and, 125, 156, 167; monotheism as religion of, 123; Moses as, 16–17; narcissistic identification with, 124–28; primal, 126–27; symbolic murder, 17–18, 123–28, 147, 204–5n25; unmasking of, 173
Father figure, in myths, 27
Father substitutes, 17
Faust, Goethe, 33
Feces, symbolism of, 125
Fechner, Gustav Theodor, 110
Femininity, 57–58; refusal of, 169

Fiction, 139; identification with hero, 117–18
Figuration process of dreams, 32–39
Figurative writing: dreams as, 30–37; of art work, 76
Five Lectures on Psycho-Analysis, Freud, 160
Flaubert, Gustave, 88
Folk tales, and dreams, 27
Fore-pleasure, 111, 114–15
Form: of art, 12–13; of dream, 36
"Formulations on the Two Principles of Mental Functioning," Freud, 134, 137, 140–41
"Four-and-Twenty Hours in a Woman's Life," Zweig, 47, 48–49, 90, 191–92
Freedom: artistic, 95; of imagination, 139–40
Frequency, dream representation, 37
Freud, Sigmund: and aesthetics, 6–13; and art, 1–5, 8–9, 21, 192–93; literary tastes, 176, 201–2n6
"From the History of an Infantile Neurosis," Freud, 71
The Future of an Illusion, Freud, 132, 154, 174

Game of life, 169–74
Genetic analysis, 74–75, 90, 98, 136–37; dream interpretation, 24–25
Genitals, 109; symbol of, 224n15
Genius, 5, 155
"Gift" of artist, 5, 142, 150–59, 164
God: as father, 170; murder of, 127, 146
Goethe, Johann Wolfgang von, 156, 165, 77; Faust, 33; Werther, 144
Gombrich, Ernst, 113
The Gothic House, Jensen, 86
Gradiva, Jensen, 40–51, 101; structural analysis, 86–87; see also Delusions and Dreams in Jensen's 'Gradiva,' Freud
Great man, 17–18, 49; artist as, 15–16, 102
Greek art, 126
Green, André, 101, 118
"Group Psychology and the Analysis of the Ego," Freud, 18

Hamlet, Shakespeare, 91–92, 116; analysis of, 29, 87; Freud's view, 12
Happiness, 145
Hebbel, Friedrich, Judith, 94–95
Hero: author's identification with, 88; biographer of, 19–20; cult of, 18; as double, 118; of Greek tragedy, 126–27; identification with father, 20; symbolic murder of father, 204–5n25
Historical memory, 62–63
History, personal, of artist, 75
Hoffmann, E. T. A., Tales, 7–8; "The Sandman," 97
Homosexuality, 164; of Dostoevsky, 87; of Leonardo, 84, 119, 166–67; and narcissism, 124, 125
Humor, 112; in childhood, 113; of superego, 173
Hypograms, theory of, 36
Hysteria, 60, 143–45; infantile scenes, 72; and poetry, 185, 190

Id, 3, 5
Identification: in art, 115–19; with father, 124–28; and narcissism, 120
Ideology, 47; Freud and, 22; traditional, 21, 170–71
Idols, in religion, 122–23
Illusion, 171, 198
Images, in religion, 122–23
Imagination, 133–41, 147, 155, 221n35; and reason, 38; and sublimation, 162
Immortality, search for, 123–24, 128
Incentive bonus of pleasure, 114, 131
Incest: as artistic theme, 99; and narcissism, 124; taboo, 56
The Incest Motif, Rank, 98–99
Inhibited drives, 163–64
Inhibition, 130; of artist, 156; of Leonardo, 167; and love of beauty, 109
Inspiration, 47, 49, 197–98
Instinctual renunciation, 22, 115, 133, 173
Instinctual sublimation, 159
Intellectual curiosity, 166
Intelligence, and aesthetics, 12
Intention of artist, 10, 12

Internal conflict, in drama, 115
The Interpretation of Dreams, Freud, 23–35
passim, 54, 58, 67, 87, 91, 116–17,
137
Interpretation: of art works, 64–75; circles of, 41; of dreams, 58; of truth,
101
Intertextual method, 26
Introductory Lectures on Psycho-Analysis,
Freud, 31, 35, 65, 78, 95, 118, 134,
138–39, 141, 155, 161; Preface to Hebrew translation, 14
Introversion, 138–39; of poets, 47

Jakobson, Roman, 36
Jensen, Gradiva, 101, 175–99; see also Delusions and Dreams in Jensen's 'Gradiva,'
Freud
Jewish religion, 122–23
Jokes, 106–7, 110; in childhood, 113;
pleasure in, 112
Jokes and Their Relation to the Unconscious,
Freud, 24, 106, 108, 110, 112, 172
Judith, Hebbel, 94–95
Jung, Carl Gustav, and Jensen's Gradiva,
177

Knowledge, 147; drive for, 165–66; of
artists, 14, 23; of writers, 40–51, 191–
92

Labyrinth legend, 54
Language play, in childhood, 113
Last Supper, Leonardo, 89
Latency period, 135
Latent content, 32, 39; of art work, 76;
of dream, 65; of Jensen's works, 86
Legend, 63; and childhood memory,
62; and dreams, 27–28; interpretation of, 54; of Narcissus, 119
Leonardo da Vinci, 107, 113–14, 125,
129, 140; Freud's views, 101; inhibition of, 156; psychoanalysis of, 165–
69; technique of, 89
Leonardo da Vinci and a Memory of His
Childhood, Freud, 19, 61, 75, 78–85, 89,
106, 119, 150–71 passim
Lermolieff, Ivan (Morelli), 10

Libido, 18, 160–61
Life, game of, 169–74
Life events of authors, and interpretation of works, 88
Limits of psychoanalysis, 4–5, 149–51,
157–59, 168–74
Literary works, censorship of, 33–34
Logic, of dreams, 30
Logical relations, expression of, 32

Macbeth, Shakespeare, 87
Magic, in art, 121–22
Manifest content, 57; of art work, 76,
97; of dream, 65; of Jensen's works,
86
Marxism, Freud's views, 22
Masculinity, 58
Masochism, in art, 107
Mastery, in art, 140
Material, psychic, 54; of art form, 31–
32; of dreams, 36
Memory, 65; art as, 75; and fantasy,
58–64; of repressed material, 68–70
Mental apparatus, 3, processes of,
137
Mental work, fantasy, 131
Metaphysical tradition, Freud and, 197–
99
Metapsychological knowledge, 46
"A Metapsychological Supplement to
the Theory of Dreams," Freud, 120
Meyer, Conrad, F., 88
Michelangelo: Freud's view, 12; Moses,
15–17, 92–94, 95
Modern art, Freud's view, 144, 222n42
Mona Lisa, Leonardo, 89, 119; smile of,
78–85; see also Leonardo da Vinci and a
Memory of His Childhood, Freud
Monotheism, 123
Morals, and Oedipus complex, 126–27
Moral suffering, in art, 115
Morelli (Ivan Lermolieff), 10
Moses, types of, 92–94, 95
Moses and Monotheism, Freud, 15–17, 62,
67, 72–73, 79, 93, 117, 123, 126, 127,
155
"The Moses of Michelangelo," Freud,
8–13, 92–94

Mother's smile, fantasy of, 79–85, 96–97, 119
Murder, symbolic: of artist, 15–17; of father, 17–18, 123–28; of father by artist, 20
Music, Freud and, 8
Mystic writing pad, 66
Myth, 46, 64, 136, 198, 204–5n25; and childhood memory, 62; of origin, 138; origin of, 100; and universal fantasy, 97
Mythological view of world, 46

Narcissism, 140, 220n18; and art, 21, 118, 119–28, 132, 173; and death impulse, 128; and religion, 146
Narcissistic stage, 18, 20
Natural reserves, 134–35
Nature: concepts of, 152–54; respect for, 171–72
Nausicaä, legend of, 27
Necessity, 17, 128, 145, 153–54, 170
Neuroses, 63, 109, 141–47; and art, 84, 190; of drama spectator, 115–16; imaginary function, 138; and Oedipus complex, 99, 127; and sublimation, 161, 159
New Introductory Lectures, Freud, 22, 54, 55, 57, 95, 163, 173
Nicholas of Verdun, Moses, 92–94
Nietzsche, Friedrich Wilhelm, 173–74, 210–11n5
Nirvana, 122, 128
Normality, and pathology, 195
"Notes on a Case of Paranoia," Freud, 152
"Notes Upon a Case of Obsessional Neurosis," Freud 45–46
Novel, as psychiatric study, 43–45
Nudity, dream of, 25–26

Object, choice, 51
Obsessional neurosis, 56, 143, 144, 190
Oedipus complex, 23–24, 27–29, 63, 91–92, 98–100, 126–27, 203n9; art and, 21; and dreams, 27–29, and neuroses, 145

Oedipus Rex, Sophocles, 27–29, 91
"On Narcissism: An Introduction," Freud, 140
"On Psycho-Analysis," Freud, 68
"On Psychotherapy," Freud, 37–38
"On the History of the Psycho-Analytic Movement," Freud, 50
"On the Teaching of Psycho-Analysis in Universities," Freud, 7
"On the Universal Tendency to Debasement," Freud, 162
"On Transience," Freud, 124
Oral tradition, 63
Originary repression, 137

Painters, psychic knowledge of, 42
Painting, 31, 32; of Leonardo, 80; see also Art
Paradise, Freud's views, 26
Paranoia, 45, 143, 144, 145, 190, 212–13n30
Parents, affective relationship with child, 18
Parmigiano, Moses, 95
Parricide, as artistic theme, 91–92
Past: of artist, 75; and memory, 61–62
Paternity, conceptions of, 170
Pathological formations, 143
Pathological repetition, 138
Pathological states, and normality, 195
Penis, symbolism of, 125
Personal history of artist, 78, 81–83, 88
Phantasmal constructions, 60–61, 63–64
"The Philological Interest of Psycho-Analysis," Freud, 30
Philosophy, and neurosis, 143, 190
Plato, 197–98
Play, 127, 133; and art, 112–14, 121
Pleasure principle, 133–37, 147–48; art and, 50–51, 107–8; renunciation of, 20
"The Poet and His Imagination," Freud, 76
Poetic license, 95, 187; in Jensen's Gradiva, 185–86
Poetry, 31, 36–37, 62–64, 117; and dreams, 26–27; and fantasy, 76;

Freud's views, 209–10n24; and hysteria, 144, 185, 190; mental work of, 131–32; pleasure in, 114–15
Poets, 11, 41, 95; material of, 46; psychic knowledge, 40, 43, 44–47
Preface to Bonaparte's The Life and Works of Edgar Allan Poe, Freud, 150, 156
Preface to Reik's Ritual, Freud, 143
Pre-text, of poetry, 36–37
Primal, 64–65
Primal father, 126–27
Primal matter of art works, 54
Primary narcissism, 123
Primary processes, 136–37; and art, 39–40, 49, 113–14; in dreams, 29–40; and imagination, 139–40; in jokes, 112; and play, 113
Primitive animism, and narcissism, 121
Primitive man, 46, 64
Probability, and truth, 72–74
Processes, in dreams, 29–40; see also Primary processes; Secondary processes
Procreation, 169–74
Proust, Marcel, 213–15n33
Psychiatry, 43
Psychic apparatus, 66–67, 137, 100; and pleasure principle, 133–34
Psychic laws, and artistic "gift," 151–52
Psychic material of dreams, 30, 31
Psychic productions, 26, 142–43, art as, 3–4; enigma of, 56; structural analysis, 96
Psychic writing, 39, 66–67
Psychoanalysis, 68–75, 71–74, 202–3n9; and aesthetics, 6–13; of art, 1–5, 11, 15–17, 20, 21, 193–94; artists and, 14; of artist's "gift," 156; and biography, 20; limits of, 4–5, 149–51, 157–59, 168–74
Psychoanalysts, 190
Psychogenesis of artist, 90
Psychological drama, 115
"Psychopathic Characters on the Stage," Freud, 107, 112, 115–17
Psychopathological drama, 115

The Psychopathology of Everyday Life, Freud, 45, 46, 60, 56

Rank, Otto, The Incest Motif, 98–99
"The Rat Man," Freud, 57, 63
Reaction-formation, 163
Reality principle, 134–36, 137; science and, 147, 148
Reason, 153; and imagination, 38
Rebellion, tragedies of, 115
"Recommendations to Physicians Practising Psycho-Analysis," Freud, 159
The Red Umbrella, Jensen, 86
Regression, of Leonardo, 167
Reik, Theodor, 14
Religion, 15, 145–47; and magic, 122–23, and neurosis, 143, 190; and Oedipus complex, 99, 126–27
Religious phase, 18, 20
"Remarks Upon the Theory and Practice of Dream-Interpretation," Freud, 72
Renunciations, art and, 133
Repetition, 129, 138, 217n51; in art, 140; of truth, 101
Replication, 187
Representation, 100–101, 219n11; and affect, 13; play, 112
Repression, 79, 102; and aesthetic pleasure, 108, 111; and art, 15, 42, 116–17, 124, 191; of artist, 142; and artistic "gift," 158–59; and beauty, 110; and censorship, 56; childhood memory, 59, 60; and distortion, 25; and dramatic identification, 117; epochal differences, 29; in Hamlet, 116; and intellectual curiosity, 166; in Jensen's Gradiva, 181–82; of Leonardo, 166–68; and Mona Lisa's smile, 81; originary, 137; in paranoia, 45–46; secular advance, 91–92; and sublimation, 164
Research, 166
Retrogressive displacement, 59
"Revision of the Theory of Dreams," Freud, 54
Riddle of Jensen's Gradiva, 176–80, 197

Role of art, 124
Rops, Felicien, 42

Sadism, of Dostoevsky, 87
St. Anne, Leonardo, 81–85, 140
St. John the Baptist, Leonardo, 84
"The Sandman," Hoffman, 97
Saussure, Ferdinand de, 36–37
Science: and art, 13; Freud's views, 14,
   22; and neuroses, 146–47; and pleas-
   ure principle, 51; and psychic knowl-
   edge, 44–45
Scientific activity of Leonardo,
   166
Scientific attitude, 173–74
Scientific method, 73
Scientific phase, 20
Screen memories, 58–60
"Screen Memories," Freud, 60
Secondary processes, 136–37; in art,
   34, 38
Self-censorship of Freud, 3
Self-sufficiency, and narcissism,
   123
Sensibility, and aesthetics, 12
Sexual aspects of beauty, 109–11
Sexual drives: and fantasy, 135–36;
   sublimation of, 130
Sexuality: and art, 130–32, 156; of
   Shakespeare, 87; and sublimation,
   161–64
Shakespeare, William, 87–88; Hamlet,
   91–92
"A Short Account of Psycho-Analysis,"
   Freud, 2–3
Similarity, association by, 56
Sleep state of infant, 137
Social function of art, 105–6,
   132
Social tragedies, 115
Society: and neuroses, 142–47; and
   Oedipus complex, 126–27
Somatic sources of dreams, 32–33
Sophocles, Oedipus Rex, 27–29, 91
Sovereign Powers, Jensen, 86
"A Special Type of Object Choice Made
   By Men," Freud, 51, 125
Spectator, identification in drama, 117–
   18

Spider, symbolism of, 57
Starobinski, Jean, 36–37
Strangers Among Men, Jensen, 86
Structural analysis, 86–100; dream
   interpretation, 24–26
Structure of dreams, 33
Style of artists, 88–90
Sublimation, 130, 159–64; by artist,
   109, 142; and artistic "gift," 158–
   59
Suffering: and aesthetic pleasure, 121;
   artistic representation, 115; in Greek
   tragedy, 127
Superego, 20, 22, 100; humor of, 173;
   and science, 147
Superstition, 46, 223–24n13
Surrealism, Freud's views, 102–3, 143–
   44
Symbol, Freud's views, 103
Symbolic interpretation of dreams, 67–
   68
Symbolism: in art, 53, 74; in dreams,
   53, 97; of genitalia, 224n15; in Jensen's Gradiva, 180–83

"The Taboo of Virginity," Freud, 64,
   94
Taboos, primitive, 45
Tales of Hoffman, 7–8
The Temptation of St. Anthony, Flaubert,
   88
Tendentious jokes, 110
Termination of analysis, 72
Texts, 9, 10, 187–88; of art, 32, 39, 47–
   49, 102, 105; of dreams, 30, 32; Jen-
   sen's Gradiva, 178, 183; as symptom,
   54–58
Theater, theories of, 208n9, 218–19n4
"The Theme of the Three Caskets,"
   Freud, 97, 153
Theological conception of art, 10, 49,
   125, 127, 154, 157, 170
Theological interpretation of Oedipus
   Rex, 28
Third object, symbolism of, 97
"Thoughts for the Times on War and
   Death," Freud, 118
Three Essays on the Theory of Sexuality,
   Freud, 109, 131, 162, 163, 165

Timon of Athens, Shakespeare, 87
Totem and Taboo, Freud, 7, 25, 46, 56, 64–
  65, 121–28 passim, 142, 143
Totemism, 64
Traces, 39, 65–67, 211–12n19; in artist,
  15; dream details, 68; in Jensen's
  Gradiva, 178, 189–90, memory, 60–61,
  64
Tragedy, 18; Greek drama, 126–27; and
  identification, 115; pleasure in, 108
Transformation of affect, in art, 106–8;
  in dreams, 34; and imagination, 140;
  play, 112
True meaning of text, 49
Truth: In analysis, 71, 72–74; Freud's
  conception, 100, 101; and illusion,
  198
Typical dreams, interpretation of, 24–29

Uncanniness, 7
"The Uncanny," Freud, 6–8, 11, 97, 118,
  123, 128, 129, 131, 139
Unconscious, 3, 5; knowledge of, 45; of
  writer, 48

Unconscious thoughts, 39
Understanding, and enjoyment of art,
  12
Uninhibited drives, 163–64
Universal fantasy, and art, 91, 96–98
Universality of dreams, 24–26
Universality of Oedipus complex, 27–
  29
Unmasking, 125, 127, 172–73

Virginity, taboo of, 96
Vocation, 129–30
Vulture, Leonardo's fantasy, 61, 85,
  97

Werther, Goethe, 144
Wish fulfillment, in dreams, 86
Women, 210–11n5; enigma of, 57–
  58
Writers, psychic knowledge of, 40–51

Zweig, Stefan, "Four-and-Twenty Hours
  in a Woman's Life," 47, 48–49, 90,
  191–92

European Perspectives:
A Series of Columbia University Press

Norbert Elias, *What is Sociology?*   1978
Raymond Boudon, *Crisis in Sociology*   1980
Arnold Gehlen, *Man in the Age of Technology*   1980
Julia Kristeva, *Desire in Language*   1980
Franz Borkenau, *End and Beginning*   1981
Bero Rigauer, *Sport and Work*   1981
Marzio Barbagli, *Educating for Unemployment*   1982
Robert Castel, Françoise Castel, and Anne Lovell, *Psychiatric Society*   1982
Gérard Genette, *Figures of Literary Discourse*   1982
Niklas Luhmann, *Differentiation of Society*   1982
Fernando Savater, *Childhood Regained*   1982
Eugenio Trias, *Artist and the City*   1982
Gilles Deleuze, *Nietzsche and Philosophy*   1983
Philippe Sollers, *Writing and the Experience of Limits*   1983
Eugenio Trias, *Philosophy and Its Shadow*   1983
Francesco Alberoni, *Movement and Institution*   1984
Julia Kristeva, *Powers of Horror*   1984
Julia Kristeva, *Revolution in Poetic Language*   1984
Richard Lowenthal, *Social Change and Cultural Crisis*   1984
Julia Kristeva, *Kristeva Reader*   1986
Daniel Roche, editor, *Journal of My Life: The Autobiography of Jean-Louis Menetra*   1986
Franco Basaglia, *Psychiatry Inside Out*   1987
Arnold Gehlen, *Man: His Nature and Place in the World*   1987
Volker Meja, Dieter Misgeld, and Nico Stehr, *Modern German Sociology*   1987
Gilles Deleuze and Claire Parnet, *Dialogues*   1988
Michel de Certeau, *The Writing of History*   1988
Julia Kristeva, *In the Beginning Was Love*   1988
Sarah Kofman, *The Childhood of Art*   1988